BETWEEN
SELF-determination
and Dependency

BETWEEN SELF-DETERMINATION AND DEPENDENCY

Jamaica's Foreign Relations
1972–1989

Holger W. Henke

THE UNIVERSITY OF THE WEST INDIES PRESS
Barbados • Jamaica • Trinidad and Tobago

The University of the West Indies Press
1A Aqueduct Flats   Mona
Kingston 7   Jamaica

04   03   02   01   00   5   4   3   2   1

CATALOGUING IN PUBLICATION DATA

Henke, Holger
    Between self-determination and dependency: Jamaica's foreign relations,
    1972-1989 / Holger Henke
    p.cm.
    Includes bibliographical references and index
    ISBN: 976-640-058-X

    1. Self-determination, National. 2. Jamaica – Foreign economic relations.
    3. Jamaica – Foreign relations. 4. Jamaica – Economic conditions.
    F1882.H46   2000   320.15   dc-20

Cover and book design by Robert Harris
Cover art by Detlef Henke
Set in Adobe Garamond 11/14 x 24
Printed in the United States of America

For Justin Leigh, my son

Contents

Tables and Figures / *viii*

Foreword / *ix*

Acknowledgments / *xvi*

Abbreviations / *xviii*

1   Introduction / *1*

2   Internal Dynamics: 1972–1980 / *14*

3   External Dynamics: 1972–1980 / *24*

4   Caribbean Tête-à-Tête: Jamaica and Cuba / *30*

5   Jamaica, the US and International Capital in the 1970s / *52*

6   Internal Dynamics: 1981–1989 / *69*

7   External Dynamics: 1981–1989 / *91*

8   Jamaica and the Caribbean in the 1980s / *101*

9   Jamaica's Relations with International Capital and the US in the 1980s / *130*

10   Conclusion / *154*

Appendix / *171*

Notes / *174*

Select Bibliography / *189*

Index / *207*

Tables and Figures

Figures

Figure 1.1:   Determinants of degrees of the dependent state's relative autonomy / *11*

Figure 1.2:   The dependent state's foreign policy / *13*

Tables

Table 2.1:   External debt in US dollars and external debt service as percent of exports of goods and services / *16*

Table 2.2:   Capital inflows into Jamaica, 1970–1977 (in J$ millions) / *18*

Table 2.3:   External trade quotient for Jamaica, 1971–1982 (at current prices) / *19*

Table 2.4:   Fixed capital formation in Jamaica, 1974–1980 / *20*

Table 2.5:   GDP indicators, 1970–1981 / *21*

Table 4.1:   Trade between Jamaica and Cuba (1972–1980) in J$ / *34*

Table 6.1:   GDP indicators, 1980–1988 / *74*

Table 6.2:   Selected sectoral performance of the economy 1980–1988 (growth rate in %) / *75*

Table 6.3:   External trade balance 1982–1988 (US$ million) / *76*

Table 6.4:   Selected balance of payments indicators / *76*

Table 6.5:   External trade quotient for Jamaica 1981–1987 (at current prices) / *77*

Table 6.6:   Selected social indicators, 1981–1988 / *78*

FOREWORD

Jamaica's modern era in development started in the late 1930s and the past sixty years have witnessed the virtual transformation of the country. First came the years of preparation for independence, which came in 1962. Beginning in the late 1930s there was the loud and clear call by the workers whose demonstrations against unacceptable social conditions and low wages awakened the country, its local authorities and the colonial power. Out of this came the establishment of political organizations and processes, the birth of modern trade unions, and the early movement towards constitutional change and self-government.

The British authorities, urged by the stinging criticisms of the Royal Commission which examined and reported on economic and social conditions in the West Indian territories, established the Development and Welfare Scheme – probably the first international aid programme of that kind, and, remarkably, in the middle of a major war.

Those early years saw significant developments in the public sector – development of an exceptional leadership corps of Jamaicans and the establishment of a number of development agencies, including a department of statistics, the planning agency, the industrial and the agricultural development corporations, social and community development agencies and, later, the Bank of Jamaica, all before independence.

Jamaica came to occupy a virtually unique position in the emerging Third World and was held in high regard, a fact demonstrated by the visits from other countries to examine the work in a variety of spheres, including planning, industrial development, community development and agricultural research.

The establishment of the University of the West Indies, with its first campus in Jamaica, and the initial movements towards regional integration created new dimensions in the experience of Jamaica and the other countries of the region. But perhaps the most remarkable and fundamental developments in those years were in the cultural field – the creative artistic output of poets, painters, writers, musicians and others – as well as in the field of sport. Through the years of independence and the very difficult experiences encountered, these have constituted sources of strength and have continued to enhance the image of the people and the country in the world.

The first ten years of independence, 1962 to 1972, gave the country its first opportunity to move fully on to the international stage and it did so with deliberate caution. The international environment of those years contributed to an atmosphere of optimism, not least because of the continued post-World War II economic boom. Those years also marked the high point in the decolonization process which brought scores of former colonies to independence and membership in the international community. This had, over subsequent years, a major impact, particularly on the United Nations. It was to influence Jamaica's posture in international affairs considerably, especially during the 1970s.

The next seventeen years, from 1972 to 1989, which are the subject of Dr Henke's examination, witnessed events that brought major changes to the international sphere, changes that affected developed as well as developing countries. The period of ten years which followed has brought the world to the eve of the twenty-first century. This has been seen as an occasion for speculation as to what lies ahead and consideration of what the requirements might be for successful existence in the new millennium and the chances of establishing them. One of the critical requirements is a thorough understanding of the past, both successes and what must frankly be acknowledged as serious deficiencies and failures.

Dr Henke's work can be seen as a welcome contribution to this effort. He approached his complex task with more than academic interest. As a young European, he brought his own personal interest in respect of a country very different from his own. This interest developed over the period of his stay in Jamaica, and this is reflected in his words of acknowledgment. He addresses "the good people of Jamaica" and thanks them for "giving an outsider the opportunity to learn about your history and culture (and thereby to become a kind of insider)".

The examination of the period of the 1970s and 1980s continues in Jamaica at different levels, and there still remain deep differences on the issues. The reactions to events of those years continue to have a strong influence.

The First Conference of Caribbean Economists was held in Kingston in 1987 and was attended by 118 economists and other scholars. Professor Norman Girvan in his Foreword to the conference report (March 1989) spoke of the intense discussion among the participants which was "a telling indicator of the sense of magnitude of the crisis confronting parts of the region". Dr Peter Phillips echoed the sentiments of the participants, stating that "there is a crisis in Caribbean economic thought".

On the subject of dependency and vulnerability, which is the centre of Dr Henke's thesis, the editor's introduction to the conference report states, "The acute degree of dependency of Caribbean economies on the world economy in general, and on the economies of their main metropolitan trading partners in particular, is a historical and contemporary fact, a dependency shared to a greater or lesser extent with all developing economies." Reference is made to a statement by one participant who labeled as a form of "romantic madness" any notion that there exists "the economy of Jamaica, Haiti or of any other Caribbean country as distinct from the world economy of which it is an integral part". Such economies, it would seem, were globalized long before the era of globalization.

Dr Henke states that "it was the intractable conditions of structural dependency in which the country was and continues to be situated, that influenced the degree of success of the two distinct foreign policy approaches" taken over the period by the two regimes, namely the governments of the People's National Party and the Jamaica Labour Party. The social and political atmosphere in the country, the deep differences, the extraordinary polarization that developed, associated with the very serious condition of the country's economy, especially during the 1970s, naturally constitute major elements in Dr Henke's study, along with the unusual degree of activism on the part of the government in the international arena in both multilateral affairs and bilateral relations.

The 1980s presented, in many respects, a very different picture. In the minds of many, both inside and outside Jamaica, it was seen as a return to sanity, orthodoxy and the democratic path. On the international scene there were also major changes, including the political movement to the 'right' exemplified by the assumption of political leadership by Margaret Thatcher in Britain and Ronald Reagan in the United States. These and other developments affected Jamaica, and the world in general, in many ways. But in spite of the progress in some spheres of the country, particularly in the achievement of some economic growth, many of the underlying problems and obstacles remained.

An examination of Dr Henke's work in the light of developments in the years that followed gives rise to a number of interesting reflections. He speaks of "the highly secret conduct of Jamaica's foreign affairs, which in itself is a part of the reason for a number of inefficiencies [which] ruled out a design [for his study] based on the dynamics of diplomatic interaction and the analysis of diplomatic notes and bargaining processes." There is no doubt some justification for this view. But there are a number of factors that can be mentioned. There has been a growing demand for greater transparency and openness on the part of the government, and the authorities have undertaken to move in that direction and, among other things, to review the Official Secrets Act. It would be interesting to know how Jamaica compares with other countries, particularly in the Caribbean, in this matter. But it must be said in the light of the considerable influence of external factors and events on Jamaica, as well as the country's own desires and efforts towards the penetration of that sphere, there is insufficient focused interest, study and reporting of such matters. The need for such effort becomes greater with advancing globalization. Such an approach calls for sophisticated arrangements involving the knowledge of the widespread sources of different types of information – on international economic, political and other topics – and the appropriate technology and the analytical capability. The information and telecommunication revolution has provided great opportunities in respect of some of these requirements.

An interesting aspect of this issue is the situation of the United Nations system which daily generates a considerable amount of information on a very wide range of subjects, these including the deliberations and decisions in its many agencies. Access to information from such intergovernmental bodies is the right of both member governments such as Jamaica and their citizens. The UN has made this information available on the Internet. There is, however, insufficient understanding of, and reporting on, the structure and operations of the UN even in situations where Jamaica's interests and concerns are directly involved. Of course Jamaica has benefited greatly from the work of Caribbean scholars in this and other spheres, including that of Dr Henke.

There has been over the years a considerable increase in the number of radio stations in Jamaica and access to foreign transmissions, mainly from the US, is now very widely available by cable television. An important feature of this is the number of local radio talk shows and call-in programmes which cover both domestic and international issues. But, on the other hand, it is unfortunate that the two Jamaican organizations established for the purpose of fostering interest in international affairs, the Bustamante Institute of Public and International Affairs and the Jamaica Centre for International Affairs, were closed in recent years due to lack of financial support.

Consideration of the very unusual experiences of the 1970s and 1980s also brings to mind the issue of the character of dialogue and the attitudes in

Jamaica, especially as they relate to social and developmental concerns. There is much evidence of serious and long-standing deficiencies in this area. There is, for example, the lack of consistent progress in the establishment and maintenance of bipartisan positions between the political parties on some fundamental issues. There are the deep differences concerning the structure and operation of the electoral system, which on a number of occasions over the years have brought the country close to a major crisis. Again, the spectre of a federation of English-speaking Caribbean countries emerges occasionally in the context of consideration of the further development of the Caribbean Community, underlining differences between the major political parties, differences which resulted thirty-eight years ago in the abandonment of the short-lived federation.

There is the failure to agree on the terms of the proposed social contract between government, the private sector and the trade unions, and the ongoing misunderstandings and differences between government and the private sector on aspects of economic policy as well as government procedures – a long-standing situation. With some outstanding exceptions, relations between employers and labour remain unsatisfactory. At the social level, tensions as well as the incidence of violence have increased and there is insufficient agreement on the main causes and on effective ways of addressing the situation. The main problem is not so much the differences mentioned as the fact that they persist year after year and in some cases decade after decade, in the face of the lack of social cohesion.

In recent years new dimensions have been introduced into the sphere of development economics. One of these is the environmental factor. Briefly, this notion is based on the proposition that conventional economic theory and practice have excluded certain critical environmental values and costs. In a similar manner, some social factors have been excluded. There is now a movement, one in which such international organizations as the United Nations Development Programme (UNDP) and the World Bank are playing a leading role, to change the situation. The introduction of these concepts might well bring about significant changes in economic and social practice and policy. Related to this is the development of the concept of 'social capital' which has been defined as "the norms, institutions, networks, organizations, traditions and attitudes which together constitute a key to a more humane and sustainable form of development". It is a question, in short, of the degree of harmony and tolerance in a community to accommodate differences, providing an environment that allows that broad consensus which is necessary for sustained progress.

Very recently there have been a number of signals which suggest that a change could be taking place in attitudes, particularly on the part of leaders in the private sector and the government, in the face of continuing economic problems. In March 1998, Douglas Orane, managing director of Grace, Kennedy Ltd and former president of the Private Sector Organization of Jamaica (PSOJ), stated that "the level of mistrust is so high in society that we cannot develop a consensus". He argues that that is a reason why the social contract has not been signed and that the major issue facing the country is social in nature and not economic. Asked why countries such as Barbados and Trinidad and Tobago have signed a social contract while Jamaica has not, he replied that "there was a deficiency in the way Jamaicans relate to each other".

The president of the Jamaica Chamber of Commerce, Howard Hamilton, has stated that the time has come for everyone "to stop pointing the finger of blame and to demonstrate that by our own efforts and ability to look at ourselves honestly we will be able to move forward as partners".

The president of the PSOJ, Cliff Cameron, expressed the view that the country has had too much discussion and that "it is time that we come together to forge links that go beyond individual interests in order to find and implement solutions which will benefit us all in the end and move the country forward". He indicated that "the PSOJ is uniquely situated to be able to fill the gap in strategic thinking". There have been other statements in a similar vein, including a call by the Minister of Commerce and Technology for the government and the private sector to join hands to bring about needed economic growth. Newspaper editorials have also been calling for a change in attitudes and in the relationships between the sectors.

There is perhaps a possibility of material change in the country in this matter, a change that might be encouraged by the approach of the new millennium as well as the dire prospect of a continuation of the current situation. For while a measure of stability has been achieved so far as some of the main economic indicators are concerned, there is a continuing absence of growth in the economy. Perhaps in this period of soul-searching it would be useful to undertake a close, critical appraisal of the past sixty years to ensure that the lessons of that period are truly learned. This could include an attempt to understand the reasons why Jamaica has failed to fulfil its early promise expressed in the performance of the society in those early years before 1962.

Comparisons with other CARICOM nations would be useful. Dr Henke, in the spirit of friendship, urges Jamaicans to study and guard well their history and culture which define their place in the greater scheme of things and can guide them in designing their future.

It seems appropriate to end these reflections with the words of the late Hon. G. Arthur Brown who served Jamaica with distinction, occupying the highest offices in public service in economic development and finance in a career that spanned a large part of this sixty year period. In his 1989 Grace Kennedy Foundation Lecture, he said "Jamaica might then ask itself, will it join those who are now setting goals for themselves for the year 2000 and can we use this target to energize ourselves and motivate ourselves to do what has eluded us up to now? Would it not be a worthwhile pursuit, not just for our political leaders, but for all sectors of our society . . . to set ourselves tough goals which they should strive to achieve? And think of what we might accomplish if an entire society were to come together and work together as a solid team. I invite our leaders to consider this and to translate affirmative decision into affirmative action."

Ambassador The Hon. Don Mills, O.J.

Acknowledgments

Undoubtedly, intellectual production is a collective process which directly and indirectly involves many individuals. It is impossible to name all the people who have contributed to this book, in a myriad of ways, ranging from critical comments to editorial and library assistance, and personal encouragement. Nevertheless I would like to mention a number of people by name whose help has greatly benefited the development of my ideas as they unfolded in the course of working on this study.

In particular, I am grateful to Rosina Wiltshire, Ambassador the Hon. Don Mills, Trevor Munroe, the late Herb Addo, R. B. Manderson-Jones, Stanley Lalta, Peter Phillips, Peter Körner, Helen McBain, and two anonymous reviewers for their constructive comments and advice at various stages in the production of this analysis. I believe that their assistance was critical in achieving a greater detachment from the subject matter. They contributed greatly to a more balanced formulation of my own ideas and opinions about foreign policy in small developing countries. Also very helpful for the progress of this particular work were Rupert Lewis and Janet Byron. For the formidable intellectual stimulation I received during my years in Jamaica in countless hours of discussion and exchange in both formal academic and informal settings, I am especially indebted to Dillon Alleyne, Ballayram, Ian Boxill, Noel Cowell, Glyne Griffiths, Damien King, and many other faculty members in the departments of government, economics, sociology, as well as the Consortium Graduate School of Social Sciences, all at the Mona campus of the University of the West Indies.

A number of politicians, business persons, and public servants both from Jamaica and the United States of America kindly agreed to be interviewed for this work and I am especially grateful for their time and permission to utilize their unique insights into the inner workings of Jamaican society, economy, and polity.

I was very impressed by the professionalism of various members of staff of the University of the West Indies Press, who made the editing of this book a pleasure. In particular, I would like to thank Linda Cameron for her accessibility and instant availability whenever editorial questions arose during the preparation of the manuscript.

To all the good people in Jamaica who made me understand that in human relations closeness and distance are not only not mutually exclusive concepts, but that they often coexist and even reinforce each other, I would like to say thank you for giving an outsider the opportunity to learn about your history and culture (and thereby to become a kind of an insider). Study them and guard them well, they define your place in the greater scheme of things and can guide you in designing the future. To live and work in your country truly was a uniquely gratifying experience which has shaped who I am today.

Last but not least, I would like to thank my wife Simone for her strength and "backative" during lengthy, and at times very difficult, periods of separation during field work. And to my parents for their support and unwavering belief in my ability to complete this work in a place far away from what used to be my home . . . I love you both.

Holger Henke
Nutley (NJ)

Abbreviations

BCCI	Bank of Commerce and Credit
CARICOM	Caribbean Community
CBI	Caribbean Basin Initiative
C/CAA	Caribbean/Central American Action
CCL	Concerned Caribbean Leaders (see also GCCL)
CDU	Caribbean Democratic Union
CME	Joint Committee of Commerce, Manufactures and Export
CNG	National Council of Government (Haiti)
CoC	Chamber of Commerce
ECLAC	Economic Commission for Latin America and the Caribbean
EFF	Extended Fund Facility
GCCL	Group of Concerned Caribbean Leaders (see also CCL)
GDP	Gross Domestic Product
IDB	Inter-American Development Bank
IMF	International Monetary Fund
JEA	Jamaica Exporters' Association
JEF	Jamaica Employers Federation
JLP	Jamaica Labour Party
JMA	Jamaica Manufacturers' Association
JNEC	Jamaica National Export Corporation
JNIP	Jamaica National Investment Promotions Ltd
OAS	Organization of American States
PNP	People's National Party
PSOJ	Private Sector Organization of Jamaica
NDI	National Democratic Institute (USA)

1

INTRODUCTION

This study examines the content and direction of Jamaica's foreign relations between 1972 and 1989. In this time period the country witnessed the ascent and fall of four governments formed by the two major parties i.e. the People's National Party (PNP) and the Jamaica Labour Party (JLP) in the context of a Westminster type democracy. Jamaica, being a typical structurally dependent "Third World" country, experienced two contrasting models of development promoted by the four governments.[1] The first endorsed an import-substitution, self-reliance oriented programme, while the second subscribed to an export-promotion, International Monetary Fund (IMF)/World Bank inspired blueprint.

The following question underlies this study: Why was it that important aspects of both foreign policy approaches did not successfully ameliorate Jamaica's condition of structural dependency but, instead, contributed to the strengthening of dependency-transmitting forces and mechanisms? Neither the attempt to openly reject and reverse this condition nor the effort to acquiescently maximize its potential benefits has led to a more viable, self-sustaining economy or greater room for manoeuvre in the conduct of Jamaica"s international relations. It is proposed that, apart from the content and execution of both development programmes, the political culture of Jamaica and the political style of both parties and their leaders in government, it was the intractable conditions of structural dependency in which the country was and continues to be situated, that influenced the degree of success of the two distinct foreign policy approaches which complemented the above mentioned development models.

Following from this perspective, the specific objectives of the study shall comprise:

1) an examination of Jamaica's situation of dependency and its development over the time period in question, showing that the country's dependency gradually deepened

2) an analysis which illustrates that the governments formed by the two parties perceived the objective condition of dependency in quite contrasting ways

3) a demonstration that the deepened dependency had a profound influence on the limits of free choice and the two parties' definition of foreign policy goals, in the sense that the former gradually narrowed and the latter did not adequately reflect an either sufficiently coherent or independent policy

4) a demonstration that, while the deteriorating range of foreign policy options in the PNP government's case was an unintended and unexpected result of its approach, the JLP government's foreign policy was a calculated attempt to re-integrate Jamaica into the political and economic dependency matrix dominated by international capital and the regional hegemony, the USA

5) the outline of some policy-oriented recommendations to address the problem of foreign policy development under conditions of dependency.

The Political Economy and Political Culture of Foreign Relations in the English-speaking Caribbean

The history of the Caribbean has made it unique among Third World regions. The revolution in Haiti led to the first black republic in the world. In other parts of the region, the Maroons[2] successfully defended their freedom and eventually forced the British to sign a peace treaty, thereby establishing the first formal foreign relations of the colonies with the colonial power. However, in the postemancipation period the colonial powers laid the "divide and rule" foundations for more informal and less coercive control over the economies and political affairs of the region. When, in the third decade of the twentieth century, the territories experienced social upheavals and demands for independence, the social basis of informal control had already been established.

After the colonial powers indicated their willingness to negotiate independence, the leaders of the labour movement tended to abandon their base. In Jamaica, for instance, the emergence of two major parties from the labour movement split labour at the organizational and political levels into two rival factions. Thus labour, of which only about a third is unionized in the Caribbean, ceased to be a class in itself, although the workers continued to constitute a potential class. This development effectively prevented either of the two political parties from forming a broad coalition between sections of the middle stratum (from which political leaders and the civil service were recruited) and a united working class which could potentially have challenged capitalist interests (Stone 1976, 191–92).[3]

Members of the Caribbean middle stratum who increasingly assumed political power in the pre-independence era were characterized by ambiguity with regard to their political goal, resulting from their attempt to satisfy bourgeois interests without alienating their populist base. Generally, their political culture displayed a lack of developmental vision, intellectual bluntness or political opportunism (James 1971, 194; Beckford 1983, 65). To the extent that they advocated economic nationalism, it usually had to be subordinated to the indicators and symbols of economic success valid in the industrially developed countries. The development model pursued by the elite in the 1950s and 1960s consequently focused on import-substitution, industrialization by invitation and policies that facilitated the expansion of both local and international capital. In order to fortify their position in the state apparatus, the ruling elite shifted from mass-based politics to class-based politics (Parris 1979, 242–59; Thomas 1988, 71ff; see also Parris 1976, 248–63; Philipps 1976, 93–119). By this approach they attempted to develop the economies without challenging the socioeconomic structure and power hierarchies in their countries.

The open door import-substitution model ran into a crisis at the end of the 1960s which increased the political pressure for a wider national and more inclusive approach to development. Parallel with this, the attention of the state elite shifted from the consolidation of their political power to the use of the state for the establishment of an economic base of their own (Thomas 1988, 192). The local bourgeoisie initially acquiesced in this new populist-nationalist drive as it aimed at enhancing social stability, thereby guaranteeing the continued viability of the peripheral capitalist project while appearing to be directed against the predominance of foreign capital in the economy.

The new states of the Caribbean had also been culturally constricted and, with the Black Power movement and decolonization in full swing at this time, attempts were also made to redefine foreign relations in a culturally more meaningful way. On the one hand, this meant closer cooperation at the regional level, while on the other hand, it created strong political sentiments for a reorientation to Africa and a new identification with the emergent Third

World movement. However, ideological questions clearly took the back seat to problems of economic development which again reflected the influence of local economic interest groups on the resources devoted to international diplomacy (Lewis 1979, 1–11; 1977, 110–30).

THE FOREIGN POLICY OF THE STRUCTURALLY DEPENDENT STATE: ELEMENTS OF AN ANALYTICAL FRAMEWORK

While Marxist imperialist theories and the world systems approach clearly tend to stress the importance of the external, they fall prey to a twofold epistemological reduction. Basically, they exhibit a broad and pervasive preference for "matter over mind". This leads directly to an overemphasis of the external structures over domestic institutions, organizations and social practices. On the other hand, they greatly de-emphasize the contingency of (relatively) independent human action at conjunctional points of history. More specifically, despite acknowledging their existence, they tend to view ideological, political, religious and other ideal factors as secondary and entirely determined by the material base on which they, in fact, rest. The analysis in this study, however, regards the material, economic factor merely as a *primum inter pares,* acknowledging the conjunctional importance of ideal factors and human action.

At its most general level, this study views the foreign policy of dependent states as a systemic process that entails fundamental functional incompatibilities within and between diverse national and international social actors who, according to their position within the structures of capitalist production, adopt policies which give this systemic process its dialectical character. Social and political forces and processes operate within a *structured* totality in which a single part (the economic) determines the *relations* among all parts. In this sense it also stresses the socioeconomic nature of foreign relations, i.e. their rootedness in the economic sphere of production and the dependent states' position within the global hierarchies of capitalist production and exchange.

Following this view, the capitalist economy by virtue of its functional requirements defines the contributions of particular interests within a society and hence the *relations* between them. In turn, the function of each part defines the form or structure of the whole, and thereby endows the former to some extent with an autonomy and logic of its own (Kubálková and Cruickshank 1989, 211). From a global perspective this viewpoint has a particular significance insofar as it regards the world as consisting of different nations, which exhibit various and variable degrees of political and economic independence, and sees the capitalist world economy (that is its substructure) as consisting of various combinations of capitalist, semi-capitalist and non-capitalist societies (Mandel 1978, chap. 2).

Strictu sensu the world economy merely exists as a dialectically structured whole, consisting of single national socioeconomic formations which at the same time are stabilizing, reproducing and undermining the whole. The single formations do not form merely economic relations under formally equal conditions. Rather, relations are comprised of various levels of interaction which are in dynamic contradiction with each other. Political, economic, social and ideological relations are not static; as they are extended and reproduced they are also transformed (Petras and Brill 1986, 8; Amin 1980, 23).

The approach adopted in this study thus offers room for the inductive analysis of concrete historical situations, i.e. stages or phases which, despite the generic and organic development of history, show distinctive characteristics clearly separating them from preceding phases or stages located in other places. Thereby, static misconceptions which are the result of non-dialectic and deterministic thinking are avoided.[4] This study therefore firmly locates itself within the broader intellectual ambit of an emergent international relations theory which emphasizes the influence of social forces as critical to an understanding of both continuity and shift in foreign relations at the national level, and the form different world orders take, at the global level.[5]

The strong impulse towards the perpetuation of dependency within this world economy is achieved through the material conditions of capitalist hegemony, which are mediated through the historical tendency of finance capital to expand into the Third World, as well as the uneven development through "biased accumulation" in these countries. The intervention of (mostly) subjective and ideal factors may *temporarily* allow certain classes or groups to take action against the constraints and pressures resulting from this structure.[6] Historical structural dependency approaches (Cardoso and Faletto 1979) identify the existence of "bridgehead elites" as the central problem of dependent countries' inability to formulate genuinely indigenous economic and political structures, processes and techniques. The local elite thus finds itself within an ambiguous double dialectic position. On the one hand, they want to exhibit loyalty towards their counterparts in the centre nations because of the profits this relation promises but, on the other hand, they are necessarily aware of contradicting interests which result from the subaltern position of the social formation from which or within which they operate:

In fact, the relation of dependence does not mean that national history in dependent nations will simply reflect changes in the external hegemonic centre, although these changes are relevant to the possible autonomy of national history. There are structural limits to possible action, beginning with the available material base of production and the degree of development of the forces of production, and including the way in which these are combined with political and juridical relations within the country and its link with the hegemonic countries. Through the action of groups, classes, organizations, and social movements in the dependent countries, these links are perpetuated, modified, or broken (Cardoso and Faletto 1979, 173–74).

The internal struggle between the classes and social groups even permeates the dominant bureaucracies which are the object of their contention (Cardoso and Faletto 1979, 172–74).

The systemic foreign policy process of a structurally dependent state can then be specified as the concrete expression of the contending priority interests of social forces of which the bourgeoisie usually has the ideological and political hegemony. The struggle for this expression is rooted in the sphere of production, i.e. the relations of production. It occurs in a sharpened form at the levels of political organization (in its widest sense), bureaucracy and the state apparatus and finds its final expression as official foreign policy in the statements of the responsible political directorate. Here, the government proclaims it as its political will and executes it in a continuous attempt to formulate and implement behavioural choices in order to adjust to the demands and constraints emanating from the external (or internalized external) environment. Although economic and political constellations in the internal and external system may allow anti-systemic options to arise from time to time, they tend to deteriorate eventually under the condition of structural dependency.

As noted earlier, the social struggle for expression of foreign relations is in its embryonic form situated in the productive sphere. In dependent social formations, elements with transnational economic interests contend with forces which (at least potentially) support national economic projects. As a first approximation, N. Poulantzas' important work has distinguished two different factions of the class which usually is the dominant force in the class struggle. First, he distinguishes the national bourgeoisie which:

. . . is the fraction of the indigenous bourgeoisie which, on the basis of a certain type and degree of contradiction with foreign imperialist capital, occupies a relatively autonomous place in the ideological and political structure . . . The national bourgeoisie is capable of adopting, *in certain specific conjunctures* of the anti-imperialist and national liberation struggle, class positions which make it part of 'the people'; it can therefore be brought into a certain type of alliance with the popular masses.

From this faction, however, has to be distinguished another faction, the so-called comprador bourgeoisie, which comprises:

. . . that fraction of the bourgeoisie which does not have its own base for capital accumulation, which acts in some way or the other as a simple intermediary of foreign imperialist capital (which is why it is often taken to include the *bureaucratic bourgeoisie*) and which is thus triply subordinated economically, politically and ideologically to foreign capital (Poulantzas 1979, 71 – emphasis added).[7]

Both factions of the national bourgeoisie usually contend for political and ideological hegemony within the state apparatus which binds the respective social formation within which both operate. The influence they exert through the power bloc, combined with their interest within the state apparatus, might be either through direct participation in important administrative positions or of a more informal nature which attempts to "pull the strings" from behind the stage.

The peripheral state's social structure, however, distinguishes itself from the centre nations (to which Poulantzas' concept is tailored) by the extremely important role which international capital plays within it. As Alavi (1989a, 297) pointed out correctly, often the metropolitan bourgeoisie even has a "structural presence in postcolonial societies and their state apparatus". This presence generally tends to tip the balance of power in favour of the comprador bourgeoisie and policies which favour their interest.

Between the bourgeoisie and the subordinated classes a third "class" is positioned which could cautiously be called the middle stratum. Very frequently this class dominates the state apparatus, where it represents its own interests which are closer to the bourgeoisie than to the subordinated classes. In this form it constitutes a technico-administrative class which frequently becomes an important part of the power bloc. In participatory societies it is subject not only to bourgeois pressure, but also to intense demands from the massive base of subordinated classes, which forms their source of political legitimacy and to which they have to cater. At certain historical junctures, it is possible, and perhaps even probable, that this bureaucratic class styles itself in a populist fashion and possibly seeks an alliance with the national bourgeoisie. As the cases of Guatemala, the Dominican Republic and Chile demonstrate, it is very possible that this situation is influenced by the coalition of the comprador bourgeoisie and foreign capital (Stavrianos 1981, 466; Niess 1986, chap. 6).

As already indicated, a study within such a historical-structural framework has to be fully cognizant of the different types of states in the capitalist world order which pursue various types of foreign policy. A clear distinction has to be drawn between Fascist dictatorship, oligarchic states and competitive democratic states. As Therborn (1980, 99; see also Richardson 1978, chap. 3; Chomsky 1987a, 331) pointed out, capitalist states dispose of (and are susceptible to, one may add) potent economic mechanisms of coercion, e.g. boycotts, blockades, political restrictions on credit. Dependent social formations, however, are more vulnerable to these mechanisms since their economies are usually comparatively weaker: their industrial sectors are not well integrated vertically, their capital base is small and fragile, their production base is extremely dependent on foreign technology, and their pool of skilled workers and professionals is small, to mention just a few factors (Alavi 1989b, 172–92). While retaliatory measures may be damaging to the developed social formation, they are likely to completely disrupt the economy of a dependent social formation.

The analysis in this study's approach remains at the level of the singular social formation as it tries to address the specific externally mediated situation of structural dependency which finds its specific form and expression within it (Hein 1985, 30). Dependency is in itself an amorphous socioeconomic phenomenon that does not exist as a homogeneous, unfragmented structure, but rather entails processes that stabilize *and* weaken its various substructures. It can therefore be argued that even where pressures from the outside dominate in these dependent states, they are rarely consistent but sometimes contradictory enough to be ignored at only a low cost or even advantageous if only perceived and exploited skillfully at the diplomatic level.

The unit of analysis of this study will be situated in three different but interactive loci of the structure of dependency: the technico-administrative (middle) class and power bloc, which is at the pivot of internal and external contradictions and which at the same time pronounces the official foreign policy line; the local bourgeoisie, i.e. its composition, its foreign policy preferences and its links with foreign capital; and international capital itself, i.e. its dynamic motion, its demands on the dependent social formation as these express themselves through the governments of the centre nations (especially the USA as the capitalist monetary hegemony) and operate through channels and institutional mechanisms such as the transnational corporations, international commercial banks and multinational financial consortia (Schubert 1985, 81–93; Mandel 1978, chap. 10; Heilbroner 1985, 94–95; Hymer 1972, 201–39). Indirectly, international capital gains and maintains access to peripheral economies through the help of international financial organizations, such as the IMF or the World Bank, which are *de facto* dominated by the powerful centre states, who themselves tend to protect bourgeois interests and bi- or multilateral free trade arrangements, such as the General Agreement on Tariffs and Trade (GATT) and the World Trade Organization (WTO).

International capital, however, is not just capital by virtue of its material properties, but rather by virtue of the social relations of dominance and subordination between the centre and peripheral nations and the relations of production therein. It is capital, as a surplus which extracts foreign investment, that retards economic development and provides the instrumental leverage for the states from where it operates to exert political influence in the dependent social formations.

The Relative Autonomy of the Peripheral State

What is the role and nature of the peripheral state within this larger picture? The state apparatus in most dependent social formations occupies a central place in the functioning of daily economic and political administration, as well as the process of development. In many countries of the periphery the state had to fill the administrative and political power vacuum that developed after the colonialists withdrew from these positions.

The question usually arises, whether the state contributed positively to overcoming the social and economic problems ensuing from dependent capitalist development, or if it served their prolongation. In other words, is the peripheral state part of the solution to the problem of dependency or rather a part of the problem itself? Dependency theories generally tend to agree that the state is indeed a part of the problem (Fagen 1983, 18; Elsenhans 1985, 141). It is at this point that the question of class antagonisms and alliances reappears in the analysis.

The objective of various dependency approaches demonstrates that the state by virtue of class alliances and antagonisms deepens capitalism in the periphery, but is unable to devise and implement strategies that would change itself or, at least, its dependent nature. Most of these approaches focus on the notion of mediation in their analyses of the structures and role of the peripheral state. An important aspect of the explanation of the nature of the peripheral state is its "relative autonomy", that is, a variable and vacillating degree of independence from the class antagonisms which permeate the state and indeed the classes which constitute its existing form. The concept of "relative autonomy" binds the study's dialectical unit of analysis into a logical unity.

As Therborn (1980, 181) pointed out, the state's specific irreducibility to extrapolitical exploitation and domination, i.e. its relative autonomy, "is governed by the problems of the relations of representation and mediation". The way these relations influence specific decisions can only be determined at the concrete level of the study of specific cases. However, the state's mediation process between its various constituencies operates according to specific modes. All these modes aim at the reproduction of the economic, political and ideological domination of the (bourgeois) ruling class and its power bloc.

Hamza Alavi is one of a few authors who have attempted to relate the nature of the peripheral state to its own peculiar class situation. His point of departure is the state as an "arena of class struggle" rather than an "actor" (Alavi 1989a, 291–92).[8] Alavi distinguishes this from Poulantzas' concept which defines the relative autonomy of the state as a consequence of conflicts within the bourgeoisie. In the context of the peripheral state he claims that this view of the state is reductionist, because it rules out "the capacity of contending *classes*, other than the 'whole' bourgeoisie to press their demands (with varying degrees of success) on the state" (Alavi 1989, 293). On the other hand Alavi correctly points out that while the metropolitan bourgeoisie tends to be more mono-lithic, the roles of different factions of the peripheral bourgeoisie tend to be mutually exclusive. Alavi's (1989a, 301–02) concept of the "over-developed state" can be seen as a useful corrective to Poulantzas' concept of relative autonomy. Indeed, the peripheral state seems to have a greater autonomy by virtue of the different audiences (alluded to above) that it has to satisfy. At the same time, it is a fallacy to conclude that this greater autonomy is anything but a formality. Primarily, it exists in substance only to the extent that the local bourgeoisie is in fundamental and open contradiction to the metropolitan bourgeoisie.

Hence, while conceding that it is in need of some adjustment, this study takes cognizance of Poulantzas' superior conceptualization of the relative autonomy of the state. Poulantzas (1974, 308; my translation) views the state's autonomy as a consequence of its relationship to the power bloc, which itself is "a contradictory unity of *dominant* classes and fractions, in which the hegemonic class or fraction dominates". However, the power bloc is divided to such an extent as to disallow its organization and integration, which would in turn allow the bourgeoisie or its dominant faction to rise to the political scene and reassert itself at this level. In this situation, it is the state which becomes the factor of the political unity of the power bloc under the custody of the ruling class or faction. It is precisely this role which allows the peripheral state to act autonomously. The actual form of this autonomy is variable and can only be determined from the analysis of the concrete phase of peripheral dependency and specific situations therein (Poulantzas 1974, 272).[9]

In order to approximate a systematic evaluation of foreign policy autonomy the following matrix (Figure 1.1) shall be applied. It charts the determinants

Figure 1.1: Determinants of degrees of relative autonomy of the dependent state

		International capital		
		Aff.	Indiff.	Non-perm.
	Aff.	n.a.	(r.a.)	r.a.
Local bourgeoisie	Ind.	(r.a.)	r.a.	(r.a.)
	N.p.	r.a.	(r.a.)	n.a.

r.a., relative autonomy

(r.a.), restricted autonomy

n.a., no autonomy

of the three basic degrees of relative autonomy that the dependent state has in particular areas. It is assumed that the degree of autonomy varies, depending on the relative importance of each issue for both the local and international bourgeoisie. Whether these determinants are perceived by the policy makers in the way that they articulate themselves is another matter. Obviously, the state's major policy makers can underestimate or even choose to ignore these determinants, but in the long run they are most likely to assert their historical force and begin to be reflected in the state's foreign relations.

The three autonomy categories derive from the dominant political mood among both the local bourgeoisie and international capital, who regard a particular policy line by a given peripheral state as desirable and in their interest (affirmative disposition); by and large, not greatly affecting their interests either positively or negatively (indifferent disposition); or detrimental or offensive to their interests as a class (non-permissive disposition). To the extent that the decision makers operate in a sense for reasons of state, the combination of these attitudes creates a corset of preconditions which circumscribe the state's room for discretionary action, the non-acknowledgment of which involves serious political costs in the medium or long run.

Along a bipolar continuum this study would then locate the following three basic autonomy degrees. "No autonomy" implies a very strong and compelling context to pursue a particular policy trajectory. This would occur as a very close and explicit agreement between international capital and the whole local bourgeoisie on a particular issue. A peripheral state's policy running against this context will sooner or later have to be terminated either voluntarily or through force.

"Restricted autonomy" points to a context in which there are only latent and comparatively weak contradictions between international capital and the local bourgeoisie, because one of them is "indifferent" towards a particular issue at stake. In this situation either the local bourgeoisie (or parts thereof), or international capital can assert their interests. However, if the state is able to mobilize the indifferent party against the other or, alternatively, demobilize the non-indifferent party it might increase its discretionary power. Vice versa, if both sides align, government finds itself in a "no autonomy" situation. Consequently, the boundary between all three categories is fluid.

"Relative autonomy" suggests relatively strong contradictions among or between international capital and the whole local bourgeoisie (or significant parts thereof) which creates a political context in which the peripheral state's regulatory function is increasingly demanded. This is necessary in order to minimize the dislocating effects of this (latent or open) conflict and to return to "normalcy". The state's intervention in such a situation might also be asked for in order to prevent a third force, i.e. populist forces or labour, from asserting itself. However, this constellation is rare and relatively unstable when it occurs. A special case of relative autonomy occurs when both international capital and the local bourgeoisie appear to be comparatively indifferent towards a particular issue which may allow the state to seize the initiative.

There is always a latent tension between the local bourgeoisie and dominant international capital which may erupt into open conflict in cases where, first, the position of the local bourgeoisie is destabilized (e.g., for social reasons or in their financial viability); second, international capital is (or is perceived to be) pushing the local bourgeoisie out of business (e.g., through dumping policies or protectionism); third, international capital is perceived by the local bourgeoisie to be vulnerable to a political offensive reducing its local influence; or fourth, a maximization of profits from an increased presence is expected. Under these conditions it may be that a strengthening of the national bourgeoisie leads to greater state autonomy vis-à-vis the international environment. Alternatively, it may be that international capital strengthens its local influence (e.g., via large scale investment; as a major creditor; through political and/or economic destabilization) which is likely to move the state to a less autonomous position since the comprador bourgeoisie will be supportive of international capital's improved position.

These re-alignments will not occur abruptly but rather take some time to develop to the point where it becomes impossible for the state to resist adapting itself to these determinants. Naturally, shifts in the sphere of production, such as technological changes, debt crises, changes in investment patterns, and new markets, take some time to mature and develop such a significance that they can no longer be ignored without negatively affecting any cost/benefit analysis at the state level.

This study then arrives at a simple model (Figure 1.2) of the dependent state's foreign policy. It has to be pointed out that relative autonomy under dependency has a different quality than the highly industrialized and more developed state's relative autonomy. Thus, it reaches a much higher plateau of restriction, i.e. more comprehensive and effective prohibitive mechanisms obstruct the dependent state's external manoeuvrability which finds its expression in the "restricted autonomy" and "no autonomy" dimensions. Assuming that every state generally attempts to maximize its utility and minimize its constraints, the proposed model suggests that the dependent state's degree of relative autonomy tends to direct its foreign policy actions to a corresponding position on a prohibitive-permissive continuum. The compulsion to adopt a particular foreign policy stance is much lower at the permissive end than at the prohibitive end where it is almost inevitable. To the extent that a dependent social formation chooses to divert its foreign policy actions from the general direction given by the corresponding degree of relative autonomy, the costs of this action are likely to increase and erode any expected long-term benefits. This erosion is effected and exacerbated by its usually subordinate position in the global economy. The sum of the actions and interactions of all social forces operating in the global and domestic economy determines the particular form and direction of a dependent state's foreign policy at a specific historical juncture.

Figure 1.2: The dependent state's foreign policy

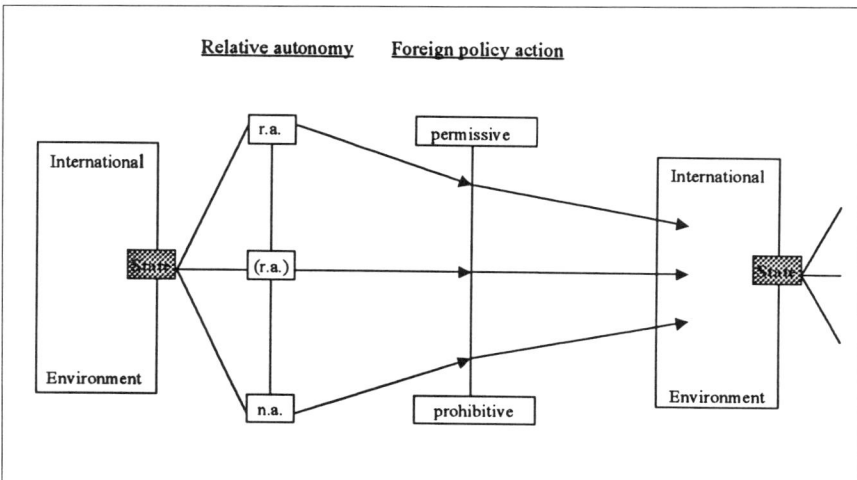

2

Internal Dynamics: 1972–1980

Government Programmes and the Constellation of Social Forces

The structural economic crisis and deterioration of living standards at the end of the 1960s was one of the main causes of the subsequent increase in social activism in Jamaica. Along with calls for more social justice and equality, an awakening of racial self-consciousness led to a greater public interest in political and cultural affairs. These developments had direct implications for the content and style of policies which would find resonance in the lower and middle strata of society. There occurred a proliferation of public anti-imperialist groups and journalism, the students were more radical and the communist movement left of the PNP was more visible (at the end of the 1970s there were two communist parties in Jamaica, the Communist Party of Jamaica (CPJ) and the Workers' Party of Jamaica (WPJ), both of which rallied only negligible support at the polls but voiced their views loudly in public).

The new PNP government which was elected in early 1972 was carried by a broad consensus and won the election with a general mandate for change. Its victory at the 1972 polls was based on the support of all classes in the Jamaican society. The strong electoral support by the lower classes indicated a greater room for autonomous government action vis-à-vis the bourgeoisie. The PNP government's composition and policies reflected the perceived and real shift in the social distribution of political power. From the start, there was a small but increasingly vocal far left faction in the PNP leadership and, after 1976, in the government. They were the main source from which the pressures for more populist policies emanated.

Both at the ideological and organizational levels the bourgeoisie was still comparatively incoherent. At the beginning of the 1970s the major private sector organizations were the Jamaica Chamber of Commerce (founded in 1779), the Jamaica Manufacturers' Association (since 1957) and the Jamaica Hotel and Tourist Association (founded in 1961); only in the course of the 1970s did the Jamaica Exporters' Association (JEA, founded in 1966) and the Private Sector Organization of Jamaica (PSOJ, founded in 1976) establish themselves as additional players among the local bourgeoisie. Due to their traditional strong influence in both parties and the state apparatus, these organizations tended to defend primarily their narrow sectoral interests, rather than formulate opinions and public statements in broader national terms (Phillips 1976, 93–119; Reid 1975). Hence, their influence on public opinion was marginal in the early 1970s. However, in the second half of the 1970s, alienated from the political process, the bourgeoisie became ideologically much more cohesive and more visible in the public debates. The government's autonomy was clearly negatively affected by this *embourgeoisement* of public opinion over pertinent economic and political issues.

The PNP's domestic programmes have been assessed by a number of authors (Kaufman 1985; Bosshard 1987; Stephens and Stephens 1986; Keith and Keith 1992) and can be said to have contributed positively to the development of the Jamaican society. However, as a point of critique it should be mentioned that various programmes were highly inefficient, due to inadequate management and/or supervision, but also due to a misunderstanding of the concept of various schemes on the part of the participants. Moreover, it appears that a number of the government's ambitious programmes (e.g. Food Farms, Special Employment Programme, free education) produced strains on the public budget. Thus, while some of these programmes could be financed at first through the additional revenues of the bauxite levy, their sustenance could only be guaranteed through higher public debt, as bauxite production decreased and the higher cost of oil imports made itself felt. The country's current account deficit rose from J$ 101.5 million in 1972 to J$ 275.2 million in 1976 and stood in 1980 at J$ 148.1 million.[1] The amount of the government's expenditure rose from J$ 471.1 million in the fiscal year 1973/74 to J$ 974.7 million in 1975/76 and stood at an unprecedented J$ 2,365.3 million in 1980/81.[2] As Levitt (1990, 5; see also Brown 1979, 6–10, 47–48 et passim) points out correctly, a financially more prudent policy would have curtailed some of these social programmes and focused on those that were efficient and socially profitable:

The failure to use the windfall gain from the bauxite levy to increase real investment in productive capacity; a rate of increase in government expenditure far in excess of the growth of revenues, resulting in the fiscal deficits of the order of 15 percent of GDP in the mid 1970s, financed largely by central bank credit; reluctance to impose tighter controls over foreign exchange transactions prior to the depletion of the country's exchange reserves in 1976, and the rhetoric of socialism and "anti-imperialism" in the context of an economy dependent on private sector confidence for investment and growth, all contributed to the economic crisis which manifested itself in the mid 1970s.

However, by this time the PNP government was so trapped in its own populist rhetoric and policies that with the upcoming elections in 1976, a socio-political "U-turn" was not considered to be feasible.[3]

After 1974 the growing public deficit was increasingly covered by borrowing from foreign private banks which in turn served to deepen the country's dependence on foreign capital. Both external borrowing and external debt grew markedly under the Manley government. Thus, the debt servicing quotient sky-rocketed from 2.9 percent in 1972 to 23.4 percent in 1979, as can be seen from Table 2.1.

The opposition of the bourgeoisie accompanied some of the government's programmes from the start. This was an instinctive reaction to the administration's attempts to break down social barriers between the classes. The upper class was opposed to the compulsory National Youth Service Programme, which they perceived as an attempt to *proletarianize* their children, and the Jamaica Manufacturers' Association (JMA) intervened on their behalf.[4]

Table 2.1: External Debt in US Dollars and External Debt Service as Percent of Exports of Goods and Services

	1971	1972	1973	1974	1975	1976	1977	1978	1979	1980
Government external borrowing	4.9	23.3	36.7	90.1	124.2	79.2	38.6	178.9	71.2	226.6
External debt	110.0	127.6	206.2	274.2	397.7	483.3	626.9	1397.8	1530.5	–
External debt service (fiscal year)	2.8	2.9	3.6	3.1	3.3	3.7	18.5	25.1	23.4*	–

*Estimate

Source: *Economic and Social Survey of Jamaica* (1975, 1976, 1979)

The ambivalence of the government's objectives regarding its domestic class relations and foreign relations was only reinforced by the contradictory variety of statements and policies coming out of the various quarters of both party and government. The single most controversial step being taken by the PNP government in autumn 1974 was the formal announcement of "democratic socialism" as the party's and government's ideological platform for the future. It was the government's intention to have a mixed economy with a "responsible" private sector (this implies a focus on what we would term the national bourgeoisie) in which the "commanding heights" would be run by an expanding public sector. This economic concept comprised a state sector operating public utilities, a cooperative sector (e.g. in the sugar industry) and a private sector operating manufacturing enterprises. The bourgeoisie's fear was not only that stigmatizing property and free enterprise might cause an unfavourable business and investment climate in the island's volatile economy, but also that expropriations and nationalization were imminent.

Towards the end of the 1970s the notion of communism in Jamaica became increasingly the focus of political opposition, which placed the government more and more on the defensive. Particularly vocal in this campaign was the local bourgeoisie. Thus, in January 1978 the eminent Jamaican business doyen (and JLP supporter) Leslie Ashenheim publicly demanded, "Fire out of the Cabinet and out of the PNP certain persons who have made plain that their goal is full Communism for Jamaica and that it is their aim to liquidate the Private Sector" (*Daily Gleaner* [hereafter *DG*], 1/1/1978, 7). A month later, Ronald Sasso from the Canadian-based Royal Bank of Jamaica Ltd warned, "I think it is time now for the private sector to launch a massive campaign to bring about a better understanding of its role in the development of Jamaica" (*DG* 17/2/1978, 11).

In early 1979, the usually conciliatory president of the Private Sector Organization of Jamaica (PSOJ), Carlton Alexander, directly warned the prime minister in an article printed on the first page of the *Daily Gleaner*, Jamaica's main newspaper, that a revitalization of the economy would become impossible, ". . . if we continue to have this fear that your Government and Party are slowly but surely linking themselves to the International Communist Movement" (*DG* 24/3/1979, 1 and 17).

Clearly, the room for autonomous manoeuvre in the government's relations to socialist countries and the Non-Aligned Movement were negatively affected by the bourgeoisie's increasing mistrust of these foreign policy ventures. The political momentum of the early 1970s was progressively eroded, as the government was put on the defensive. The refusal to sufficiently integrate

Table 2.2: Capital Inflows into Jamaica, 1970–1977 (in J$ millions)

	1970	1971	1972	1973	1974	1975	1976	1977
Capital (net)	137.1	160.7	59.9	124.5	221.7	189.9	41.9	51.7
Direct investment	234.5	146.8	21.2	20.2	20.6	1.7	-0.5	-6.4
Private long-term	3.1	7.6	10.8	68.9	101.9	72.8	10.0	4.3
Private short-term	-2.3	2.3	9.2	2.1	16.2	6.4	-37.6	59.2
Central government	-1.3	4.0	18.7	33.3	81.7	112.4	72.3	6.4

Source: Hofmann 1984, 209.

bourgeois claims into its domestic and foreign policies, however, only meant a deferment of their cumulated impact on the state's relative autonomy. Thus, its relative autonomy in the second half of the 1970s was only borrowed and the political "interest rate" rather high. But even this artificially enlarged state autonomy was not unaffected by the contradictions between the social forces, as we shall see later.

As a consequence of the combination of leftist overtures and the rejection of the IMF, the influx of capital into Jamaica started to peter out after the re-election of the PNP in 1976. Table 2.2 gives an impression of this drain.

ECONOMIC PERFORMANCE AND SOCIETAL COUNTER-STRATEGIES

One of the elements of Jamaica's economic dependence stems from its open economy. To what extent the Manley government was aware of the role of foreign investment and the pressure of the local bourgeoisie is not easy to determine. Manley has said that the PNP's foreign policy agenda in the 1970s "was very upsetting to the private sector and was one of the reasons why we had extremely bad relations with the private sector at that time."[5] One particularly negative spin-off of the PNP's emphasis on "self-reliance" was the continued priority given to import substitution at a time when this strategy had clearly reached its limits for expansion. The PNP's failure to fully appreciate the importance of exports contributed to the foreign exchange crisis which developed after the first oil crisis. However, it was not a priority of the Jamaican bourgeoisie to venture into these highly competitive markets.

Table 2.3: External Trade Quotient for Jamaica, 1972–1980 (at Current Prices)

Year	Expected ETQ	Real ETQ
1972	45.3	36.9
1973	45.1	36.0
1974	44.9	40.5
1975	44.8	40.0
1976	44.5	33.4
1977	44.4	32.1
1978	44.2	41.3
1979	44.0	48.9
1980	43.8	51.9

Source: *National Income and Product* (1981 and 1988) – author's calculations.

The extent of Jamaica's increasing integration into the world economy rather than the success of the government's proclaimed economic self-reliance, can be proved by taking Jamaica's external trade quotient (ETQ) into consideration. Jamaica had by 1972 a relatively low ETQ compared to other countries like Trinidad and Tobago with 56.4, Nicaragua with 52.0, or Taiwan with 43.5.[6] Up to 1977 (with the exception of 1974 and 1975, the year of and after the bauxite levy) there seems to have been a trend for a further decline of this already low world market integration. After 1978 we find a sharp increase, however, from 41.3 in 1978 to 51.9 in 1980.

When one contrasts the real ETQ (Table 2.3 above) with the one which is to be expected theoretically, it is apparent that Jamaica approximated this index only towards the end of the 1970s.[7] While in the early 1970s the large gap between the real and theoretical quotient was probably still due to the import substitution strategy pursued during the 1960s, the 1970s reveal a more mixed picture.

However, the clear upward trend after 1978 indicates that the way the Jamaican economy developed implied, contrary to the PNP's self-reliance rhetoric, a growing integration into the world economy.

The reaction of the bourgeoisie to the government's economic management and performance was either migration or disinvestment. Both took on crisis proportions in the second half of the 1970s. The illegal export of capital was estimated to amount to several hundred millions of dollars which, as Stephens

Table 2.4: Fixed Capital Formation in Jamaica, 1974–1980

	1974	1975	1976	1977	1978	1979	1980
Gross fixed capital formation	478.2	524.8	370.8	263.5	281.0	267.6	206.9
GDP (in purchasers' values)	2159.2	2152.6	2013.6	2013.6	1965.7	1940.5	1829.5
1% of GDP	22.1	24.4	18.4	13.4	14.2	13.8	11.3

Source: *National Income and Product* (1988, 36/37).

and Stephens (1983, 32) point out correctly, "could have made the difference in whether or not to go to the IMF" (see also McBain 1981, 102). As Table 2.4 indicates, fixed capital formation as a percentage of the gross domestic product (GDP) dropped in 1976 below the sustainable 25 percent barrier and continued to decline thereafter. Apart from the fact that the government was overspending its resources, its failure to design a coherent investment programme contributed to the financial drain of the economy. The crucial role new investments could have played in revitalizing the economic slump which made itself felt by the mid 1970s was not sufficiently perceived by the government (Brown 1979, 14).

It is useful to consider some of the broad national indicators of socioeconomic development on the basis of which one then can proceed to analyse the nature of the economy and the trends it went through during the 1970s. The most common indicator is the GDP and its composition.[8] A look at Table 2.5 indicates that in the early 1970s the growth of Jamaica's GDP began to stagnate and after 1975 a marked downward trend began. The only sectors that managed to grow during this period were the financing and insurance sector, the manufacturing sector (until 1975), the mining/quarrying sector (except in 1975, 1976 and 1979) and the agriculture/fishing/forestry sector, although the latter showed mixed results. Moreover, the government sector expanded during this period, indicating the degree to which public sector enterprises were inserted into the economy.

The progressive depletion of the resources available to the state resulted not only in further opposition from the bourgeoisie. In the context of Jamaica's clientelist political system, the failure to deliver to the electoral mass base also resulted in the withdrawal of political support from the lower classes (Edie 1986, 71–94). This had a negative effect on the state's autonomy vis-à-vis the bourgeoisie.

Table 2.5: GDP Indicators, 1970–1981

	1970	1971	1972	1973	1974	1975	1976	1977	1978	1979	1980
Real GDP per capita in J$1974	1060	1069.2	1144.3	1137.2	1076.6	1066.3	985.8	952.2	947.4	919.7	858.2
Rate of growth in % at constant prices:											
Agriculture	5.9	11.8	1.8	-6.0	1.4	-0.4	2.7	2.8	9.2	-10.9	-2.9
Mining/ quarrying	29.1	6.9	6.4	14.3	8.5	-20.2	-20.5	17.5	2.6	-1.6	10.3
Manufacturing	6.1	2.3	11.7	0.7	3.4	2.4	-4.9	-7.1	-4.9	-5.5	-12.4
Construction/ installation	20.9	0.5	-2.9	-1.7	-5.5	-1.3	-20.0	-20.8	3.6	-0.8	-30.3
Distribution (retail & wholesale)	5.6	2.8	17.0	-3.5	-16.8	2.7	-18.2	-3.9	-5.1	-4.6	-6.7
Transport/ storage/ communication	11.4	6.0	6.1	1.5	10.0	4.1	-3.7	-5.1	-0.5	0.4	-3.4
Financing/ insurance	6.4	-1.1	10.9	6.5	-0.1	1.3	2.7	6.0	0.1	-6.2	8.6
Real estate/ business services	12.8	-1.5	3.5	5.6	-2.1	3.6	0.5	1.8	-2.9	2.7	-0.3
Producers of government services	19.5	0.9	14.0	21.1	0.2	5.5	15.9	6.9	4.8	6.6	-1.2

Source: *Economic and Social Survey* (various years); *National Income and Product* (1980)

The Bauxite Levy

By 1972 a certain amount of dissatisfaction had developed with the role of the bauxite/alumina industry in the national development process and the PNP established the National Bauxite Commission, chaired by businessman Mayer Matalon, which was to concern itself with the question of increasing the state's input in this industry. By 1973 several objectives for negotiations with the companies had been worked out in detail: an increase of revenue from bauxite production, a 51 percent share in ownership of the mining operations, the repatriation of bauxite lands, the establishment of a Jamaica Bauxite Institute (JBI), the formation of a producer cartel of bauxite mining countries, and the development of an aluminium smelter complex in cooperation with Mexico and Venezuela (Manley 1982, 98). After extended and difficult negotiations, a well prepared Jamaican team failed to secure the demanded increase from the bauxite companies who apparently kept assuming that ultimately an agreement on their terms would be settled (Manley 1982, 101).[9] The government subsequently imposed the so-called Bauxite Levy unilaterally by law on May 15, 1974.

The PNP's renegotiation of the terms of the extraction of the country's main raw material was, as Manley pointed out, a matter of "national, economic interest" and therefore primarily a domestic policy (Manley 1982, 100). Nevertheless, it clearly had implications for the country's foreign relations. From the point of view of this study, however, one important fact, which is usually mentioned only *en passant*, contributed to the success of the whole renegotiation process. The tacit and open support of the national bourgeoisie was the cornerstone on which the government's freedom of bargaining and unilateral imposition of the levy ultimately rested. Indeed, the negotiations were led by two prominent members of the local business community, Mayer Matalon and Pat Rousseau. The support of the local business elite was also underscored by the attitude of the JLP Opposition which clearly supported the move. Even the conservative sector of the Jamaican print media, the *Daily Gleaner*, approved the move (see *DG* 16/5/1974, 8).

However, the support of the local bourgeoisie and also the government's receptiveness to their assistance seemed to fade by early 1977, after Manley had been re-elected with what was widely (especially among the left) perceived as a mandate to go ahead with the implementation of democratic socialism. As a consequence of the subsequently growing influence of party politics on the negotiation process which so far had "a cold analytical approach", Matalon and Rousseau resigned from the Bauxite Commission and later confessed that the national bourgeoisie, among other things, had become dissatisfied with the imprudent spending of the government (*DG* 26/2/1985, 8). As Rousseau reported, one of the reasons for by-passing him with the Soviet bauxite deal was the government's attempt to put itself in a better light by not letting capitalists negotiate with the Soviets (Rousseau 1987, 103ff).[10] Another reason was that the intraparty left had to be satisfied in their demands for stronger assertion of democratic socialist goals (see McDonald 1982).

From the perspective of this study, the negotiation of bauxite contracts for the Jamaican economy reflects not just the deep involvement of the national bourgeoisie in the foreign relations of the state. The dynamic interplay between their involvement, political shifts in the PNP leadership and the nature of the new trading partners shaped the specific way in which these negotiations were conducted. The bourgeoisie's general approval of expanded state activity in this particular sector of the economy guaranteed the state room for initiative on this specific issue. The government's subsequent attempt to sever one aspect of its foreign policy from the direct participation of members of the local bourgeoisie proved to be disadvantageous to the maximization of this specific foreign policy goal. Thus, the break-up of the original negotiation team led to a bauxite deal with the Soviet Union, the terms of which were so detrimental to Jamaica's trading interests that it had to be renegotiated.[11]

3

EXTERNAL DYNAMICS: 1972–1980

DEVELOPMENTS IN THE Global ECONOMY

Several developments in Jamaica's external environment exerted great influence on the country's economy and polity. The official termination of the fixed exchange rate for the US dollar, the first oil crisis in 1973, the worldwide recession between 1973 and 1975, the second oil crisis in 1979 and the increasing indebtedness of many structurally dependent countries were only a few of these global developments.

For international capital and the bourgeoisie, the crisis in the world economy in the early 1970s had manifold consequences. However, for analytical purposes one will have to distinguish between finance capital and productive capital. Finance capital (and the finance bourgeoisie) certainly emerged strengthened from the economic turbulence of the 1970s. The boost which the abundant availability of petro-dollars gave to the banking business in the so-called offshore facilities allowed international finance capital ever increasing levels of transnational mobility. In other words, finance capital became more and more independent of national boundaries and legislation, allowing it to shift rapidly from places it considered unfavourable for business to more profitable locations (Schubert 1985, 29–34; Gill and Law 1989, 186–88). This in turn tremendously increased competition between different social formations for this finance capital.

For national productive capital (i.e. manufacturing and service firms/enterprises) the world recession, its stagflationary tendencies and the (temporarily) increasing prices for raw materials, certainly meant that it would be more keenly watching its own interests, which in turn meant more rationalization, unemployment, and above all, a stronger call for protectionist measures. In April 1972, US President Nixon initiated a comprehensive new trade act which allowed improvement of the deteriorating US trade balance through the imposition of import restrictions (Sweezy and Magdoff 1973, 11–12; Tancer 1976, 93).[1]

Transnational productive capital was in a somewhat intermediary position. Although it was also affected by the recession, its high horizontal and vertical mobility allowed it to react in a very flexible way by relocating and/or diversifying its production. Therefore it was able to effectively circumvent geographical, structural or cyclical disincentives.[2] This, in turn, made it increasingly sensitive to measures restricting transnational mobility, as it relied more and more on international freedom of movement. However, its fixed assets would not allow it to shift its activities as easily as finance capital. Thus, a second strategy of the Nixon administration was to give stronger incentives for increasing foreign investments by American enterprises, which seemed to contradict efforts to halt the deterioration of the US dollar. Apparently it was expected that profits made abroad would compensate for this. To the extent that international capital strengthened during the 1970s, the limitations on labour, restricted by national jurisdiction in its mobility and bargaining strength, became more and more evident.

Although the process cannot be said to have been straightforward, the increasing transnationalization of finance capital and productive capital motivated the political elites of the industrial world to increasingly press for liberal trade agreements and codes for investment and profit transfers. Thus, in October 1976, William E. Simon, in his function as the US governor of the World Bank and IMF, warned:

The American partnership with developing countries and development prospects of all countries depends . . . on our trade and investment links. The world-wide demands for capital in the period ahead will be massive and the competition fierce. Countries which wish to attract investment capital will find that establishing the proper domestic climate is essential. Countries which raise impediments to capital flows will not be able to meet the competition.

And, repeating one of his standard formulae:

Development assistance should be thought of, not as an international welfare program to redistribute the world's wealth, but as an important international investment program to increase the rate of economic growth in developing countries . . . (International Bank for Reconstruction and Development et al. 1976, 189–190).

This policy line was also pursued by the industrial countries in the Tokyo round of the GATT negotiations which were concluded in 1979. This implied that industrial countries place the onus of development on economic production and de-emphasize the role of other factors (e.g. human resource development, technology transfer and social care) as preconditions for both growth and improvement of general living conditions.

The New Assertiveness of the "Third World"

By the beginning of the 1970s a new determination to grow economically started to emerge in the developing countries (Rothstein 1977, chap. 5; Opitz 1984, 11–44). The conventional economic wisdom in the countries of the South at that time emphasized the importance of self-reliance and South-South cooperation. The subsequent process of political amalgamation of a comparatively large number of countries from all regions of the developing world culminated in their demand for a New International Economic Order (NIEO), which was pressed for in a UN resolution of May 1974 and a plethora of international conferences.

However, negotiations in international conferences between North and South made only very slow progress. The negotiations were impaired by several logical inconsistencies and tactical shortcomings on the side of the Third World. In the view of one informed observer, one of the biggest problems in the negotiation process was exactly the point on which the Non-Aligned Movement (NAM) and the Group of 77 prided themselves most, namely their unity (Rothstein 1979, 155–56 and 271). This situation, however, seemed to give rise to an inbuilt radicalization mechanism, for only extreme and comprehensive demands promised something to everyone. The initial preparedness of developed industrial countries to negotiate some selected items vanished, as they became increasingly aware of the extent of the South's intransigence and, especially, the deterioration of the latter's bargaining position.

Observing these counter-rotating tendencies in the bargaining process and keeping in mind the development in the global economy, one can safely conclude that towards the end of the 1970s there occurred a convergence of positions between the political representatives of international capital and what seemed to become an increasingly "de-nationalized", and hence transnationalizing, bourgeoisie in the Third World. The political and ideological platform of this merger was the reformed old international economic order based on neoliberal free-market principles and the notion of "interdependence" (a favourite phrase of US representatives) and its corollaries (Amin 1977, 20).

Détente and Confrontation

After the predominance of intense political and military tensions between the former World War II allies, the USSR and the USA, there occurred a slow and measured warming of relations at the beginning of the 1970s. On the international scene, the Soviet involvement in the liberation war in Angola posed, for many American policy makers, a problem for the continuation of the détente process, although it was not so high a priority as to threaten the substantial US grain sales to the Soviet Union at that time.

However, the new foreign policy approach adopted by the Carter administration promised not only to continue détente but, actually, to expand its geographical and political width and depth. President Carter's insistence on human rights and a case by case evaluation of each country's specific circumstances as new cornerstones of US Third World policy were widely welcomed and interpreted as the beginning of a new phase in North-South political relations. Thus, it was the rule rather than the exception that administration officials throughout 1977 echoed, in one or the other form, Carter's publicly expressed intention "to win the friendship of nations that in the past have not been close to us who may have been heavily influenced by or very closely friendly with the Soviet Union and who may still be" (quoted in Garthoff 1985, 634). This was, of course, a most promising but equally deceiving statement.

There would have been sufficient reason to be suspicious of the US reclamation of her "city-upon-the-hill morality" in international affairs; thus, the two-sidedness of the Carter administration's approach became increasingly apparent. Indeed, due to congressional sentiment and the opposition of the American Bar Association, the US did not embrace those documents on economic and social rights of most concern to the majority of UN and Organization of American States (OAS) member states (Vogelgesang 1980, 184). As such, Carter's "newly detected morality" had both a domestic and an external dimension:

The lack of labor-backed opposition and the integration of labor bureaucracy within the capitalist system preclude anything but symbolic, 'moralistic' changes. From the viewpoint of the corporate ruling class, this is the cheapest and most effective fashion for avoiding any challenges to their authority and profits. On the contrary, the 'moralism' abroad is an effective distraction from problems at home. Both serve to buttress corporate authority while attempting to provide an apparently new basis for political authority (Petras 1977, 48; Herman 1978, 43; Brzezinski 1973, 712).

Towards the end of the 1970s, US neoconservatives actually managed to appropriate the moralistic rhetoric of the liberals and employ it for the promotion of their own interventionist agenda (Ajami 1978, 452; Bauer 1976, 31–38; Petras 1980, 15–27).

The Continuing Relevance of Cuba: American Angst and Caribbean Aspirations

From a political and ideological point of view, Cuba was widely perceived in the US as posing a destabilizing threat to its plurally organized society with its emphasis on individual liberty.[3] Cuba's socialist ideology was perceived as the antithesis of the "American way of life" and the existing hegemonic order in the region, which *ipso facto* meant a negation of US hemispheric hegemony.

From the viewpoint of international capital, and specifically the US bourgeoisie, the Cuban revolution had a slightly different significance. The social and economic implications of the Cuban development model, her successful (albeit only through Soviet help) withdrawal from the capitalist world economy, and, in the 1960s, her revolutionary/subversive activities in the Caribbean and Central America were, from this perspective, of far greater importance than any political and national security concerns (Stavrianos 1981, 752).

The determination of the US to suppress the rise of a "second Cuba", and thereby limit its attractiveness as an alternative development model, provided strong political motives for interventionist action throughout the 1960s and 1970s. Several regional developments in the second half of the 1970s contributed to a hardening of President Carter's initially "dovish" foreign policy. Although his policy was somewhat ambivalent when the Nicaraguan Sandinistas finally ousted dictator Anastasio Somoza, it was ultimately guided by traditional goals of US policy in Central America, i.e. the maintenance of internal and regional order and keeping any Soviet-Cuban influence from spreading (Chace 1985, 75–80). A situation similar to that in Nicaragua seemed to develop in El Salvador where an illegitimate military government was under siege from several revolutionary guerrilla movements, which toward the end of the decade followed Castro's advice to form a united front. Here, too, the Carter administration supported the status quo, as well as its defenders in the military and among the big landowners. Finally, in the Caribbean, the Grenadian revolution in 1979 boosted Cuban influence in the region, which in Washington's perception, established the third pillar of an intolerable "red triangle" in the Central American/Caribbean region. Without doubt, these developments in the mid to late 1970s gradually changed US perceptions and policies to a position of zero tolerance towards any socialist experiments in its sphere of interest.

4

CARIbbEAN TÊTE-À-TÊTE: JAMAicA ANd CubA

Jamaica's relationship with Cuba evoked much attention and emotion from political and economic observers and decision makers at both the domestic and the external levels. The issue led to intense disputes, the arguments of which were regularly warped by subliminal political antipathies and manifest utterances of disdain, which increasingly prohibited the rational exchange of arguments and a fair acknowledgement of the other side's point of view. This dialogue of the deaf elevated the essentially quite plain and sober relationship with Jamaica's neighbour to a level where Cuba became a mere metaphor for a wider political credo. The ensuing situation created great damage for Jamaica's foreign relations *in toto*, but also served to distort the proper implementation of domestic political and socioeconomic programmes. Indeed, it is no exaggeration to say that the issue of Cuba was the most critical and controversial of all the Manley government's foreign policy ventures in the 1970s.

OVERTURE: RApprochEMENT

In an act of coordinated foreign policy, the governments of Jamaica, Barbados, Trinidad and Tobago and Guyana established diplomatic relations with Cuba on December 8, 1972. Initially it seemed that, for the new PNP government, entertaining relations with Cuba was mainly a "Third World affair". In his first budget speech Manley had affirmed that:

. . . Jamaica is a part of the Third World and to me and to us, the Third World is not a matter of political ideology but of economic survival . . . We will go boldly into the Third World, retaining our traditions and friends and committed to our systems but determined to build bridges of understanding between the Third World with which we are going to be associated and of which we are a part.[1]

This wider view of Third World identity and solidarity was also to be introduced into regional fora. Thus, Jamaica sent an early signal to the OAS about what her guidelines regarding intra-regional affairs and, implicitly, her relationship with Cuba would be. As the Minister of State (with special responsibility for foreign policy) in the Prime Minister's Office, Dudley Thompson, pointed out to the OAS early after the election which brought the PNP into power:

If the Organisation of American States is not now to abandon its original ideal . . . it must decide afresh what its relationship will be in the immediate future to those countries in the hemisphere of different ideological persuasions or which are choosing different forms of social organisation. The question whether a particular American state should have restored to it full rights and responsibilities within the Organisation is entirely distinct from the question whether the Organisation of American States should assume the right to determine for its members what diplomatic relations they may establish or maintain with any other state. There are dangers in the tendency to treat them both as one (*DG* 20/4/1972, 10).[2]

After Jamaica had restored her diplomatic relationship with Cuba, the US State Department indicated that it had a different opinion. Stating that it found the OAS embargo on Cuba still necessary and that individual countries should not engage in diplomatic relations with Cuba outside of the OAS, it deplored the step of the three OAS members (Guyana was not a member of the OAS) as an "unfortunate development" (*DG* 14/12/1972, 1 and 8).[3] It is noteworthy, however, that since 1973, the OAS embargo was increasingly being circumvented, transforming it more or less into an insubstantial policy. At this time, even the US Department of Commerce granted US firms in Argentina permission to export to Cuba (Mesa-Lago 1979, 215).

In May 1973, a Cuban delegation under the Deputy Minister of External Affairs visited Jamaica for discussions on the improvement of relations and an evaluation of an earlier exchange of agricultural experts. A highly symbolic event in this year, which attracted a lot of attention and criticism, was Manley's acceptance of an invitation to travel with Castro to the NAM summit in Algiers (in September) in the Cuban president's private jet. With regard to the bourgeoisie, public objections to the trip came mainly from the Jamaica Manufacturers' Association (JMA) which, however, focused its criticism mainly on Manley's offer in Algiers to symbolically support African liberation struggles with volunteer fighters and money (J$ 50,000) (*DG* 13/9/1973, 1).[4] It has to be understood that the close relationship with Cuba emanated almost completely from Manley who eventually developed a very friendly relationship with Fidel Castro. Thus, the decision to fly to Algier was entirely Manley's own and did not come as a result of consultation with the party leadership.[5]

Despite Manley's attempt to explain his decision to the bourgeoisie, the trip led to a first rift between the government and the bourgeoisie. Manley had assigned his special assistant O.K. Melhado, one of the principals in one of the eminent business families in Jamaica, to convince the president of the JMA (Douglas Vaz) that the fact of his travelling with Castro did not make him a communist. However, he did not find the support he had hoped for. Indeed, the trip apparently contributed to Vaz's decision to withdraw his PNP membership and join the JLP.[6]

The Warming of Relations between Jamaica and Cuba

In spring 1974, the relationship with Cuba started to intensify. In retrospect, it appears as if the entire pattern of future actions and reactions was set out in the first few months of this year. Upon the Cuban ambassador's taking office in Kingston in January 1974 (i.e. *before* the announcement of democratic socialism in Jamaica), the *Daily Gleaner* published an article which considered the possibility of a communist coup d'état in Jamaica (*DG* 28/1/1974, 10 and 19).[7] Considering the extremely low profile of the relationship at that point in time, this comment was certainly grossly out of proportion and raises legitimate questions about the newspaper's observation of the journalistic code of ethics at this point in time.

During this period, the US were trying to improve their relations with Latin America and for this purpose had convened a conference with the intention to promote a "new spirit". It was at this particular meeting that Jamaica came forward with a rather undiplomatic and untimely statement which attacked US Secretary of State Kissinger personally for his intolerant attitude towards Cuba. The statement, issued by Dudley Thompson, a man of distinctly leftist convictions, complained that Kissinger had not commented on Cuba which he, Thompson, had "demanded, not asked"; the exact, and quite blunt, wording of the statement was: "Cuba is a four letter word as far as this conference is concerned. To ignore Cuba is sheer stone-age stupidity. Jamaica refuses to join anyone who takes an ostrich stance" (*DG* 24/2/1974, 1).

The mere fact of the establishment of closer relations with the Castro regime created new external constraints for the Jamaican government at this early stage, as was to be seen by the public statement of the conservative and US influenced Inter-American Press Association, which asked the prime minister to "initiate whatever efforts he might deem feasible for gaining the freedom of . . . political prisoners, especially of the newspaper men . . ." (*DG* 6/4/1973, 2). Thus, it was brought home to the government quite clearly and early that subsequently it could hardly avoid becoming entangled in contentious human rights questions, such as the freedom of the press and political prisoners in Cuba.

During 1974, several bilateral meetings discussed and subsequently agreed on various technical cooperation and exchange programmes. Cuban assistance took the form of establishing operations of Air Cubana through Jamaica; sending technical personnel and equipment for the construction of a micro-dam scheme in the rural areas; providing doctors and medical personnel to serve in Jamaica; construction of four gift schools; providing language training and training in construction as well as a large number of scholarships in several fields (*DG* 27/2/1974, 1; *DG* 28/2/1974, 2). Jamaica, in turn, supplied Cuba with technical information on agriculture, coffee and cocoa seeds, semen from Jamaican Hope Bulls and information on the processing of sugar, among other things.

According to a report from the Jamaica National Planning Agency, the technical assistance received in 1976/77 amounted to a significant J$ 3,179,400.[8] However, the costs to Jamaica of taking advantage of the exchange programme with Cuba were comparatively high, at J$ 1,825,697.[9]

Despite several talks between both countries in order to identify trading possibilities with Cuba, no significant trading developed. To a large extent this was due to punitive legislation in the US. To the local bourgeoisie this must inevitably have signalled that, from an economic point of view, the relationship with Cuba would be negligible. The low level of economic exchange indicated the extent to which the relationship with Cuba was of *political* significance to the PNP government. In Table 4.1, the exact level of bilateral trade is set out. By and large, trade had developed unevenly and the export of Jamaican products to Cuba gathered some momentum only after 1975. Considering that the level of exports to Cuba as a percentage of all exports to the (relatively insignificant) non-Commonwealth Caribbean averaged only a minuscule 3.2 percent, it is tempting to conclude that Jamaica-Cuban trade in the 1970s was virtually nonexistent.

In 1975, some major developments marked the definite ending of the "take-off phase" in Jamaica-Cuban relations. In July of that year, the Jamaican

Table 4.1: Trade between Jamaica and Cuba (1972–1980), in J$

Year	Imports	Exports	Balance of visible trade	Exports as % of total domestic exports to non-Commonwealth Caribbean
1972	16.800	56,982	40,182	n.a.
1973	n.a.	6,282	6,282	1.2
1974	1,822,390	94,875	-1,726,215	1.9
1975	2,097,193	249,800	-1,809,424	4.7
1976	914,633	126,827	-752,020	1.9
1977	39,436	933,357	924,187	12.1
1978	5,176,301	633,045	-4,436,152	4.2
1979	6,413,579	410,144	-5,352,026	0
1980	1,622,151	511,916	-342,301	2.4

1) Without re-exports

Sources : External Trade (Dept. of Statistics), various years; various monthly Summary Tables of
        Tables of External Trade (Dept. of Statistics)

prime minister was the third Commonwealth Caribbean Head of Government to visit Cuba, following visits of Prime Ministers Burnham and Williams. On this occasion the Cubans conferred their highest national order on Manley, who took the opportunity to speak of the "natural alliance between Jamaica and Cuba in international affairs", an interesting utterance which will be addressed later (Manley 1975). In the joint communiqué Jamaica expressed, besides the anti-imperialist, anti-capitalist, non-aligned and national liberation rhetoric, for the first time publicly outside the UN, her support for Puerto Rican self-determination, a particularly sensitive issue with the US. In the UN, the issue had been on the agenda again since 1972 and in this forum diplomatic treatment of this issue enjoyed the sheltering aura of legitimacy qua UN item. However, to support this issue outside the UN and in close cooperation with the Cubans would certainly have aroused attention and consternation in Washington. For the Cubans, the reference to Puerto Rico meant support for an issue of their foreign policy agenda which was at that time in danger of losing its forcefulness. Since it had been reintroduced into the UN mainly as a consequence of their own initiative, it was in danger of becoming too closely identified with the Cuban government (Linsley 1979, 125).

During his trip the Jamaican prime minister also made negative references to capitalism, equating its historic role with that of a handyman of colonialism (*DG* 13/7/1975, 1). This was likely to have repercussions within the Jamaican private sector. About a fortnight after the prime minister's return, the president of the new Jamaica Exporters' Association (JEA), Winston Mahfood, publicly criticized the prime minister's statements made in Cuba, indicating that the initial climate of confidence between the private sector and the government "is now weakened": "We cannot help but note . . . that references made in Cuba in the last two weeks by our Prime Minister have created a situation in Jamaica where a part of the private sector is frightened, worried, uncomprehending and deeply concerned" (*DG* 26/7/1975, 1).

The Question of Cuban Troops in Angola

Before the year ended, the government came to face what can be regarded as its single most difficult and momentous political decision regarding Jamaica's international relations during that period – the question of whether to support the presence of Cuban troops in Angola. The liberation struggle in this country, which was becoming a full-fledged civil war, had been in the making for years but reached its peak in mid 1975, when the interference of several foreign countries on behalf of one or the other of the three liberation movements intensified. The involvement of Cuban troops in Angola had the greatest international repercussions and ultimately tipped the balance in favour of the Marxist Popular Movement for the Liberation of Angola (MPLA).

As Valdés (1979, 88) has pointed out, Cuba had developed after the revolution a foreign policy concept of "integral coexistence" which stipulated that all states should live in peaceful coexistence.[10] A precondition for this, however, was that Third World nations be free and independent of interference from the industrial states and that the latter recognize the rights of the former. This principle would entail Cuban solidarity with the oppressed and active support for liberation movements. The Cuban involvement in Angola was no new feature in her foreign policy as was so often contended. In fact, Cuba had supported the MPLA since the early 1960s and especially after 1970. However, the magnitude which the Cuban military involvement reached in late 1975/early 1976 had not been attained before.

In the "balance-of-power mind" of US Secretary of State Henry Kissinger, Angola became a geostrategic litmus test in which an internally and externally battered US would have to reassert her determination to exert influence and leadership as a world power and, more specifically, to prove that even under US-Soviet détente, she would not allow the other side to take advantage of geopolitical inattention and/or domestic politico-military moods of retention (Robbins 1983, 213).[11] For the US, Angola had implications for the process of détente which was then under way, if temporarily stalled. In his autobiography, written several years later, Kissinger (1979, 1257) was still not willing or able to view Angola outside of a Cold War context and charged the Soviet Union with "aggressiveness and adventurism in Angola".

According to several well informed observers, there was a very strong possibility that the United States may have encouraged South Africa "to come on the side of UNITA (indeed, South Africa believed it had a promise of US military and economic help)" (Hanlon 1986, 154).[12] Indeed, Kissinger and other officials in the State Department admitted later that both countries had exchanged "intelligence data", which was not denied by the expansionist South African apartheid regime (Marcum 1978, 271). Valdés' (1979, 99; see also Hanlon 1986, 154) concise summation is therefore entirely correct: "The interests of Zaire, South Africa, the FNLA, UNITA and the United States were the same: to defeat the MPLA."

Through the summer of 1975 military aid continued to flow to all movements, with the US, South Africa, China and some Western states supporting the FNLA and UNITA, and the Soviet Union supplying the MPLA. Although the respective amounts will probably never be determined exactly, it has been stated that "there was no significant difference in the amount of outside assistance to the two sides (MPLA versus FNLA/UNITA) between July and October" (Marcum 1978, 263).

Already in late spring 1975, Cuba had reportedly begun to send military advisers to MPLA training camps inside Angola. Castro possibly imparted some of the details to Manley during his July visit in Havana. However, at this point in time there was no need yet for Jamaica to take an official stance in favour of one or the other movement. Indeed, it would have been an act of premature recognition to embrace officially any of the three movements before Angolan independence from Portugal had been gained (which was planned for November 11, 1975).

The situation changed, however, when the South African army started to occupy Angolan territory near the Namibian border, especially in October when they started an offensive which threatened to overthrow the then dominant MPLA movement. Around May 1975, the FNLA and UNITA leaders had contacted South Africa, an alliance which translated into an active military coalition during August. On August 9, South African troops took positions inside Angola and proceeded to move forward in early September. On October 14, South Africa started her offensive on the capital Luanda towards which they subsequently moved at a fast pace. In the North, the FNLA attacked with the support of South African weaponry. By mid November, FNLA/UNITA/South African troops were close to Luanda where the MPLA had set up a government on November 11 (just as the UNITA and FNLA had done). Around or on November 5, the Cuban government decided to respond to a plea by the MPLA to send regular combat troops to resist the two rival movements fighting alongside the South African white supremacists' army. From November 7, Cuba began airlifting troops from Havana to Luanda, at a time when the MPLA was rapidly approaching its military defeat.[13]

An important question is whether the Cuban government was in fact responding to the legitimate call for help by a legitimate government. Certainly the MPLA had during the summer commanded authority and control of viable parts of Angola, including the capital, basically on the grounds of its own superior organizational and infrastructural capabilities. But this did not yet mean that the two other movements, on strict principles of international law, could be discounted. However, from a moral and political point of view one could argue that their pact with the internationally isolated, racist regime in Pretoria had disqualified them from their legitimate claim. On the grounds of this argument, this study tends to agree with those who would argue that the MPLA constituted the de facto government (see Valdés 1979, 103).

The question of Cuban planes on their way to Angola refueling in Barbados indicated for the first time that the pro-Cuban "lobby group" in the Caribbean (i.e. Barbados, Guyana, Jamaica and Trinidad and Tobago) had started to break up. On December 17, the Barbadian government stated that it could no longer "countenance use of its territory for the purpose of interference in the internal affairs of Angola" (*DG* 18/12/1975, 1). Two days later, the Trinidad and Tobago government rejected a Cuban request to allow its planes to refuel and informed the Cubans that it "will not under any circumstances intervene in Angola's affairs or contribute to the intervention by any country into Angola's affairs" (*DG* 20/12/1975, 1; Jones 1979, 135–36). Hence, both governments strongly repudiated Cuba's involvement in Angola.

Towards the end of December, the Jamaican government found itself pressed to make a decision on whether or not to adopt an explicit, official stance towards the question of Angola and the Cuban role there. The question as it presented itself was two pronged; first, what would be the official position of the government regarding the role of the MPLA and second, would it condone the involvement of the Cuban military (fighting, as it was, with Soviet military equipment)? As it approached the decision, the government, which had just reaffirmed its excellent relationship with Cuba, found itself exposed to mounting domestic criticism coming from the conservative sector of the printed media and the opposition (*DG* 24/12/1975, 8; *DG* 19/12/1975, 1; *DG* 2/12/1975, 10; *DG* 3/11/1975, 1 and 2).

Some PNP left wingers who had just returned from the Cuban Communist Party's Congress in Havana opened the public debate. In a public statement there (which was later carried by the *Daily Gleaner*), the PNP's secretary general, D.K. Duncan, had expressed the party's support for both aspects of the Angola question. In a carefully worded statement he declared:

The People's National Party (PNP) considers the MPLA as a genuine liberation movement. We think it has the right to fight for freedom and to ask for assistance from any source . . . The PNP, as distinct from the Jamaica government, is totally opposed to the entry of South Africa into internal affairs of Angola and opposed to the role by the United States and Central Intelligence Agency (CIA) in Angola.

He had also expressed ". . . total support to (*sic*) the position of Cuba to help our brothers of Africa fight for the liberation of Angola" (*DG* 27/12/1975, 1). This was, of course, a *party* statement expressing mainly the sentiments of the party left. Different opinions from within the PNP were not publicly voiced and hence it can be said that the left wing had occupied the PNP's position in the public debate.[14] This was also evident in the presence of an MPLA "team" which had accompanied Duncan and Senator Arnold Bertram (parliamentary secretary in the Prime Minister's Office) from Cuba to Jamaica. Apparently, a deliberate attempt was made by the party left wing to coax the government into pursuing the direction it desired. Thus, the PNP left took a quite unorthodox step by drafting a resolution addressed to the government in a public meeting of several left organizations (e.g. the PNP Youth Organization; WLL; Rastafarians). This popular resolution, 'framed and passed unanimously', reflected the MPLA's request and can be seen as an example of the PNP's left wing trying to corner the government on a question of foreign relations, through pressure from the street (*DG* 29/12/1975, 1).[15]

The publicly displayed cautiousness of the Jamaican government (as well as of the PNP representatives receiving and presenting the MPLA team publicly) to distinguish between government and party, and not to evoke the impression that representatives of the government had received the MPLA, had primarily two reasons. First, US Secretary of State Kissinger had arrived on December 26 in the island for a private holiday and was due to consult with high-ranking government officials.[16] Second, an official reception of the MPLA would have been interpreted as a tacit recognition of one of the contending forces in

Angola.[17] The second point is significant, in so far as Kissinger must have been aware of the MPLA's Caribbean tour for recognition, and would have felt particularly embarrassed by the Jamaican government, if it had officially received them and thereby recognized the MPLA de facto.[18]

However, this cautious approach was soon abandoned when on January 1, 1976, the Office of the Prime Minister issued a statement regarding the visit of the MPLA delegation. This statement doubtlessly has to be read as the definite de facto recognition of the MPLA as the legitimate government of Angola. The prospect of technical cooperation which was offered implies that the government was expecting to assume diplomatic relations with the "People's Republic of Angola". Admitting for the first time now that the MPLA delegation had "very friendly and useful discussions with Prime Minister Michael Manley and other government leaders", the statement embraced the MPLA, although stopping short of explicit recognition:

A friendly delegation of the MPLA of the People's Republic of Angola visited Jamaica from December 24–28 . . . The delegation received assurances of friendship and sympathy for the great struggle in which the MPLA is engaged. Both sides vigorously condemned the continued intervention of South Africa in Angola . . . Initial discussions were held on future technical co-operation between Angola and Jamaica, and it was agreed that early in 1976, a meeting be held between representatives of Angola and Jamaica to finalize a technical co-operation agreement (*DG* 1/1/1976, 1).[19]

With the de facto recognition of the MPLA as effective government of Angola, the government had cleared a logical obstacle to the support of Cuba's military presence in Angola. The justification of their presence there might have been questionable if the MPLA was not recognized as the legitimate government.

After the government had de facto recognized the MPLA, the prime minister had talks with US Secretary of State Henry Kissinger, who had already been in Jamaica for several days already. No substantial information was released for the public about the contents of the talks except that they were "friendly" (*DG* 4/1/1976, 1). It should be mentioned at this point that the position of the US government had been complicated by the refusal of Congress to grant further aid to the FNLA or UNITA. Manley revealed later that he was pressed very subtly by Kissinger who apparently said that "he would appreciate it if Jamaica would at least remain neutral" on the question of Cuban military involvement in Angola (Manley 1982, 116). To this, Manley replied that the government was still in the process of gathering information, monitoring the effects of both the South African and Cuban armies, as well as trying to determine the view of the African states. He further stressed the Jamaican government's concern about the fact that South Africa had invaded Angola. Afterwards, Manley recalls, Kissinger raised Jamaica's request for a one hundred million dollar credit and said somewhat ambiguously that the US would be looking at it.

By this time, the Jamaican private sector had started to express objections to what it perceived as a revalorization of the Jamaica-Cuba relationship. The issue that the private sector began to publicly comment on at this point is noteworthy, for it is a good indicator of the extent to which the state's relative autonomy over foreign policy began to be directly affected. In late December, the conservative media had already expressed its view that the government should "wait until the civil war in Angola is resolved before recognizing the group which is in control of the government then, be it Communist or non-Communist" (DG 30/12/1976,10). In January, the president of the Jamaican Chamber of Commerce, Winston Meeks, expressed his objection to the Jamaican involvement in the Angola issue (DG 21/1/1976, 1 and 21).

In mid-January, the JMA knocked that aspect of the technical assistance agreement which provided that 280 Cuban construction workers would come to Jamaica. The manufacturers saw "no necessity" for this provision, while there was unemployment in the construction industry (DG 16/1/1976, 1). This critique was later reiterated by the JMA and reinforced with the demand to renegotiate the agreement: "While tens of thousands of highly trained, highly skilled Jamaican workers are unemployed, the JMA calls on the Government to re-negotiate this gift and utilise Jamaican labour to build the school" (DG 24/1/1976,1 and 2). However, the sincerity of this critique is reasonably questionable. No employer in a capitalist system of production is really interested in the elimination of unemployment, as long as it does not reach the level where it threatens the stability and smooth operation of his or her individual business or the whole economic system as such. Not very surprisingly, neither of the two large Jamaican trade unions spoke out in favour of securing 280 (temporary) jobs for Jamaican workers. It seems, therefore, that the JMA's argument was crafted in order to drive a wedge into what tended to be perceived more and more as a Cuban-PNP/labour movement coalition: "The JMA has no intention of standing by and watching fuel being added to the current raging social and economic fires" (DG 24/1/1976, ibid.).[20]

Despite this criticism, which was given broad coverage in the Daily Gleaner, the Jamaican government expressed its support for Cuba's action in Angola publicly. In February, Foreign Minister Thompson expressed his gratitude to Cuba, calling Cuba's help a "salvation". He also characterized Castro as "one of the greatest men of our life-time" who was already absolved by history (DG

21/2/1976, 1). On March 2, the prime minister's response to a question in Parliament as to whether the presence of Cuban troops in Angola was interference in the internal affairs of that country, was that he would "not regard that as interference" (*DG* 4/3/1976, 1 and 18). Apparently aware that this brief answer might only invite more probing questions in future, the government found itself pressed to issue a clarification the next day. On this occasion it finally came out publicly with an explicit statement on its position on Cuba's presence in Angola. It did so by putting it in the context of the perceived sequence of events in Africa:

All the evidence available to us makes it clear that Cuban troops are present in Angola at the specific and open invitation of the MPLA which is recognised by the majority of African states as the legitimate Government of Angola. The evidence available to us makes it quite clear that South African troops invaded Angola on October 23, 1975, and had advanced to within striking distance of Luanda, the capital of the country . . .

The evidence available to us indicates that the Cuban troops assisted our black brothers in Angola to defeat the forces of the white racist regime of South Africa, thereby removing the threat of a disastrous extension and expansion of white supremacist power in South Africa. On basis of these facts, the Cuban presence in Angola is neither clandestine nor subversive . . . (*DG* 5/3/1976, 1 and 21).

Several inferences can be drawn from this statement. First, the government was apparently aware that it had not yet explicitly and *de jure* recognized the MPLA as a legitimate government, which consequently weakened its attempt to legitimize the Cuban involvement. It therefore had to point out that the MPLA is recognized by "the majority of African states". Thereby, of course, it suppressed the fact that the MPLA had not been the legitimate government at the time, when it extended the "specific and open invitation" to Cuba.

Second, considering this objective situation, a logical consequence to an admission of this legal fact would have demanded that the government take either of two positions: either reject both South African/Zairian and Cuban involvement as foreign interference or admit that South Africa's presence in Angola was on the same illegal basis as the Cuban military presence. This logical quandary, however, was solved "politically", first by stating that South Africa had "invaded" the country (which was correct in so far as South Africa had sent regular combat troops into Angola before regular Cuban combat troops entered Angola), and second, by drawing upon South Africa's morally and diplomatically isolated international position due to her brutal, racist suppression of the black majority of South African people through apartheid.

Third, although the statement above is certainly explicit enough to be called open support for the Cubans, it again stopped short of saying precisely this in unambiguous terms.

The political artifice pointed out above became obvious when the Opposition called Manley's attention to the point that the MPLA had been only one of three contending liberation movements at the time when they asked the Cubans for assistance. Manley's response to this, again avoiding the issue of the legal implications, was:

There were in fact three groups. Two of these groups had *made a deal* with South Africa to have white South Africa coming to assist them to consolidate their position. Therefore we regard the assistance that Cuba gave to anti-apartheid forces of the MPLA as honourable and in the best interest of all those who care for African freedom and above all freedom from white supremacy rule (*DG* 5/3/1976, ibid. – emphasis added).

The somewhat colloquial language of this statement reflects the government's difficulty in justifying its position *on strictly legal grounds*. Following Manley's statement to Parliament in which he supported Cuba's role in Angola, the government evidently perceived the necessity to recognize the MPLA *de jure*, which it did a few days after.

The above argument does not cast doubt on the fact that, both politically and morally, the Jamaican government was perfectly right in taking a supportive stance for Cuba and the MPLA. There is no way that the international community could condone expansionist schemes of fascist and racist regimes on the basis of technico-legal interpretations of international conventions or formal positions of non-alignment. However, the legal and technical implications, as well as their relevance for the diplomatic style in which a specific position is expressed, have to be discussed. Another aspect is, of course, that after 15 years of MPLA rule Angola had still not found peace, but in the early 1990s found itself in a situation where it had to put half of its yearly export earnings (more than US $2 billion) towards a civil war with the US-backed UNITA forces of Jonas Savimbi (*South*, June 1990, 77–79).

Looking at the chronology of the recognition of the MPLA and the support for Cuba, the following can be said. The analysis has revealed that in both instances the government did issue its position somewhat reluctantly and only gradually. The government's support was clearly not as unequivocal, spontaneous and outspoken as the party's support, especially that of the left wing. With regard to the recognition of the MPLA, it seemed that it was the visit of an MPLA team in Jamaica that tipped the balance to come out in indirect and de facto support of this movement. Public support for Cuba was only given very tentatively, after Foreign Minister Thompson, in an interview with Cuban journalists, had characterized Cuba's help as "salvation".

There seems to have been a point in the decision making process when it was no longer possible to avoid support of this issue. Thus, rather than the emphatic defence of principles as Manley and others tried to depict it later, Jamaica's public support for the MPLA and the Cuban presence in Angola was largely due to "mishaps" (Manley 1982, 116). Indeed, as a consequence of Duncan's statement in Cuba, which indicated that the party supported Cuba's presence in Angola, the Cabinet was "very upset".[21] Contrary to Manley's own account (see above), it appears that Kissinger had succeeded in convincing Manley not to support the Cuban presence in Angola publicly, but Duncan's statement on the eve of Kissinger's arrival in Jamaica had complicated the situation.[22] As it turned out, the Jamaican government stalled the decision to support Cuba and the MPLA for almost three months, and Jamaica was one of the last countries to formally recognize both. Together with the rivalry between different party factions over the issue, the surprisingly detailed and far-reaching opposition from parts of the local bourgeoisie and the US Department of State (representing interests of international capital) definitely affected the style and sequence of the government's decision to recognize the MPLA and give legitimacy to Cuba's military presence in Angola.

Despite this, the outcome was a truly non-aligned foreign policy stance which reflected solidarity across different Third World regions and repudiated superpower hegemony. The price, however, was a rapidly growing alienation and, indeed, hostility towards the Manley government coming from the local bourgeoisie, the Opposition, and international capital. The insistent stance against domestic and foreign opposition to autonomous action regarding this issue ultimately had negative consequences for Jamaica's economic development and, evaluated against this wider background, contributed negatively to its struggle for a comprehensive national independence.

DESTABILIZATION AND RESISTANCE

In the weeks and months after the government had taken the decision to lend diplomatic support to Cuba and Angola, the US media reported extremely negatively about Jamaica. For this they used criticism publicly expressed in Jamaica by representatives of the private sector and/or Opposition. As a consequence, the government started to perceive a US destabilization scheme similar to the one employed in Allende's Chile, and tried to countervail these comments with statements that were likely to be interpreted as growing anti-Americanism and rising pro-Cubanism.

From about April 1976, therefore, a new phase of Jamaican foreign relations commenced which witnessed an increasing internationalization of domestic factors. In this phase Jamaican foreign relations became very reactive as a consequence of the external constraints which started to make themselves felt now. Internationalization also refers to active attempts by the political opposition to gain political support abroad by free-riding on anti-communist and anti-Cuban sentiments in the US society and polity.

A series of anti-Jamaican articles in the US press began in mid March with a suggestive article in the *New York Times* by James Reston, a close confidante of Kissinger, who quoted high officials of the Ford administration charging Cuba with having "entered into agreement to train the police forces of Jamaica."[23] Minister of National Security, Keble Munn, was very quick in denying the report on the very same day of its publication; however, he had to admit that indeed two security officers (out of a total of 163 being trained abroad) were going to Cuba (*DG* 18/3/1976, 1). Arguments and criticism originating from the Jamaican bourgeoisie were willingly echoed in the United States, thus, the following statement is highly reminiscent of the Chamber of Commerce critique quoted earlier above. "With 20 percent unemployment", the article asked suggestively, "you wonder why they need Cuban construction crews" (*DG* 27/3/1976, 14; *DG* 17/4/1976, 12 and 22).

Foreign Minister Thompson made several statements which repudiated the allegations of the US media and the sources in the US government that stood behind them. Mentioning "insidious approaches" made to Jamaica's ambassadors in an attempt to make them disloyal, the foreign minister told his heads of foreign missions of a hysterical campaign and of "what I am convinced are deliberate attempts by external forces through the medium of local situations to destabilise the economy of Jamaica" (*DG* 9/4/1976, 2).

The long expected and delayed visit to Jamaica by Fidel Castro took place in mid October, to the surprise of the Opposition, the public and even parts of the PNP and Cabinet. The visit occurred at extremely short notice – it was announced only two days in advance – and the Opposition decided on a boycott.

The leader of the Opposition's protest campaign built on the dissemination of "information" assembled from an adroit combination of half-truths with carefully formulated appraisals and speculation about the potential significance of the Cuban link from an utterly anti-communist perspective. Thus, while in London on an unofficial visit, the leader of the Opposition, Edward Seaga, called a press conference during which he chided the government's relationship with Cuba. According to Seaga, the influence of Castro in the Caribbean seemed to have reached its zenith:

Traditionally, Cuba has never had any real influence in the English-speaking Caribbean countries. It is only through influence established in Jamaica and Guyana that there will be any real spillover into the English Caribbean countries who will take their cue from Jamaica and Guyana. [. . .] Mr. Manley is deliberately furthering Cuban designs (*DG* 19/10/1977, 1).

For the media and interested persons this was a remarkable news item delivered by the leader of the Opposition in the Jamaican Parliament. Indeed, it could be argued that the work of the Jamaican Opposition in the United States was an important, and hitherto underestimated, factor in the resurgence of a Cold War-inspired West-East perspective in the official foreign policy of the United States and her public political discourse (Cuthbert 1979, 93–109). Seaga claimed that, while in the 1960s Cuba attempted to covertly export its revolution to Latin America (why did the JLP then maintain consular relations with Cuba during that time?), in the 1970s "the Cuban influence is by direct invitation which puts it in a far stronger position".[24] Guyana and Jamaica were portrayed as manipulating public opinion, through massive propaganda campaigns, into accepting an alien philosophy and development model (*DG* 7/11/1977, 12 and 15).

Implicitly, his hyperbolic message to the congressmen was that the very roots of Jamaican (and Caribbean) democracy were at stake at the present juncture. Great irregularities would paralyse the election system, thereby making it most difficult for the legal opposition to get into power again. Reviving the Cold War's domino theory, Seaga suggested that, ". . . we are in fact losing it [the fair election system] on the present basis of manipulation. It succeeds in one country, it becomes a model for the rest" (*DG* 7/11/1977, ibid.; *DG* 29/11/1977, 1).

On the economic side, Seaga pointed out that all indicators since 1972 had deteriorated, relating this result exclusively to the "Cuban anti-business development strategy" of the PNP government. The context in which he placed these deteriorating indicators reduced the variety of reasons for the economic slowdown to a monocausal explanation, namely Cuba and her (direct or indirect) influence on the PNP and the government.

In reply to a question concerning future US aid, the leader of the Opposition explained that financial aid would not necessarily help Manley and the United States ". . . will have an interest in seeing that democratic rights are maintained . . ." (quoted in *DG* 7/11/1977, ibid.). The fact that this inflammatory "information" came from the leader of the Opposition in Parliament added credibility and conveyed a sense of urgency. In future deliberations about the constitutional definition of limits to the role of leader of the Opposition, this kind of conduct should raise questions about future amendments to Jamaica's constitution.[25]

Seaga's overseas campaign, however, was part of a broader offensive which started to incorporate the private sector and conservative elements of the local and foreign press. Thus, the comprador bourgeoisie's Leslie Ashenheim publicly asked the government to "play down the Cuban connection and phase it out as early as possible. We have little to gain from it and plenty to lose" (*DG* 1/1/1978, 7; see also *DG* 8/1/1978, 11; *DG* 17/2/1978, 8; *DG* 18/3/1978, 1; *DG* 19/3/1978, 12).

GOVERNMENT DEFIANCE AND THE POLITICAL SHOW-DOWN

By late 1978, the coalition between the political opposition and the private sector was more united than ever before. Seaga sealed the new coalition with a formula which tied the political and economic aspects of all opposition forces in Jamaica into one unsolvable knot:

. . . the extent to which the mixed economy and market system was able, as a strategy to produce the expected benefits for the Caribbean population, would be the extent to which it would keep the society open to the democratic principles which it has respected (*DG* 18/10/1978, 1 and 13).

While PSOJ President Carlton Alexander only a month earlier had proclaimed that no one could quarrel over the Manley government's conduct of the country's foreign affairs, in late March 1979, he reached out to the JLP, saying that a revitalization of the economy would be impossible, ". . . if we continue to have this fear that your government and party are slowly but surely linking themselves to the International Communist Movement" (*DG* 24/3/1979, 1 and 17).

In mid April P. J. Patterson travelled to Cuba. In the joint communiqué issued later, Jamaica sided with Cuba on the Guantanamo Bay issue. Although the Jamaican government had endorsed this question before in the deliberations of the Non-Aligned Movement (NAM), it had not yet made the US naval base an issue of its statements outside of this forum. The issue had also not been brought up in the communiqué of Manley's visit to Havana in 1975 (*DG* 28/4/1979, 15). Hence, as with the Puerto Rico issue, Jamaica now went a step further and sided with the Cubans on this extremely controversial issue.

Of course, the government's pertinacity at this point only served to further amalgamate the coalition between the Opposition and the bourgeoisie. Aaron Matalon, member of the eminent (pro-PNP) Matalon business family, clarified what the private sector's difficulties with the government's relations were, going straight to the point:

... when the Government pursues diversification at the expense of existing relationships, one begins to wonder about its objectives. This latest set of statements about a principled relationship of balanced trade are the strangest thing I have heard from this Government. We have to buy from Hungary and the U.S.S.R. goods and services equal to what they buy from us. Apply this principle to the U.S. and the U.K. and we would find ourselves in serious trouble because they buy more from us than we buy from them. [. . .] Why are we setting one set of rules for our traditional friends and another for our newly discovered friends, thus jeopardizing existing relationships? Does this mean that the Government is pursuing a policy of diversification at any cost rather than diversification in the interest of Jamaica? Perhaps the Government hasn't even bothered to work out all the implications of its policy and the diversification strategy will go the way everything else has gone (DG 5/8/1979, 19).

This was clearly a justified and legitimate critique of this aspect of the Manley administration's foreign policy. The fact that it came out of the national bourgeoisie should have alerted the top directorate of the government, before all others the prime minister himself who often acted as a conciliator.

Apparently the Cubans also perceived that in 1979 a new phase in their relations with Jamaica had been reached. In a rather malicious way a member of the Cuban communist party's central committee called Jamaica's *Daily Gleaner* "ultra-reactionary" and accused the leader of the Opposition of a "fascist style" (DG 8/8/1979, 1). Only a few weeks after this incident, the Cuban ambassador to Jamaica, Ulises Estrada, lashed the JLP and the *Daily Gleaner*. Estrada's comments were certainly neither *de rigueur* with regard to diplomatic conventions, nor did they harmonize with the requirements of international law.[26] Indeed, the Jamaican government could have advantageously used the opportunity to request Estrada's replacement, a step that would have been covered by international law and which would have proven internationally and domestically that Jamaica was not simply an uncritical pro-Cuban sycophant. The PSOJ, CoC and JMA unanimously demanded the expulsion of Estrada on the basis of a *persona non grata* declaration (DG 21/9/1979, 1; DG 24/9/1979, 13; DG 22/9/1979, 1 and 19; DG 29/9/1979, 10). The JLP also tried to gain political capital from the Estrada affair.

Two weeks before this Jamaica had made another step on the international scene which signalled that it had tightened its relationship with Cuba. Cuba, occupying the chair of NAM, hosted the Sixth NAM summit in Havana (3–9 September 1979). During the preparatory meetings, it had become apparent that Castro was trying to bring together NAM and the Eastern bloc countries. Castro apparently sought a final communiqué that would stipulate a "natural alliance" between both blocs. As demonstrated earlier (page 34) Jamaica had spoken already of a "natural alliance" between Cuba and Jamaica, and also been involved in the preparatory meetings of the summit. The question was now: would Jamaica endorse the Cuban thesis?

Manley did not explicitly embrace the thesis of a "natural alliance". However, a content analysis of his speech strongly suggests that an alliance was implied. Defining his government's perception of non-alignment along the lines of the traditional view of the movement, Manley said:

Looking back to the genesis of the Movement, we . . . agree that we are opposed to military alliances and blocs . . . while we oppose blocs as such, our first concern must be power alliances that seek to entrench a world order characterized by exploitation of the weak by the powerful (Sixth Conference of Heads of State or Government of Non-aligned Countries 1980, 335).

With regard to his support for Puerto Rican self-determination and independence, he added that this was "regardless of whether they [i.e. the Puerto Rican pro-independence movement] are in the minority at this time, because that principle is fundamental to our Movement and its beliefs" (Sixth Conference 1980, 337).[27] This indicated a radicalization of Jamaica's position in so far as three years earlier, then Foreign Minister Thompson had declared that as a point of difference between Cuba and Jamaica, Jamaica had never supported the Puerto Rican independence movement because the majority of the people were in favour of association with the USA (12/10/1976, 8 and 17).[28]

Manley's speech caused consternation in Washington. According to then Jamaican ambassador to the US, Alfred Rattray, the relations between Jamaica and the US ran into 'difficulties' immediately after the speech.[29] Considering other available evidence, this is a polite euphemism. With the Havana speech, the Manley government had clearly overstepped the point of no return. Little difference did it make in January 1980 that the Jamaican government condemned the Soviet Union on the issue of intervening militarily in Afghanistan. All the signals emanating from the US indicated now that the government was reassessing its relationship with Jamaica. The *Daily Gleaner* quoted an unidentified source from the US Department of State, claiming that "there is a hit

list for the worst act in Havana, and guess who is head of it?" (*DG*
20/9/1979, 6). In October 1979 the US Senate requested a freeze on US$
34.6 million which had already been granted to Jamaica, because, as Senator
Richard Schweicker put it the "recent public statements by its current Prime
Minister at the Non-Aligned nations meeting in Havana and the recent lead
he took in criticizing US action vis-à-vis Soviet troops in Cuba are no less
than complete acceptance of the Cuban line on many important foreign
policy matters of interest to the United States" (quoted in *DG* 8/12/1979, 1;
DG 27/11/1979, 6).

Meanwhile, there were indications coming from the US that a harder
policy line towards Jamaica, suggested in particular by Brzezinski and
Robert Pastor, prevailed over the softer line advocated by the US State
Department. Allegedly, one secret memorandum to Cyrus Vance stipulated
that Manley had close contacts to the KGB: "While Manley's KGB contacts
are disturbing, his paranoia about the Opposition in his own country and
possible activities by the CIA is well known. He may simply be looking on
the KGB as another source of information on these activities" (quoted in
DG 30/10/1979, 1 and 15).[30] Seaga, who, as several Department of State
officials admitted, was a major source of US intelligence on Jamaica,
reportedly supplied Pastor and other National Security Council officials
with a document that purported to connect more than four dozen of
Manley's staff to the KGB and the Cuban secret service DGI (*DG*
27/11/1979, 6; see also *DG* 16/12/1979, 11).

In a militant mood, JMA President Winston Mahfood unreservedly linked
foreign policy issues to the success or failure of any attempted revitalization of
the economy:

I don't see how this economy is going to turn around until our politicians stop talking
about imperialism and North-South dialogue; or until they realise *that nothing is going to
take place* until there is a new economic environment in which nations can talk and work
together rather than behave in a spirit of confrontation (*DG* 16/12/1979, 1 – emphasis
added).

The government, or more precisely the prime minister, did his best to
minimize the damage done already, but his excuses came close to farce. Despite
these desperate attempts, the private sector called upon the government to
resign; both the JMA and, shortly after, the PSOJ issued statements to this
effect (*DG* 12/11/1980, 1; *DG* 15/1/1980, 1).

Conclusion

Above all, it should be apparent that although (or rather, because) the government pursued an independent and sovereign foreign policy with regard to Cuba in the face of severe internal and external criticism, this relatively autonomous approach had extremely high economic and political costs. The issue of Cuba became the rallying point around which political and economic opposition forces fused and which helped to validate and cross-fertilize their criticism which essentially sprang from distinct motivations. While the bourgeoisie was concerned primarily about the state of the economy and the dwindling profit margins, the political opposition utilized the issue as a convenient catalyst for their anti-government campaign. The bourgeoisie was not noticeably split in its opposition and towards the end of the 1970s increasingly harmonized its criticism with the political opposition, especially the JLP. Thus, the bourgeoisie increasingly dropped its economic arguments and directly attacked the government's foreign policy.

As Manley recalls, the Cuba issue was frequently discussed with potential foreign investors:

. . . there were constant references. I think every time one went to try to discuss foreign investment . . . and would point out our record of scrupulous legality and propriety in dealing with foreign capital. [. . .] I can't recall that I ever discussed foreign capital without everybody wanting to know "But what's your relationship with Cuba?" Everybody did.[31]

Certainly Jamaica's close involvement with Cuba contributed to a drying up of various sources of international finance. When Finance Minister Eric Bell failed to renegotiate Jamaica's debt with some of the creditor banks in New York, one banker reportedly commented that it is "not so much Manley's social democracy we mind as the Castro thing" (*Nation* 31/5/1980, 652).

On the political front, the JLP acted in a substitute function, expressing and amplifying (in its own interest) the concerns of the private sector. The opposition in no way hesitated to internationalize its campaign against the government's foreign policy. The ultimate outcome of this campaign was that it induced the US government (to a far greater degree than hitherto acknowledged by the literature) to change its Caribbean policies from an accommodative stance to one of revitalized Cold War thinking.

Finally, considering the ideological hegemony of the bourgeoisie in Jamaica the political and military hegemony of the United States in the Caribbean and the global political economy, it is also suggested here that Jamaica's (justified, because desirable) diversification of economic links was conducted against the background of the wrong political discourse. In other words, dealing with socialist countries and Cuba would hardly have become such a political and economic problem, if the attendant rhetoric had not made this process of diversifying the economy so visible. Had it occurred in the twilight of a utilitarian pragmatism and without the vociferous, defiant zest for changing at once the entire structure of rules governing the global economy, diversification of the Jamaican economy would probably have been much easier to achieve.

5

Jamaica, The US and International Capital in the 1970s

As the Jamaican government attempted to diversify its external relations, it did not perceive this process to be accompanied by a parallel alienation of and opposition by Jamaica's traditional external partners. Indeed, resistance from international capital or the US was conveniently rationalized as an inherent feature of the evil of imperialism and, by extension, of the fight of small developing countries, like Jamaica, against it. The applied rhetoric obstructed any collective understanding of the fact that a qualitatively radical reorientation of Jamaica's internal class and external relations could be anything but a long, tedious and carefully directed exercise of economic nation building in the same order of magnitude of what took most developed or newly industrializing countries decades to accomplish. Jamaica's multilateral foreign policy, even in its treatment of economic issues, placed particular emphasis on politics, i.e. questions of democratic participation and distribution of power. There was a clear tendency to replace pragmatic, economic details, involving trade-offs, with broad political considerations of Third World unity. This emphasis on the political, however, was not as pronounced in her bilateral relations.

Testing the Waters

The last point mentioned was discernible from the very start of the Manley government in 1972 and was exacerbated as the 1970s drew to a close. Only four months after the election, the then minister of industry and tourism,

P.J. Patterson, informed potential foreign investors in New York about the government's new attitude towards foreign capital:

I wish to emphasize that my Government continues to welcome foreign investment. In doing so, however, we cannot sacrifice the sovereignty of of (*sic*) our people and must ensure that the level of foreign investment never places us at the sole mercy of external interests or make our people subordinate in our own country" (*DG* 4/7/1972, 14).

Acknowledging the importance of private foreign investment in the process of technology transference, Patterson assigned highest priority to the joint venture mechanism which was seen as the most profitable arrangement for both host country and foreign investor. Despite this unequivocal invitation, Patterson pointed out that in future the government would approach foreign investment with a different strategy: "It will first determine the industries we need to establish in the country and then go out and seek the investor, both foreign and local, who can establish those industries by vigorous and dynamic promotion" (*DG* 4/7/1972, 14). With regard to American enterprises, the government expected that they "commit themselves to the task of providing new skills and the accumulation of an adequate pool of technically qualified personnel" (*DG* 4/7/1972, 14).

This new policy was, from foreign capital's perspective, somewhat ambivalent, particularly in comparison with the JLP's policies of the previous decade. For, while Patterson guaranteed them profitability and security of their property, he also hinted that circumstances might change this. While such a statement would have caused no great problems in Europe, careful listeners in the US became alerted when they heard the minister, a trained lawyer, uttering what sounded like precognition: ". . . there comes a time when *despite the laws*, if the people find the arrangements unacceptable and repugnant, the sanctity of the laws themselves comes under question and its validity is impugned" (*DG* 4/7/1972, 14 – emphasis added). However, while exhibiting some ambiguity, the proposed policy certainly was not more than a policy 'skeleton' which was awaiting more concreteness through specific regulations. This was probably a factor which induced the influential *Daily Gleaner* in Jamaica to recommend Patterson's maiden speech abroad as "both sensible and straight-forward" (*DG* 7/7/1972, 10).

In retrospect it is clear, however, that the government should have made a better organized attempt to establish a continuing dialogue with foreign capital. Speeches like Patterson's remained scarce. From the government's viewpoint it was certainly important to point out the rights and aspirations of the Jamaican workers and entrepreneurs, but it was a mistake to confine all explanations to these issues. While foreign investors are usually aware of these aspirations and may even find them legitimate and worthy of support, they are primarily interested in their own profits and the specific economic programmes and policies a new government intends to implement. The need for greater detail and straight business talk would have been particularly critical at this time and location, since investment levels had steadily declined towards the end of the 1960s.

Since the main investment thrust of the 1960s had largely petered out at this time for economic reasons, the discriminative approach to investment seems to have sent the wrong signals. In the face of global competition, the numerous political qualifications foreign investments were now expected to fulfill put the government's invitation to investors in a different perspective. Consequently, the renewed thrust of foreign investment which the government had sought did not occur. Actually, US net direct investment in Jamaica stagnated, reaching in 1973 the same US$ 618 million as in 1971 and, despite an increase in 1975, dropping to US$ 577 million in 1976 (Palmer 1979, 14).

The local bourgeoisie, on the other hand, exhibited an even higher level of resistance to the government's foreign economic policies. When in June 1972 the government invited the JMA to participate in a mission to China and some Eastern Bloc countries, it was turned down (*DG* 20/6/1972, 1). Although at this point political motives did not explicitly play a role in the manufacturers' decision, political predilections obviously weighed heavier than strictly economic considerations such as the exploration of (large) new markets for Jamaican products or the search for cheaper or more suitable production inputs (e.g. raw materials, technology).

In 1973, the US ambassador to Jamaica, Vincent de Roulet, was declared *persona non grata*, after he told the US Congress that he had promised Manley not to interfere in the 1972 elections if he would refrain from making the foreign bauxite investments an issue during the election campaign. The expulsion of de Roulet, who had also publicly uttered racist remarks, did not damage the relationship between the US and Jamaica.

By and large, however, the relations with the US were remarkably relaxed during the PNP's first three years in office, although the Jamaican government pursued foreign (and domestic) policies which would have been very difficult to implement during the 1980s. Although the PNP was determined not to "accept our dependence as a natural and permanent condition" and to disengage from "a slavish obedience to the US", the US itself, by its relative tolerance, encouraged further challenging foreign policy initiatives (Manley 1982, 68).[1]

THE REACTIONS TO THE BAUXITE LEVY

The implementation of the bauxite levy was flanked by a number of diplomatic activities at the international level. Before the implementation of the levy, Manley had talked to the governments in Ottawa and Washington. In Washington, he assured Secretary of State Kissinger that the levy was "purely economic in its implication" and that, recognizing the strategic importance of the metal, Jamaica "would never seek to affect US access to our bauxite through the legitimate channels of its multinational corporation" (Manley 1982, 100).

Five weeks before three bauxite multinationals appealed to it for a settlement of the dispute which evolved over the levy's imposition, the government had informed the World Bank's International Centre for the Settlement of Investment Disputes (ICSID) in Washington that, according to Art.25(4) of the ICSID's constitution, disputes relating to investments in mineral resources industries were not subject to the jurisdiction of the centre (United Nations 1975, 365). Prior to this, the UN had drafted a report which claimed that Jamaica had reneged on its obligation to settle the dispute with the ICSID. A protest by the Jamaican delegation led to the withdrawal of this draft.

In March 1974, the International Bauxite Association (IBA) was founded, with its headquarters in Kingston. Again, this venture was actively supported by the national bourgeoisie, in particular by Mayer Matalon who was close to the negotiations. Thus, Matalon, together with other skilled and high-profile negotiators, made sure that the overseas promotion of both the bauxite levy and the IBA was convincing and successful (Rousseau 1987, 39). Although Manley had tried to avert the impression of a cartellization which was an important concern in Washington, the IBA and Jamaica's attempt to have its members follow Jamaica's lead created the impression of a new level of international solidarity among bauxite producers. With Jamaica occupying the initiating role, this was likely to promote a perception among international capital of the PNP government being not just a political trouble-maker, but actually the source of future profit reductions.

Due to the government's circumspect and well prepared diplomacy, official reactions in Washington were very moderate. Although the bauxite multinationals had approached the State Department in order to get some sort of retaliation, the US government did not officially condemn the Jamaican initiative. Considering the financial windfall gains resulting from the levy, the initial drawbacks (i.e. withdrawal of foreign investments, political costs) have to be considered comparatively minor. In the medium term, however, the multinationals shifted their production away from Jamaica. Although the US did not condemn the bauxite levy at the official level, foreign policy makers in Washington were nevertheless indignant at Jamaica's initiative. Apparently it was perceived as a negative precedent for other Third World nations which was not to be condoned.[2] It has to be pointed out that, as an important shortcoming of the bargaining process, Jamaica's diplomacy did not utilize the UN's Charter of Economic Rights and Duties of States in order to give greater legitimacy to its cause.[3]

Although a few elements of the comprador bourgeoisie (as will be seen later) opposed the levy, the majority of the bourgeoisie supported it, since it promised relief for the treasury and hence a reduced probability of sharp tax increases and a greater stake for Jamaicans in an economic sector formerly completely controlled by foreign interests. The PNP government's bauxite levy was therefore in the interest of the national bourgeoisie and even parts of the comprador bourgeoisie.

One Step Forward, Two Steps Backward: The IMF Path

Towards the end of 1976 when the PNP was campaigning with the enthusiastic support of the party left and on the basis of populist slogans, Manley had sent Finance Minister Coore in September 1976 to secretly commence negotiations with the IMF. At the same time, the prime minister defiantly proclaimed at a mass rally in Kingston, "We are not for sale" and "We know where we are going". Hence, there was a fundamental and unresolved antagonism, epitomized in the political persona and ambiguous statements of the prime minister, between the populist left and the more moderate mainstream of the party.[4]

After the election, both domestic and foreign policies were primarily a reflection of internal party debates and only secondarily a reflection of the objective power relations within the Jamaican economy and society. In other words, since the large majority of the Jamaican bourgeoisie (with the exception of the Matalon family) had withdrawn its support from the Manley government, their benefits from or influence over government policies depended almost entirely on the decisions of the Cabinet and the prime minister, who desperately tried to keep an equilibrium between the different wings within the PNP and the populist appeal which had won him the election in 1976.

Before the election, Jamaica had already secured a broad consensus on the terms of the IMF agreement, which was to be announced by Manley immediately after the polls had closed. At the same time, however, he had commissioned some exponents of the left and economists from the University of the

West Indies to draft an Emergency Production Plan based on the premises of non-IMF self-reliance (see also Kaufman 1985, 130ff; Stephens and Stephens 1986, chap. 5). The rationale of this manoeuvre was twofold: first, to enhance Jamaica's bargaining leverage with the IMF and second to distract the party left and its followers by giving the impression that the government was doing everything to avoid the IMF option which, however, among Cabinet moderates and by Manley himself, had already been agreed upon in principle.[5]

The proposed non-IMF path was based on a serious and detailed plan which, by all means, could have been implemented rationally, provided that it had attained the consensus and active support of the majority of the Jamaican people. From the point of view of this study, however, this option was foreclosed even before it had become a reality. The exertion of power by, and on behalf of, the local bourgeoisie, the party leadership, the US foreign policy establishment and international capital contributed to this foreclosure. The abandonment of this option, which was decided by the prime minister alone, was taken contrary to the political mandate the PNP had obtained from the electorate. This popular support indicated that the achievement of a "non-IMF consensus" might not have been entirely out of reach if it had been prepared more thoroughly.[6]

The decision to seek IMF assistance already having been taken in principle does not mean that Manley did not have problems with the measures suggested by the Fund. Thus, in a speech on January 19, 1977, prior to the agreement, Manley announced a series of measures which implied greater austerity but appeared to be leftist. The onus of the measures was put on the middle strata and upper class, yet the increase in petrol prices implied a reduction of living standards by the lower classes as well. Neither the planned nationalizations, nor the price freeze and the rejection of devaluation were favourites of either the IMF or the local bourgeoisie (e.g. Caribbean Cement was owned by the powerful Ashenheim family which also owned the *Daily Gleaner*). The curbing of foreign exchange availability implied increasing problems of raw materials and spare parts supply for local manufacturers.

As one aide to D.K. Duncan pointed out in her reflections on the decision making process which led to the rejection of the Emergency Production Plan, some representatives of the national bourgeoisie played no small role in the decision to become involved with the IMF. Manley, finding himself under the spell of both the PNP's left wing and the moderate segment, influenced by international considerations (e.g. the prospect of warming relations with the new Carter administration), conferred the task of 'tipping the balance' to industrialist Mayer Matalon, after moderate economist Alister McIntyre had supported the IMF path in principle, but left the ultimate decision to Manley. In fact, Manley stated that unless Matalon could be convinced of the prudence of the decision then it would be unworkable. The crucial role of Matalon was not only his control of local capital and capitalists but his "in" with Jewish financial circles externally and the bauxite companies (Henry n.d., 24).[7]

Thus, while the turn to the IMF had been motivated by an economic downturn, compounded by government overspending and, above all, the withdrawal of local and foreign capital, the ultimate decision to adopt an IMF programme seems to have been made by a member of the Jamaican bourgeoisie. In its turn, the IMF option enhanced international and local capital's leverage over domestic government programmes which it perceived detrimental to its interest.

In the period before the government commenced the negotiations, it sought to improve its relations with the US under the new Carter administration but, at the same time, continued to test the scope and limits of this new relationship by trying to avert some of the policies based on the tenets of international finance and traditional US foreign policy. On the one hand, Manley's foreign relations sought to develop a better dialogue and friendly diplomatic relations with the US, but on the other hand, his government attempted to institute policies which violated the capitalist tenets to which the United States adheres. By virtue of the incompatibility of these two policy objectives, the outcome could only be expected to be limited. It was probably for this reason that the PNP government also sought to draw the Callaghan and Trudeau governments in the UK and Canada on its side. They both "promised to help and did" (Manley 1982, 156).[8]

US support for an agreeable IMF programme did not come cheap. The US took the opportunity to put forward some of her demands regarding Jamaica's foreign relations, as well as the reconstructive aspects of the island's internal development process. For example, US officials had private discussions with Manley pertaining to the alleged ineffectiveness of the new Ministry of National Mobilization.[9] In direct talks with the minister, D.K. Duncan, the US Deputy Assistant Secretary of State of Inter-American Affairs William H. Luers referred to the ministry as an "irritant" and a "throw away line" and made clear that it had no future. Luers also made it plain to Duncan that economic relations with the Soviet Union "were not on in any serious way". He pointed out that the government should proceed with caution in nationalizing enterprises and that institutions such as the State Trading Corporation were regarded as economic deformations in the US (Henry n.d., 42–43).

Whatever the precise arguments of US officials were, by agreeing to enter an IMF agreement the PNP right wing reasserted itself, steering economic development away from a path of collective self-reliance and diversification of external trade relations which by then had been perceived as the twin pillars of independent national development (Henry-Wilson 1977, 186).

The mood among the Jamaican business community during the first few months of 1977 was, at the public level, a "wait-and-see" attitude mixed with fear and uncertainty about what the future might bring (*DG* 17/3/1977, 12; *DG* 24/7/1977, 7). At the private, family level, however, there prevailed "almost panic", as could be seen in the steadily growing numbers of business persons and professionals who migrated abroad and the concomitant disinvestment in the Jamaican economy (Stephens and Stephens 1983, 6–8).

Due to general approval by the local business sector and the nature of international support for the IMF path, the government was able to negotiate a comparatively lenient agreement with the Fund. In April 1977, Manley announced the (revised) Emergency Production Plan which was supposed to facilitate the agreement with the IMF. In this plan the prime minister called for the establishment of a dual exchange rate, with the old rate applying to government transactions, basic food imports, petroleum, medical supplies, fertilizers, feeds and the bauxite-aluminum industry. The new rate, devalued by 37.5 percent, would apply to all other sectors. Wage increases were to be limited to $10 per week. Although the Fund's technocrats had not been comfortable with the dual rate and despite the fact that the government reneged on its commitment to put a ceiling on wage increases, the IMF agreement did not demand either a further devaluation or unification of the exchange rate. It also accepted the government's policy on wages (Ministry of Finance 1977; Bernal 1988, 272ff). However, the agreement stressed deflationary demand management which directly contravened the government's programme of expanding the public sector. Particularly disappointing was the low level of overall commitment of only US$ 74.6 million over a two-year period. Of this sum, US$ 44.4 million was to be disbursed during the fiscal year 1977/78. This sum has to be contrasted with the depleted net international reserves position of J$ 154 million in March 1977 (Ministry of Finance 1977, 4; see also Brown 1981, 38).

Potential foreign investors were apparently not satisfied with the scope of the IMF stabilization programme. Foreign capital remained a mere trickle and Manley had to realize that it takes a country more than just the formal approval of its economic policies by the IMF to achieve a steady flow of foreign capital. International capital seeks not only a "favourable investment climate", but also likes to see policies in place which promote private sector development, relatively uninhibited flows of factors of production, free profit remittances and general assurances against "undue" involvement of the state. All these, however, were issues subject to some amount of uncertainty and fears in Jamaica at that time.

As a consequence, Jamaica missed the domestic assets target of the IMF in December 1977 by a narrow 2.6 percent (or J\$ 9.1 million) (Bernal 1988, 279). Due to the failure, a World Bank loan and a loan package from a private bank consortium could not be drawn. Indeed, the default meant that the Jamaican government had now lost whatever small credibility regarding economic management it had formerly enjoyed with friendly quarters of the business communities in the US, the UK and Canada. Considering the very small margin by which Jamaica defaulted the test and the fact that some foreign credits already had been delayed, the IMF could have granted a waiver on the basis of a 'guilty with explanations' interpretation. However, the Fund immediately suspended the programme, which meant that Jamaica was now in a worse position than in early 1977. Manley, describing the situation as "nothing short of a disaster", was apparently completely surprised by the failure of the test (Manley 1982, 159). The Fund technocrats, however, had not forgotten the diplomatic pressure which the little island had brought to bear on them a few months earlier, which had compelled them to moderate their standard loan conditionality.

The PNP government's unsteady relations with international capital and the US after 1977 are often conceptualized in terms of a power struggle between different factions in both the party and the government, which essentially left both without a workable consensus for its policies (Lewis 1983, 141). While this contention is basically correct, it does not take sufficient cognizance of the fact that at the root of personnel policies are often disparate perceptions and interpretations of reality and the facts which constitute it. This study, therefore, regards the unfolding scenario of relations between Jamaica, international capital and the US after the termination of the first IMF agreement rather as a reflection of the collective, societal understanding and admission that neither an accommodative nor an aggressively defiant foreign policy were able to generate sufficient levels of economic growth and development. The fact that this collective insight was not synthesized into a broad consensus about which objectives and interests a Jamaican government should pursue with regard to its foreign relations, is testimony of the abysmal disparity of views on development in Jamaica and its profound economic and cultural openness as a social formation deeply penetrated by conflicting value systems.

This fundamental cleavage pervaded the PNP, the government, the Cabinet and the elite, and was, ultimately, epitomized in the personality of the prime minister who stood at various times for different incompatible societal and state interests which were not traded off against each other and thus created all kinds of friction.

One of the cardinal errors during this phase was the Jamaican government's overestimation of the political leverage it had with the US political system, particularly the US administration itself. Based on close formal and informal ties to the Congress' Black Caucus, UN Ambassador Andrew Young and even President Carter himself (through his wife who visited Jamaica in May 1977), by late 1977 the Jamaican government mistakenly regarded the tainted Jamaican-US relations as restored and healthy.[10] Thus, Foreign Minister P.J. Patterson perceived the result of the continuing bilateral dialogue as a "clear improvement in our relationships without any compromise of basic principles on either side" (*DG* 22/11/1977, 16).

When Jamaica commenced negotiations with the IMF for an Extended Fund Facility in early 1978, the government was in a worse bargaining position than before. There existed a dire need for short-term foreign currency loans, but international commercial banks had become very wary and suspicious of the Manley government and now started to emphasize debt repayment over disbursement of new loans. Thus, the government was forced to negotiate advances on the following year's bauxite levy and Tate & Lyle's sugar proceeds (see also Bernal 1988, 280ff; Bank of Jamaica 1991, 26/27). This situation, of course, demonstrates the precariousness of the country's financial position at that time. With the local bourgeoisie continuing to withhold its material and political support, international capital was now able to dictate the terms of the new agreement. When some international commercial banks decided to give Jamaica a short-term loan of over US$ 40 million in March 1978, this was only done to keep the country financially afloat during what turned out to be a protracted period of negotiations with the IMF (Bernal 1980, 51/52).

Prior to the commencement of negotiations, the IMF gave Jamaica two preconditions, a 10 percent devaluation and monthly mini devaluations tied firmly to its wage policy (see also Girvan, Bernal, and Hughes 1980, 124). The negotiations during January and February were extremely difficult, although the government had devalued the Jamaican dollar. According to three authors who were close to the negotiations, the IMF team was less interested in figures and performance tests than in the government's "readiness to undertake a radical change in the nature of its policies, and to follow this through with political determination" (Girvan, Bernal, and Hughes 1980, 125). By the end of April agreement seemed imminent after the government had acquiesced to all IMF demands, giving up its earlier opposition to the size of the devaluations.

However, subsequent to a meeting between IMF officials and representatives of some international commercial banks the Fund hardened its position. This was obviously in response to demands from these banks that the Jamaican government be put under more pressure and show more concrete signs of a politico-economic turnaround (Girvan, Bernal, and Hughes 1980, 125; Bernal 1980, 56). The emphasis was now on the first year of the three-year programme, including a further 30 percent devaluation which was asked for without any technical justification, a wage guideline of 15 percent, tax increases on oil, alcohol and cigarettes, a guaranteed 20 percent profit margin for the private sector, limits on the activities of the State Trading Corporation and Jamaica Nutrition Holdings, and reductions in government spending. The government had little choice but to accept this extraordinarily harsh programme.

The programme contributed to a great extent to a new upsurge of anti-IMF sentiments in Jamaica, thus laying the foundation for the eventual break with the IMF in early 1980. Manley points out that "in the final days of the negotiation, the most conservative and pragmatic members of the Cabinet were in revolt . . ." (Manley 1982, 160). Hugh Small, who in 1980 became minister of finance, claims that "the IMF people did not really consider their plans to be realizable in Jamaica" and that it was their aim "to prevent the Jamaican economy from moving before a winding down of the political process."[11] Even the minister of finance in charge of the negotiations, Eric Bell, who had often represented the IMF's point of view against his colleagues in the Cabinet, termed some of the programme's conditions "unduly harsh" (quoted in Girvan, Bernal, and Hughes 1980, 126).

Members of the local bourgeoisie, having been promised 20 percent profit margins, apparently saw the agreement still as the lesser evil. Thus, the Chamber of Commerce complained only lukewarmly that the terms of the agreement "were much too binding" (*DG* 23/4/1978,1). However, the Jamaican manufacturers were more concerned, as the compression of demand and foreign exchange availability was likely to affect their production and sales.

An unwritten condition of the second IMF agreement was that the government would amend the Labour Relations and Industrial Disputes Act in order to strengthen the state's capacity in the mediation process between labour unions and employers (see also Stephens and Stephens 1986, 204–05). Hence, the agreement effectively sought to diminish the political and economic influence of the trade union movement and, thereby, to diffuse both the political and economic class struggle. Considering the enormous social burden which the agreement caused for the lower and marginalized classes, it can be concluded that its contribution to the political weakening of the Manley government was not an entirely undesired side effect for the IMF and international capital, on whose behalf it was operating in Jamaica.

Closing the Accounts

Some time between mid 1978 and early 1979, perceptions about the viability of the IMF path changed among the leadership of the government and party. A consequence of this collective change of perceptions about the viability of the IMF solution can be seen in Jamaica's intensifying relations with Cuba and the Soviet Union in 1979. Thus, Manley went off to Moscow in early April and traded Jamaican alumina for Soviet goods and services. Besides the fact that the alumina deals with Hungary and USSR violated CARICOM agreements and upset Jamaica's partner Trinidad and Tobago, the US became increasingly concerned about Jamaica's latest moves in the direction of the socialist bloc (*DG* 21/4/1979, 1 and 15; *DG* 24/6/1979, 1). In July, Hugh Small was on record as claiming that "anyone who offends the people of Cuba offends the people of Jamaica" who would be "at one with the heart and mind of the Cuban people" (*DG* 1/7/1979, 1).

Apart from this resurgence of rhetoric, obviously being promoted by the party leadership, Manley himself indicated that the experience of the past one and a half years left the impression that the government's actions were otiose: "I am going through an enormous reappraisal in my own mind . . . neither diplomacy, nor reasonable argument have got us anywhere in this system" (*DG* 29/7/1979, 1). Clearly, Manley seemed to approach the position of the party left, especially that of D.K. Duncan, who had earlier argued that consensual populism would have to be abandoned now for the benefit of a policy that would heighten class antagonisms, but at the same time benefit the Jamaican *hoi polloi* and thereby widen the PNP's electoral base. With regard to foreign relations, the left argued that only a decidedly pro-socialist foreign policy (although, like Cuba, in the framework of non-alignment) would generate the kind of COMECON assistance the country required in the absence of support by local and international capital (Jamaica Hansard May 16, 1978, Aug. 1, 1978, 29ff). When Manley supported Duncan's reelection to the post of PNP general secretary, it was evident what the "reappraisal" of his mind meant in practical terms.

The PNPs increased anti-imperialist rhetoric and the government's accelerated pace of broadening its relations with the Eastern bloc and other countries, however, stood in curious contrast to its request to the IMF in June 1979 for an increase in its lending. Obviously, both steps, which were likely to cancel out each other, were dictated by the government's dire need for foreign exchange and the split within the party. This apparent inconsistency reflects a collective conviction of the non-viability of the IMF path, only tempered by a perceived "not-yet-viability" of a non-IMF path. Thus, Manley in his message to the North-South Conference on the International Monetary System and the New International Order in Arusha (June/July 1980) pointedly stated that "the notion that with IMF approval international commercial banking institutions will supplement the funds made available by the IMF is a fallacy" (Manley 1980, 5; see also Girvan, Bernal, and Hughes 1980, 130).[12] However, considering the nature of the politics in Jamaica at this time, the government's attempts to talk other Western governments into believing that the investment climate was "favourable" in Jamaica speak of an extraordinary mixture of professional optimism, economic naivety and political delusion (see also *Die Welt* 7/9/1979).

The reasoning of international capital seemed to mirror this evaluation of the situation. Top-level technocrats in the IMF were evidently split about the prospects of successfully continuing the current programme and the need to discontinue and negotiate a new agreement (International Monetary Fund 1979a, 1). According to the Fund's projections the net foreign assets test would not be met in December. Besides technical economic reasons such as the government's missing the targeted real GDP growth of 3 percent for 1979, the inflation rate which was higher than projected, the annual rate of wage settlements which was higher than estimated and a number of fiscal and monetary concerns, the IMF was clearly concerned about Jamaica's domestic and foreign policies and raised these issues in discussions with the government. Thus, in a confidential internal briefing for the IMF mission which was to visit Jamaica on November 19, these objections were elaborated:

... the mission will stress the unfavourable impact on local and foreign investment, capital flows, and migration of skills, of the deeply entrenched suspicion that the government is not seriously committed to its economic program, judging from perceived inconsistencies between its foreign policy and domestic political stances on the one hand, and the dictates of the program on the other (International Monetary Fund 1979b, 5).

The Fund's objective of a complete turn around of Jamaica's foreign policy was remarkable in so far as the IMF always projects the image of a non-political or politically neutral institution. Its attitude, however, was fully consistent with the US foreign policy interests at that time which tied in with the interests of international capital.[13] Total USAID assistance fell from US$ 32.2 million in 1977 to US$ 18.1 million in 1979 and US$ 14.6 million in 1980.This was, in the words of one IMF official, notably ungenerous to Jamaica in terms of bilateral aid (*Times* 6/6/1980).

After the government had failed another net international reserves test in December by almost US$ 130 million, IMF officials told the ministry of finance that the banks had even further hardened their attitude to Jamaica because of the Havana speech and the return of D.K. Duncan (Bernal 1980, 56). It has been pointed out that internal and external factors beyond the control of the government accounted for about 60 percent of this fiscal shortfall (Girvan, Bernal, and Hughes 1980, 129). Jamaica applied for a waiver which the IMF countered with new conditions, among them a reduction in public expenditure of $300 million in 1980/81, a contraction of roughly 25 percent in real budget expenditure, excluding debt service, relative to 1979/80. In the ensuing discussions with the IMF the government resisted the IMF's demand to cut the budget. The party, meanwhile, had commissioned an alternative economic programme which was to be discussed subsequently. The general mood in the party favoured a break with the IMF. On March 8 and 9, the National Executive Council (NEC) of the PNP met, accepting the non-IMF programme.

However, it was still not decided at what point the break with the IMF should occur. The alternative was between an immediate and a phased break with "a final IMF agreement to cover the next year as far as the economy was concerned and provide time to put in place an alternative foreign exchange strategy" (Manley 1982, 187). This option was proposed by Manley himself:

I counselled that to break with the IMF with no period of preparation, with no attempt to satisfy yourself that you had your economy in shape to cope with the tremendous pull-out of foreign exchange . . . and say that I would counsel campaigning in the election on the basis, if we win we are going to embark upon a process of disengaging from the IMF. . .[14]

Negotiations with the IMF still continued after this meeting. At this stage there were "frantic discussions sometimes by telephone between Washington and Kingston to try to get the particular target adjusted".[15] Despite minor changes by the Fund, the view prevailed that it was unlikely that Jamaica could meet this target by September.

The near absence of foreign investments and loans from international commercial banks, as well as the very limited official assistance from the US and other Western countries, indeed constituted a compulsive incentive for the government to continue its relationship with the IMF in order to avoid national insolvency. There was a real danger that the smaller banks around the world that had lent to Jamaica would lose their patience and call Jamaica into default (*International Herald Tribune* 6/5/1980). This was a direct consequence of Jamaica's subsequent late decision in March to break off talks with the IMF and delays in the disbursement of loans negotiated with Libya (US$ 50 million), Iraq (US$ 10 million) and Venezuela (US$ 97million).

When the NEC met again on March 22, suspicions about the Fund's intentions and considerations regarding the upcoming elections in October had the majority of the centre joining with the minority left and voting with a two to one majority for an immediate break with the IMF. This vote was opposed by Manley and a majority of the Cabinet, but nevertheless formally approved by it two days later.[16]

Conclusion

The substance of Jamaica's relations with international capital and the US in the 1970s was greatly affected by both the local bourgeoisie and international capital whose interests increasingly converged towards the end of the 1970s. Both then mutually complemented each other in the influence which they sought to exert over the PNP government, which narrowed the state's relative autonomy in foreign policy considerably. The government's attempts to put up resistance to these aspects of capitalist development in Jamaica and the North-South relations in general complicated its foreign policies, but were unable to change the substance of the international economic relations effectively. Despite its rhetoric and diplomatic manoeuvres aimed at giving a new quality to Jamaica's relations with the US and international capital, they essentially remained determined, directly or indirectly, by the stewards of the domestic and international economy.

Because the government's bauxite offensive had the broad and active support of the local bourgeoisie, it was able to successfully negotiate against international capital's opposition and to unilaterally impose and internationally defend its position. However, its flanking diplomatic strategy, albeit successful, was rather apologetic, which also indicates the desperate resistance that some parts of international capital offered. When the government phased out its cooperation with the national bourgeoisie, the subsequently negotiated deal with the Soviet Union (the supposedly fraternal socialist brother nation) was so detrimental to the country's interests that the government eventually had to request a renegotiation. This would seem to indicate that at the technocratic level the country was not in the position to renounce bourgeois interests in foreign policy.

Relations with the IMF were fully embraced and actively initiated by the local bourgeoisie. Consequently, the government was able to put effective diplomatic pressure on the Fund and receive a relatively favourable agreement. Nevertheless, the US and international capital were eventually able to utilize the IMF lever to demand the downgrading of some of the government's new institutions aiming at greater public sector involvement and political mobilization. The Fund used the first opportunity to impose stricter conditions on the government. The social strain resulting from these measures served to erode the government's popular support, but did little in terms of inducing international private banks to support Jamaica financially. Without doubt, this attitude was facilitated by the increased economic disengagement and political opposition of the bourgeoisie, which was amplified and even carried overseas by what D.K. Duncan sardonically used to call "Her Majesty's loyal Opposition".

On the basis of the perception that according with the rules of international capital (while attempting to change them) did not effectively address Jamaica's economic problems, particularly the foreign exchange shortage, the government radicalized its foreign policies after the failure of the second IMF agreement. Rather than trying to accommodate the government's resolve to resist the interfering political conditions posed by international capital, the IMF, the US, and international finance capital explicitly opposed Jamaica's foreign policies at the political and economic levels. Indeed, the IMF was fairly sure that Jamaica would continue to be its customer "whoever wins the election" (*Times* 6/6/1980). Consequently, the country's impending international insolvency forced the government to make the ultimate decision, that is either full surrender to IMF conditionality or pursuit of a completely self-reliant and quasi-autarkical development path.

By the time the government called for election, the bourgeoisie and the Opposition were determined to bring about its defeat by all means considered necessary. The unprecedented level of political intimidation, death threats and violence, on the one hand, and the dire islandwide shortages of even basic foods, on the other hand, made the defeat of the PNP at the polls virtually unavoidable.

The fact that Jamaica engaged in rhetorical battles in the context of pursuing de facto capitalist relations with the external environment and, indeed, being in a number of ways very dependent on them, left the attempt to formulate a democratic socialist/non-aligned foreign policy doomed to failure from the start.[17] Occasional attempts to rationalize certain policies, especially by the prime minister himself, ignored the power of perception in politics and simply amounted to intellectual sophistry. To sum up, it seems fair to say that to pursue such a level of independence in foreign affairs simply requires a much higher level of economic viability which has to be competitive and productive enough to withstand a certain amount of opposition and/or economic disengagement from local and international capital. As long as business is good, investors, producers and consumers will not interfere unduly with the conduct of foreign policy.

6
Internal Dynamics: 1981–1989

The Political Climate and Reorganization of the Public Discourse

After the PNP's IMF *débâcle* the JLP won the October 1980 election with an overwhelming majority. The party's populist campaign slogans, which promised to make "money jingle in your pockets" and generally emphasized "deliverance", were as successful as the PNP's "Better must come" campaign in 1972. As usual during this highly partisan period of Jamaica's history, the election was followed by a purgative atmosphere in which the new ruling party persecuted members and supporters of the opposite party, in order to further widen its leverage against the opposition. In this purgative phase of the early 1980s, criticism and even public debate about Jamaica's foreign relations was extremely limited. There was no way that one could have compared this political atmosphere with the intensity of public and internal party debates of the 1970s.

Similarly, the relations between the new government and *Daily Gleaner* were clearly much better throughout the 1980s. Thus, there were no negative commentaries or any sustained public campaigns to be found, whenever government members verbally attacked this newspaper, which happened several times (*DG* 29/10/1988, 1; *DG* 23/4/1988, 3). Nor were any protests heard when one of its reporters was abused at a JLP function, which in the 1970s would have been branded as a sacrilege against the freedom of the press (*DG* 24/11/1988,1).

However, support for the government went to much deeper levels than taking a public position for or against its policies. The thrust of the whole public discourse on economics and politics operated to a much greater extent in favour of the Seaga government than most political analysts have realized. Compared with the period of the 1970s, there was a fundamental change of focus in the media. Most commentaries now concentrated on macro- and micro-economics, the functioning of markets, etc., with very businesslike, pragmatic and clear anticommunist under- and overtones. This new focal point of public analyses had at least three consequences which operated in favour of the JLP government: first the uprooting of any general and sustained discussions in terms of power relationships among and within classes. Hence, there was a "torsion" of political class struggle promoted by the state. Second, a reinterpretation of the period of the 1970s, with the apparent side effect of a foreclosure of any evaluation of historical alternatives. The public discussion became utterly "unscientific" through its tendency to refute historical experience without sufficiently testing the validity of its alternative options. Third, the local version of what Habermas (with reference to Peter Sloterdijk) has termed a "stop of reflection and firm values" (*Reflexionsstopp und feste Werte*) (Habermas 1985b, 62). This neo-conservative scheme of ideological planning is characterized by the deliberate omission of critical questioning. Thus, questions pertaining to what kind of democracy and human rights development Jamaica would favour, or a general discussion of the role of the state, were almost completely displaced in the public debate. They were clearly superseded by short-range questions, concerning themselves with immediate day-to-day and small-scale problems of economic management (as opposed to national development).

Arguments of the dependency schools were flatly denounced as ideologically biased. Thus, unequal exchange was regarded as nothing but the ideological version of comparative advantages in the productive sphere. Trade in any form, therefore, was unequivocally welcomed. With remarkable simplicity, a leading Jamaican intellectual twisted complex and valid arguments about the distorted nature of dependent economies in, for example, Samir Amin's writings. Instead, he pointed to the stereotyped success stories of Japan and a number of newly industrialized countries:

When he is taken on his own terms his version of the dependency theory has some merit. But you have to believe in what he does. If like me you believe that there is nothing sinful about the occasional bowl of Kellogg's cornflakes, much of his argumentation will seem frankly bizarre (*DG* 17/7/1983, 13).[1]

Questions about the possible viability of national (or regional) cornflakes production (to stay within the picture), perhaps with adjacent possibilities for local farmers, naturally fall outside of this neoliberal frame of rationalization. The whole question of foreign consumer taste patterns and the high import dependency of the Jamaican food sector are completely neglected.

In the short run, the impact of the new frames of reference in the public discourse translated itself only to a limited extent into tangible room for greater manoeuvrability in foreign relations. Thus, in 1981, only 41 percent of the population approved of Jamaica's diplomatic break with Cuba, while a majority of 48 percent opposed it (*DG* 6/12/1981, 18). Certainly, there was no way that the new discourse could prevent the *hoi polloi* from perceiving the effects of economic austerity measures and blaming the incumbent government for them. In 1986, 65 percent of the population were of the view that conditions in the island were worse than in 1980, while only 23 percent thought that they had improved (*DG* 1/6/1986, 3). In the medium to long run, the public's attention was shifted from acute political awareness to a deeper, albeit preoccupying, understanding and interest in economic affairs.

Mood changes and focus in public discussions on national affairs led to the foreclosure of any far-reaching and general public evaluation of development alternatives. As the parts of the state apparatus, e.g. the University of the West Indies, strengthened their infrastructure only with regard to management and business accounting studies, economics, and natural sciences research, critical reflection about alternative schemes of production such as, for example, workers' participation and share ownership of enterprises, job sharing, part-time work or technology copying, were completely neglected.[2] Instead, a myopic mystification of export orientation in the so-called newly industralized countries was promulgated by the media and the government. This kind of debate did not attempt to transcend the limits of dependent capitalism, but readily provided an intellectual environment in which both positive and negative external forces could easily play an important role (Payne 1988, 111–130).

The new economic and political discourse in Jamaica in the 1980s (and early 1990s) exerted its influence at an even deeper level of social communication. Thus, through the introduction of neoliberal vocabulary into the public discourse, the ideas and concepts of economic neoliberalism were not only expressed *through* language, but even *within* language. They were therefore operating much more forcefully on a subconscious level. Both aspects constitute what could be termed the new discursive dependency of the 1990s.

Thus, in the 1980s it was the Jamaican "private sector", not the "bourgeoisie", which was squarely declared the "motor of development", without any further analysis of its historical role, capabilities or motivational preparedness to accept the responsibilities of this role. Similarly, it was no longer fashionable to speak of specific "industries" which in turn might allow class assignment, but rather one would talk about specific "sectors" (e.g. agricultural sector; garment sector; tourism sector).[3] In this way, the issue of class antagonisms was sublimated and chloroformed in its function as the womb of social pressure from the lower class. This ideological submersion of language went rather unnoticed in Jamaica (cf *Money Index* Aug. 1988, 25).

If the public discussion was already narrowed to such an extent, it can be reasonably assumed that among the decision makers themselves the consideration of alternative development options would have amounted to political heresy. Indeed, one senior civil servant in the ministry of foreign affairs admitted that he put his career at risk when he challenged Prime Minister Seaga publicly by suggesting that the NIEO had some justification and merits.[4]

The new prime minister and his Cabinet colleagues routinely referred to the era of the 1970s as a period of chaos which effectively excluded a historical perspective for the analysis of the genesis and structural causes of Jamaica's economic crisis. Although references to this period were made from time to time, they treated the economy in an abstract and superficial manner: "The economic and ideological misadventure of the Marxist system was not acceptable to a people accustomed to the lifestyle and expectations of the market system" (Seaga 1980a, 8). The surgically neat separation of the previous period from that of the 1980s allowed the JLP to legitimize a completely new economic programme. This programme sought to "adjust" the Jamaican economy to the requirements of the global environment. The proposed "structural adjustment" of the economy was depicted in such a way as to suggest that it would be the *only* possible way of making the economy more beneficial to the development of every and all Jamaicans.

Economic Performance and Structural Adjustment

There is no way that either developments in the economy or Jamaica's foreign relations in the 1980s could be understood without consideration of the various IMF "stabilization" programmes which the country underwent, or the World Bank's structural adjustment loans which it received. The very extensive, if not excessive, utilization of funds from both organizations resulted in a tight exogenous network of socioeconomic cross-conditionality to which the country had to adhere.

Usually, the Fund's textbook analysis of a country's permanent balance-of-payments deficit diagnoses inflation as the fundamental economic problem, caused by "excessive demand". The "excessive demand", that is, too much money chasing too few products with a consequential rise in prices, is mainly caused by faulty monetary policies of the state (Körner et al. 1987, 55). Thus, the IMF analysis usually criticizes the levels of expenditure for public services, subsidies of basic goods, high costs of unproductive and/or inefficient state enterprises, and the "excessive" provision of social services by the state. A (relatively) poor export performance is usually blamed by the Fund on an overvalued currency. This overvalued currency obstructs the chances to increase exports in order to earn more foreign exchange, which could balance the expenses from increasing imports. The resultant balance of payments gap has to be bridged with foreign loans which leads to a deterioration of the country's international reserves position.

Following this analysis, IMF economists usually prescribe a standard set of monetary measures. Three basic principles on which these measures rest can be identified: 1) market economy principles, 2) deflation of the economy through demand control and 3) integration into the world market (Körner et al. 1987, 56). Addressing primarily the domestic economy, the Fund often prescribes a strict credit policy, limiting the money supply within the economy through measures such as increasing the interest rates. Here the IMF usually draws a clear distinction between the private and public sectors. The allocation of credits to the state is normally very restricted, while the private sector will (despite reductions) still receive funds on a preferential basis. But, as Gerster points out, in the private sector, "occasionally, some business branches are explicitly mentioned and restricted" (Gerster 1982, 129). The IMF often asks for a comprehensive tax reform aimed at increasing revenues. However, these reforms are usually designed in such a way as to provide incentives (e.g. tax holidays, reductions on profit taxes, etc.) for what they consider potential investors, i.e. the local bourgeoisie and international capital. Finally, there is an insistence that the state puts a ceiling on wage increases in order to prevent the trade unions from attempting to catch up with the increasing consumer price index which results from the above mentioned measures. If wage increases are on par with increasing costs for consumer products and social expenses, this would wipe out the anticipated stabilization effects and simply heat up inflation.

Table 6.1: GDP Indicators, 1980–1988

	1980	1981	1982	1983	1984	1985	1986	1987	1988
Real GDP (J$ 1974)	1828.8	1875.5	1898.7	1942.2	1925.6	1836.1	1867.2	1983.4	2012.6
Growth rate (% of GDP)	-5.7	2.5	1.2	2.2	-0.9	-4.7	1.7	5.9	1.5
Real GDP (per capita)	858.6	868.3	867.0	870.9	848.3	798.3	794.6	–	–

Source: Computed on the basis of *Economic and Social Survey* (various years);
        Anderson and Witter 1991, Appendix I.

However, in spite of the broad application of these measures in Jamaica, the expected improvement of the economy did not materialize. The overall performance of the Jamaican economy in the 1980s, as reflected by the GDP, tells the following. As Table 6.1 indicates, the average annual growth rate was merely 1.2 percent. In 1984 and 1985, the economy actually contracted. At the end of the JLP's term in office, in 1988, the real GDP (in J$ 1974) had still not reached a higher level than the GDP of the second year of democratic socialism (i.e. 1976). In fact, in 1987 the level equalled that of the year 1970. If compared with the growth of the population, the picture looks even worse. In per capita terms, there was a clear downward tendency between 1980 and 1986. According to these data, the economy operated at the end of the 1980s at a comparable level to that of the early 1970s.

The sectoral performance of the economy also showed mixed results (Table 6.2). Thus, the agricultural sector grew by 6 percent over the 1981–1988 period. Export agriculture, one of the emphases of the JLP government's economic plan, was almost stagnating, while the domestic agriculture also grew very slowly at an average annual rate of less than 1 percent. The declining relative importance of the mining sector is evident in its negative growth over the time period. The growth of the manufacturing sector was steady with an average of 2 percent yearly. A clear boost was given to construction and finance. Finance and real estate services in particular succeeded in expanding their relative share in the GNP (Davies and Witter 1989, 79). These numbers might be seen as the first statistical sign of an increasingly speculative and rather unproductive nature of investment, which very visibly engaged in the construction of office buildings and shopping plazas all over the island. The available

Table 6.2: Selected Sectoral Performance of the Economy, 1980–1988 (Growth Rate in Percent)

	1981	1982	1983	1984	1985	1986	1987	1988
I. GOODS								
Agriculture	2.2	-7.9	7.3	10.0	-3.6	-2.1	5.2	-5.4
Exp. Agri.	1.2	-1.6	-3.1	3.5	-3.0	-2.9	-1.4	8.5
Dom. Agri.	3.6	-12.0	8.6	15.8	-1.6	-4.0	5.3	9.7
Mining etc.	1.3	-29.0	0.6	0.7	-19.5	6.6	4.9	-4.7
Manufacture	1.1	6.7	1.9	-4.2	0.4	2.4	6.3	2.0
Construction	0.4	15.9	6.7	-7.1	-8.3	3.1	13.9	14.7
II. SERVICES								
Distr. Trade	5.0	6.7	-5.0	-0.7	-9.1	5.8	11.0	1.0
Finance	8.8	-2.4	21.4	-8.5	-7.0	16.6	3.3	16.4
Real estate	3.1	2.6	2.9	-1.8	-1.9	2.6	5.2	3.3
Producers of Govt. Service	2.5	2.3	0.5	-4.2	-5.8	3.6	0.6	3.5

Source: *Economic and Social Survey* (Planning Institute of Jamaica), various years.

office or shop space was often rented out at horrendous costs or the whole building profitably resold after a short period of time.

Shifting the focus from production to trade leaves an equally mixed impression on the observer. As Table 6.3 shows, the balance of trade remained negative throughout the 1980s. In 1988, the last year of the Seaga administration, the balance of trade was still operating at the same deficit level (approximately US$ 600 million) as in 1981 and 1982. Although there was some improvement in the mid 1980s, when the deficit went down to US$ 380 million, which was largely due to falling oil prices, the data indicate that the JLP government could in no way claim to have even approached its own stated objective, namely, to enable Jamaica to earn its way out of the debt crisis. Since the notion of adjustment suggests a period of restructuring (i.e. "inward" oriented growth), it may be still too early to formulate a definite assessment of this phase. However, the data presented so far suggest that the 1980s were indeed in many aspects of social and economic development a lost decade.

One of the economy's few bright spots was the tourism industry, which replaced the bauxite industry as the most important net earner of foreign exchange. As Table 6.4 shows, inflows improved from US$ 406 million in 1984 to US$ 607 million in 1989. Investment income outflows steadily increased, largely due to debt repayment and losses in the mining industry.

Table 6.3: External Trade Balance, 1982–1988 (US$ million)

	1982	1983	1984	1985	1986	1987	1988
USA	–	-284.3	-181.4	-292.5	-287.2	-310.8	-385.1
Canada	–	28.7	39.0	51.4	44.0	27.6	15.7
UK	–	63.3	35.1	35.5	46.0	39.6	59.5
Netherlands	–	0.1	-3.4	-2.5	28.6	68.4	66.4
Norway	–	–	20.8	8.9	12.8	20.7	3.5
FR of Germany	–	-17.1	-16.4	-8.1	-13.4	-23.3	-20.7
USSR	–	–	33.4	24.7	19.9	21.5	25.7
Trinidad & Tobago	-3.7	27.4	7.5	-17.5	-2.8	-20.2	-9.9
Barbados	1.6	3.0	5.2	8.2	8.5	8.5	9.7
TOTAL	-607.4	-595.2	-437.9	-575.0	-379.6	-525.1	-601.1

Source: *External Trade (Statistical Institute of Jamaica), various years; Economic and Social Survey* (Planning Institute of Jamaica), various years.

The net international reserves account declined by more than US$ 100 million between 1984 and 1989, indicating the state's precarious payment position in the face of growing external debt payment obligations.

Jamaica's external trade quotient clearly reached significantly higher levels than in the 1970s. While in the 1970s it had averaged 40.1, the average in the 1980s was 52.6. As Table 6.5 indicates, it peaked in 1985 with 63.6. Thus, Jamaica's integration into the global economy in terms of trade was clearly higher than in the previous decade. This suggests a greater vulnerability to

Table 6.4: Selected Balance of Payments Indicators

	1984	1985	1986	1987	1988	1989*
Foreign travel	406.6	406.8	516.1	594.9	527.1	607.4
Investment income	320.6	340.6	332.2	404.7	417.6	480.2
Changes in reserves (minus = increase)	-225.7	72.6	24.0	208.2	-143.2	170.4

*Preliminary.

Source: *Economic and Social Survey*, various years.

Table 6.5: External Trade Quotient for Jamaica, 1981–1987 (at current prices)

Year	1981	1982	1983	1984	1985	1986	1987
	52.5	44.0	43.5	56.3	63.6	53.7	54.7

Source: Calculated from *National Income and Product 1987* (STATIN), Kingston 1988.

economic changes in the international environment, as well as a greater susceptibility to the political terms of participating in it.

The Social Conditions

The combination of economic stagnation and fiscal austerity led to a deterioration in the social conditions of the majority of Jamaicans, with the poorest section of the population bearing the brunt of these measures. Two intermediary factors acted as buffers and prevented the country from imploding. First, the high and increasing numbers of Jamaicans migrating to the USA, Canada or the UK and, second, the rise of the so-called informal economy in Jamaica (Deere et al. 1990, 70–80; Witter 1989).

The JLP's policies of devaluation and demand reduction, through wage restrictions and fiscal cutbacks, brought to Jamaica the familiar pattern of social hardships experienced by scores of countries under IMF and World Bank supervision. Poverty and maldistribution of income, malnutrition, rapidly deteriorating health and education standards, poor public transportation and prohibitive costs for housing were the most salient features of the general deterioration of living standards in Jamaica during the 1980s. As Table 6.6 indicates, the standards of public health services and education deteriorated, especially after the mid 1980s. While real per capita outlays on health declined by 42 percent from US$ 44 in 1982/83 to US$ 25.6 in 1986/87, per capita public expenditure on education declined from US$ 84 to US$ 57 (Levitt 1990, 27). The average inflation rate as expressed by the consumer price index increased by an annual average of almost 14 percent. Anderson and Witter (1991, 70) pointed out in a survey that, in 1985 and 1989, 60.6 percent and 46.1 percent, respectively, of employed workers "earned no more than a half of the minimum family income" (see also Antrobus 1989, 145–60). This compares unfavourably with the level in 1977 when only 35.4 percent of the workers earned these low wages. At the same time wealth became more

Table 6.6: Selected Social Indicators, 1981–1988

	1981	1982	1983	1984	1985	1986	1987	1988
Unemployment	25.4	27.9	26.9	25.6	25.6	23.6	21.0	18.9
Cases of								
1) Murder	490	405	424	484	434	449	442	414
2) Robbery	4617	3618	3989	4950	4989	4721	4903	4433
No. of Government								
Doctors	370	416	414	388	317	365	397	367
Nurses	1869	1918	–	2086	1815	1640	1548	1411
Consumer price index (% change)	4.6	6.5	16.7	31.2	23.1	10.4	8.4	8.5
Net migration (in thousands)	5.9	9.8	4.3	10.5	13.4	20.1	30.9	38.9
Migration rate (%)	13	20	9	24	32	49	77	88
Public expenditure on health/ education (%)	21	21	19	21	17	18	17	–

Source: *Statistical Abstract (STATIN), various years; Economic and Social Survey, various years; Anderson and Witter, 1991, 70.*

concentrated among those who earned twice or more than the minimum family income (Anderson and Witter 1991, 70; Levitt 1990, 21ff).

The compression of wage levels was supposed to make Jamaica more attractive as an investment site for international capital, since it enhanced what both the IMF and the JLP government perceived to be Jamaica's main "natural" comparative advantage, namely cheap labour. For the government, the compression meant that it had an additional incentive to offer to potential foreign investors. Thus, it could boast that the average wage per hour for its workers in export industries (especially the so-called "Free Zone") was US$ 0.63 or 1/22 of the comparable wages in the US (Dominican Republic: US$ 0.79; Haiti: US$ 0.58).[5] The income of workers continued to fall and the suppression of demand through lower wages indicates that workers' consumption was afforded little importance. Thus, while after 1985 more jobs were created, this did not amount to an economic resuscitation or social development. As some authors pointed out, "the trade off from structural adjustment was that where employment increased, job adequacy in terms of earnings decreased" (Anderson and Witter 1991, 23; *DG* 4/1/1988, 8).

For its political survival and the sustainability of adjustment programmes biased in favour of the bourgeoisie, the government also became more dependent on handouts from international agencies and donor countries. As Levitt (1990, 23) points out in her comments on Seaga's Food Security Programme which financed the government's distribution of food stamps:

The food for this programme is imported in the form of food aid from USAID, the EEC, the World Food Programme etc. . . . The actual level of government expenditure on food stamps was J$45m; a sum sufficient adequately to cover the 'food deficit' of only 76,000 of the total number of 317,000 registered persons eligible to receive food stamps . . . the 'food deficit' remains enormous and will increase as further price increases come into effect, and the last remaining general food subsidies are removed in compliance with the IMF programme.

The continued availability of an industrial reserve army and a reservoir of marginalized people (especially youths) would suggest that in general, public health services were only a secondary consideration of both international and local capital. A similar conclusion can be drawn for the standards of education in Jamaica with regard to its relevance to international capital. As indicated already, qualification is more often than not, no primary concern of foreign investors in dependent social formations. However, to the extent that the local private sector wishes to successfully compete in local and overseas markets, it would need to fully recognize and appreciate the singular importance of a highly skilled, knowledgeable and technologically up to date labour force. It can therefore be concluded at this point that the government's IMF induced cutback of expenditure for education clearly operated to the medium and long term disadvantage of the local bourgeoisie, especially the national bourgeoisie. The Jamaican bourgeoisie, throughout the 1980s and in the early 1990s, has not fully understood the increasing importance of education, specialized research and development and the necessity for material support of these critical areas of national economic development for the achievement of international competitiveness in an increasingly knowledge driven world economy (Carnoy et al. 1991). This shortcoming is the direct result of the discursive dependency to which the JLP government yielded by its adherence to the basic premises of the IMF/World Bank conditionality. Thus, Jamaica's insertion into the production structure and trade markets of the global economy did not promote a dynamic growth process (such as in some Asian countries), but served only to consolidate her dependent capitalist status.

Although the prime minister dutifully insisted that his tenure in office was a success, it is clear that even by some of its own objectives the government had failed.[6] At the end of the 1980s, money certainly did not "jingle in everybody's pockets" and the large accumulated debt was programmed to kick off an avalanche of further social pressures. The government, however, was not unaware of the social costs of adjustment. As the election year 1989 approached, it planned to embark on a 'social adjustment' programme which intended to focus on the health and education sectors. However, the late timing and the subordination of these programmes to a specific economic growth target demanded by international capital indicated that by no means would these programmes have a priority status. Thus, Seaga himself eventually had to admit that his social plan had been reviewed by the IMF, the World Bank and major bilateral agencies and been ". . . given the support of all these agencies, *in terms of closing the financial gap that exists in order for us to be able, in the medium term, to carry out the programme of maintaining sustainable growth at 4 percent*, while embarking upon those two programmes of social adjustment and the reduction of the debt service ratio."[7] Seaga also cautioned that "much of what we've planned for the future is based upon the world economy continuing to show at least the same levels of performance, if not improved levels."[8] In other words, if exogenous shocks should happen to threaten the primary objectives of domestic fiscal stabilization, there would be hardly a chance for the continuation of what was probably perceived as luxurious charity programmes.

Inter- and Intraclass Relations

The temporary and/or unstable absorption of labour by new export-oriented industries (mostly owned by foreign capital) and the informal economy had several consequences. To the extent that informal commercial importers (ICIs or "higglers") became owners of their means of production, the expanding informal economy became more receptive to the interests of the local bourgeoisie (e.g. calls for lower interest rates and import taxes; greater availability of credits). Their greater flexibility made it easier for them than for wage labour to absorb the socioeconomic consequences of IMF policies, e.g. devaluation. Generally speaking, this shift led to an increasingly outward oriented focus of the working classes.

The bourgeoisie was well aware of this new nexus, as became evident in 1988 when six private sector organizations (PSOJ; JEA; JMA; CoC; JEF; SBAJ) reprimanded calls for greater social justice in the "export free zone". Warning that these demands would court "disaster", they argued: "If we persist in unrealistic demands now we would only damage our competitive position and, more directly and painfully, jeopardize the economic prospects of the thousands who are still unemployed and unskilled" (*DG* 13/7/1988, 3).

More than ever, the interests of the working class and international capital were portrayed here as being complementary. Nevertheless, the expressed concern for competitiveness reveals the real concern of this class.

Since the mood to articulate grievances was relatively submerged among non-unionized labour and the population in general, the question of how far political class struggle in the 1980s was articulated on the level of the trade unions arises. As Deere et al. (1990, 98; see also *DG* 24/4/1981, 1) point out, the regional approach of trade unions towards the adjustment exercise was one of "critical support". Thus, they promoted tripartism and the qualified inflow of foreign capital. Initially, the National Workers' Union (NWU) (related to the PNP in opposition) tried to assert itself. Public opinion and intervention by the judiciary, however, resisted their demands. Thus, when the NWU resisted certain aspects of the first IMF agreement and advocated unconditioned wage bargaining, opinion leader Carl Stone criticized the union (*DG* 29/4/1981, 6; *DG* 4/1/1987, 3; *DG* 12/7/1981, 15).However, as a look at the statistics indicates, both work stoppages and industrial disputes clearly decreased over the period. While in 1981 there were 706 industrial disputes and 145 work stoppages, in 1986 these dropped to a low of 391 and 40, respectively.[9]

However, this seems not so much a reflection of the trade unions' commitment to national economic growth (as they depicted it), but rather a testimony of their inherent political weakness which found its expression in a rather accommodating stance towards the economic policies of the government and the IMF. Thus, even after the austerity programmes had begun to bite large chunks out of the real wages of the workers, the tone of trade union presentations was decidedly moderate. The soft line taken can be seen in a presentation by a leading trade union representative to the Jamaica Employers Federation (JEF) in May 1987. Pointing out that between 1983 and 1985 real wages had already fallen by over 30 percent, the union representative lamely warned: "It cannot be expected that workers' support for wage guidelines can be maintained forever if measures concerning prices and profits are not introduced" (Joint Trade Union Research Development Centre (JTURDC) Newsletter Sept. 1987, 6; see also *DG* 22/1/1987, 8).

Concerning the social wages of workers (i.e., social services provided by the government), he pointed out that, in per capita terms, social expenses by the government fell from J$ 51.58 in 1982/83 to J$ 13.50 in 1984/85. Regarding the data for the following year, the union representative simply stated that "we really hope that it did not fall too much further" (JTURDC Newsletter Sept. 1987, 6). This hardly seems to be the kind of language to coax the representatives of the local bourgeoisie into actively supporting policies in the interest of the workers.

Hence, in the 1980s the ideological penetration of the Jamaican workers' movement by the prevailing economic paradigms reached a higher level compared with the 1970s, which is epitomized by the frequent usage of the notion of "national economic units", replacing the now outmoded "classes" (JTURDC Newsletter Sept. 1987, 7).[10] On the political level, therefore, and with direct relevance to the substance of foreign relations, the movement in the 1980s became "compradorized" and failed to offer an alternative vision of economic development. With regard to local capital, the union movement obviously perceived itself to be in some kind of junior partnership with the government and the bourgeoisie.

More than ever, it became apparent in the 1980s that the Jamaican bourgeoisie's generic nature was organic, but not homogeneous. By and large, the bourgeoisie supported the tenets of the new government's economic policies, especially the economy's ultimate subordination to the conditions and requirements of international capital. On the other hand, sections of the bourgeoisie that were hard hit by the structural adjustment exercise became fierce critics of *sectoral aspects* of Prime Minister Seaga's policies. Despite their criticism, they nevertheless clearly stayed within the basic policy matrix of the government's and international capital's neoliberal economic philosophy.

On the organizational level, the bourgeoisie clearly strengthened itself, increasing its visibility in society and public affairs. Founded in March 1976, the umbrella organization of the entire bourgeoisie, the Private Sector Organisation of Jamaica (PSOJ), in 1986, in an obvious act of political symbolism, established its headquarters opposite the entrance to Jamaica House, the seat of the Prime Minister's Office. This, as well as a number of other projects, was the direct result of close cooperation between the PSOJ and the USAID, the overseas development branch of the US Department of State. The support was anything but coincidental, as it is an explicit aim of USAID to increase the influence of the Jamaican private sector.[11] In 1985, for example, the PSOJ received a US$ 750,000 grant which was designed "to assist the company to strengthen its role in co-ordinating the efforts of the Jamaica Private Sector to take advantage of the business opportunities presented by the government's structural adjustment programme and the Caribbean Business Initiative" (PSOJ n.d., 17).

The infrastructure of the PSOJ was refurbished in several ways. Internally, its structure was diversified (with USAID support) into a number of committees and departments responsible for matters of public policy, security, economic policy, etc.; the board of directors was enlarged, with the president responsible for information, public relations, unity and consensus, as well as international relations (*DG* 11/4/1984, 23; *DG* 3/5/1986, 1; *DG* 13/11/1988, 18). With such a broad range of specialized concerns, it is hardly surprising that the PSOJ claimed to be speaking "for all sectors of society" and even "in the national interest", a theme that was frequently invoked (*DG* 23/3/1986, 1; *DG* 29/9/1986, 13; *DG* 9/3/1986, 21). Foreign aid was also involved in the PSOJ's venture to establish an export credit insurance company (*DG* 14/3/1985, 13).

Through the PSOJ, the local bourgeoisie also extended its outreach into the North American subcontinent. Thus, it established branches in Miami, Hartford (Conn.), New York, Washington DC, Toronto and London (e.g. *DG* 4/10/1985, 19). A good example of the smooth cooperation between parastatal agencies, the local bourgeoisie and overseas interests was the establishment of an "information brokerage office" by the PSOJ in Dallas (Texas), which was financed with a USAID loan and earmarked in collaboration with the Jamaica National Export Corporation (JNEC) and the Jamaica National Investment Promotions (JNIP) (*DG* 3/8/1984, 30; see also McAfee 1991, chap. 4).

Throughout the 1980s, the PSOJ organized public meetings and lectures with prominent conservative North American scholars and businessmen, sent Jamaican businessmen to US Department of Commerce seminars and made regular presentations in the media (*DG* 11/4/1984, 23; PSOJ n.d., 3; *DG* 6/10/1986, 1). However, despite all the financial support from USAID and the new buoyancy of the local bourgeoisie in general, the PSOJ's rhetoric was betrayed by its own fiscal negligence. Thus, the organization's deficit amounted to $456,000 in 1988 which was $300,000 more than in the previous year (*DG* 23/11/1988, 18). Nevertheless, the bourgeoisie was fully aware that, in the words of the PSOJ's President Mahfood, "a strong PSOJ means a strong collective private sector" (*DG* 11/1/1987, 9).

More important, in terms of political substance, was the PSOJ's economic programme which elaborated the interests of the private sector, but was conspicuously quiet about the sector's economic responsibilities. Echoing Prime Minister Seaga's recurrent repulsion of IMF critics, it unambiguously stated that any non-IMF or debt default strategy would make the current hardships look like Eden (PSOJ 1985, 11). Consequently, the private sector, like the IMF and the Jamaican government, identified the negative balance of payments as the root cause of all ensuing economic problems. However, it also tended to perceive this problem as a temporary imbalance rather than as a structural one.

The remedy therefore would be to export more – an idea to which the bourgeoisie by and large subscribed. This export bias is clearly reflected in its programme and epitomized in the PSOJ's candid admission: "New industries and business firms will form, old ones will disappear, as is to be expected in any dynamic economy" (PSOJ 1985, 14). Beneath this apparent subscription to economic dynamism and entrepreneurship, however, lay the reality of a bourgeoisie which for decades had been pampered by various forms of state protectionism that shielded the local manufacturers and agriculture from external competition. Besides the few who had read the signs of the times, there remained a sizeable portion of the local bourgeoisie which continued to expect special benefits, incentives and protection by the state from international competition.[12] The inherent tension between the different factions of the bourgeoisie was eased, albeit not resolved, by the PSOJ's demand for a phased adjustment to export-led development which would allow those members willing to shift their production to make the necessary investments and organizational adjustments. The local bourgeoisie, particularly segments of the national bourgeoisie, had a point insofar as a transitional period of structural change always requires extra amounts of finance.

Considering the role of the IMF, all sectors were implicitly and explicitly in agreement with the Fund's presence in the island. Even the manufacturers, who stood to lose most in the adjustment exercise, congratulated the prime minister in early 1981 for his agreement with the IMF, since it would help the sector to take its place in a new economy (*DG* 16/2/1981, 2; *DG* 24/4/1981, 1; *DG* 25/2/1981, 14; *DG* 20/7/1982, 11). In this early phase, however, expectations were tremendously inflated, especially with regard to private foreign capital. Large numbers of the Jamaican business people simply thought that the new inflow of potential investors would mean that they came to Jamaica "to give us some money".[13] Hence, expectations of the local bourgeoisie and international capital clearly did not fully coincide.

The commitment of the private sector in material terms was quite disappointing notwithstanding all rhetoric to the contrary. Potential foreign investors reportedly often left the island, frustrated by the attitude of the local business community indulging in skepticism rather than exhibiting entrepreneurial impetus and vision. In 1984/85, the level of private sector investment in Jamaica as a percentage of GDP reached only about a third of what it had been in the sluggish year 1970 and only about half of what it had been in 1974 (*DG* 27/3/1985, 8). Equally disturbing was the local bourgeoisie's low propensity and lack of preparedness to engage in joint ventures. The Jamaican business community was disinclined to reveal their programmes for expansion into third markets and in many cases such medium term business planning probably did not even exist. In 1986, the outgoing JNIP overseas director, Audley Shaw (JLP), commented on this state of affairs: ". . . one of the things that we have found most difficult was even to get the most rudimentary information from our private sector, basic information that you would want to provide a potential foreign investor as a joint-venture partner" (*DG* 3/10/1986, 22/23; *DG* 29/6/1984, 14; *DG* 23/6/1985, 23).[14] To the extent that international capital became increasingly aware of, and frustrated with, such stalling attitudes of the local bourgeoisie, the Jamaican state became less inclined to accept the PSOJ's call for phased "structural adjustment".

The national bourgeoisie did not get tired of warning against the advantages foreign producers had and, particularly, the flood of illicit imports (*DG* 23/2/1982, 1). Over the years, manufacturers clearly developed a perception that they were bypassed by a government which, in their view, operated on a timetable primarily worked out between the World Bank and the IMF, on the one hand, and the government itself, on the other. One former president of the JMA squarely laid the blame at the feet of the World Bank and IMF technocrats whom he termed:

". . . failed Third World refugees operating in the World Bank scenario . . . They have migrated to the World Bank, having failed in their own countries . . . They are here, trying to impose on us solutions that themselves don't work in their own countries . . ."[15]

However, as pointed out already, this criticism occurred *intra muros* of a general private sector consensus on "structural adjustment".

Although the exporters (qua producers), like the manufacturers, were also concerned with the scarce and expensive money supply, they were much more supportive of the IMF programmes, which they explicitly welcomed (*DG* 24/4/1981,1; *DG* 20/8/1988,14; *DG* 16/6/1985,11; *DG* 2/2/1985, 2).[16] The different degrees of support could be seen when, in the light of foreign exchange shortages, both exporters and manufacturers separately proposed a classifica-tion of the essentiality of imports, or rather the allocation of foreign exchange funds for these imports. While the manufacturers somewhat opaquely suggested that the prioritization should relate to "their ability to be paid for on a cash/sight basis or require extended supply credit relating to the budgeted availability of foreign exchange", the president of the JEA was much more specific: "We once again reiterate our position that foreign exchange supplies can only be increased if *earners of foreign exchange* are given priority access to available supplies of what is available" (*DG* 23/11/1984, 24 – emphasis added).

As it became more and more obvious that a number of Jamaican entrepreneurs were not prepared, able or willing to follow the new impetus towards export production, the importance of the organizations representing the different and competing interests within the local bourgeoisie shifted even more. The Chamber of Commerce, representing those trading activities which under "structural adjustment" became almost obsolete, clearly lost its former importance. On the other hand, the Jamaica Exporters' Association greatly enhanced its political leverage.[17] As a result of the new focus on export-led development cum externally financed fiscal stabilization and adjustment, the small national bourgeoisie, focusing on commercial trading and production for the local market, was on the retreat. This trend was also reflected in the institutional arrangements of the Jamaican bourgeoisie. Thus, in 1987 the JMA was hit by a financial crisis and avowedly had $300,000 debt which led to the dismissal of a quarter of its employees; moreover, 15 percent of its members were reportedly "financially delinquent" (*DG* 30/12/1987, 2). Thus, its viability as the exponent of a section of the local business community during the 1980s suffered.

Although JEA's president, Prakash Vaswani, denies that on the part of the exporters there was any antagonism towards the JMA, the JEA was certainly not interested in a merger with the JMA (*Money Index* June 23, 1987, 8). When the JMA in early 1988 made such a bid, the JEA proved to be quite uninterested, stating that it might dilute its focus on the export sector and "weaken its strong financial base and thereby its ability to perform efficiently and independently" (*DG* 22/4/1988, 2). Shortly after, the JMA and CoC formed a Joint Committee of Commerce, Manufactures and Export (CME). Obviously designed to harmonize their policies with regard to exports, the JEA shunned the CME despite an invitation to join it. Thus, the committee was the manifestation of concrete conflicts of interests between merchant capital and actual exporters. Moreover, it did not play any important role, certainly not from the point of view of the exporters:

The CME was a flop from the word go. Basically it was a move by the trading sector to get more power, because their power was being eroded . . . So they were trying to get focused on exports without the earning base. So it was more of an egotistical move and I think it was one of the more stupid moves by the private sector in the 1980s.[18]

Thus, the comprador bourgeoisie clearly understood that its word was weightier than that of any other segment of the local bourgeoisie. The new entente between the old rivals, the merchants and the manufacturers, on the other hand, gives an impression of the apparent sense of desperation of both subsectors of the local bourgeoisie.

The Role of the State

Interpreting the PSOJ's vision of the legitimate role of the state, its president, Peter Thwaites, attributed security and freedom for all citizens, the maintenance and improvement of the basic infrastructure of the country, public health services and basic education for all to the sole domain of the government (*DG* 17/5/1987, 1 and 2). However, the government ought to divest all or most of the public enterprises and put in place a comprehensive tax reform.

In early 1987, the state's role in relation to the proportion of forces between different factions of the bourgeoisie was illuminated. In summer 1986, Seaga had reshuffled the Cabinet and abolished the ministry of industry, which was integrated into the extended ministry of foreign affairs, trade and industry, with Douglas Vaz becoming a junior minister without portfolio in this ministry. This reshuffle was apparently in anticipation of the impending new IMF agreement which called for an accelerated adjustment process. The abolition of the "manufacturers' ministry" indicated the further displacement of the national bourgeoisie and reflected the increasing pressure of international financial organizations on the government at that time. Apparently aware of the loss of power and the imminent hardships for domestic producers, Vaz wrote a letter to Seaga in which he warned him of the detrimental consequences to the manufacturing sector of the new agreement. Justifying his warnings to the prime minister, the letter partially read:

I have legally and faithfully sought to communicate and implement government's stated policies of deregulation and structural adjustment, even to my own personal detriment, as after lifelong commitment to the manufacturing sector, many who saw in me a potential benefactor at the time of my appointment, soon felt I was a traitor ruthlessly administering a policy for their destruction (*DG*11/1/1987,2).[19]

In public, Vaz admitted that he had made his presentation indeed qua manufacturer and on behalf of the manufacturing and commercial factions of the local bourgeoisie (*DG*10/1/1987, 1; *DG*13/1/1987, 3). His immediate dismissal from office by the prime minister forcefully drove home the point that – with regard to the specifics of the government's economic policies – Seaga was disinclined to succumb or even be subjected to pressures from the national bourgeoisie, even where they manifested themselves at the level of the state. This diagnosis appears to be corroborated by Seaga himself, who indicated that he generally did not take much note of what he saw as particular interests of specialized lobby groups:

Most of the opinions that come from those kind of sources are really interest groups expressing their own *narrow viewpoints* for the purpose of any particular type of problem that they may be facing at the moment. They certainly don't . . . need to be considered on a basis for policy.[20]

This kind of attitude, which certainly helped to increase the relative autonomy of the state, was encouraged by international capital, which thereby sought to enhance its own leverage with the Seaga government. Thus, J. Todd Steward from the US Embassy advised the government to be patient and not to give in too easily to public pressure (*DG* 25/11/1984, 8).

While Seaga tried to block pressures emanating from the bourgeoisie, there was also a clear tendency by the state to limit the trade unions' ambit of free collective bargaining on behalf of the workers. Thus, the 1986 Amendment to the Labour Relations and Industrial Disputes Act intervened in at least three ways in workers' rights: 1) it undermined the bargaining process between the parties by allowing the minister of labour unilaterally to refer disputes to the Industrial Dispute Tribunal at any time, even before the negotiation process between the parties involved had a chance to commence; 2) it sought to reduce the opportunity of the legitimate strike weapon in the negotiation armoury of the workers; and 3) it permitted the entry of the judiciary in a penal way in the industrial relations involvement (Rattray 1986). In effect, the amendment ended the legal right of free bargaining over wages, social conditions, benefits, etc. in Jamaica. However, except for a handful of speeches warning somewhat vaguely against the erosion of workers' rights, the trade union movement acquiesced in the amendment (*DG* 27/5/1983, 17; Munroe 1990, 247). Therefore, their *political* significance clearly decreased during the 1980s and they only remotely resembled Georg Lukács' (1986, 665) characterization of trade unions as the "systematizing coordination of individual revolts against capitalism to one of the subjective factors of its limitation as a force".

The government's determination to act as autonomously as possible was also reflected in the fact that despite some consultation with the private sector, the latter repeatedly complained that it was not sufficiently involved in decision making and was only informed after decisions had been taken and implemented by the government (*DG* 22/8/1981, 8; *DG* 23/2/1982, 11; *DG* 29/10/1985, 2; *DG* 3/1/1986, 1 and 21; *DG* 21/3/1984, 8). At one point it actually went so far as to no longer invite the JMA to take part in the regular meetings the prime minister had with the private sector.[21]

Conclusion

There was a fundamental consensus among the whole local bourgeoisie that Jamaica should operate within the framework of an IMF stabilization programme and a parallel World Bank "structural adjustment" programme. The extent of this basic agreement left virtually no room for autonomous government action on this question. The autonomy of the Jamaican state was effectively confined to micro-economic fine tuning within the broader framework of tight IMF-USAID-World Bank cross-conditionality. The scope and content of this exercise were defined by the differing priorities of the various factions of the local bourgeoisie operating under these new conditions.

The rise of the comprador bourgeoisie, which began in the late 1970s, continued in the 1980s. The concomitant export oriented development strategy, promoted by the Jamaican state (through its new government) and international financial organizations, led to a further opening of the country's fragile economy. Scores of foreign consultants, managers, and 'experts' entering the country, increasing foreign debt, and a modest upturn of foreign investment were some of the immediate consequences of this development.

On the other hand, international capital, as one of the audiences the JLP had to cater to, could not expect to form more than a loose coalition of interests with the comprador faction of the Jamaican bourgeoisie. To the extent that exporters were also manufacturers, they suffered from import liberalization, tight money supply and protectionism in major international markets. These problems, of course, put the export sector in a junior position within the international economy. Thus, even JEA President Vaswani in 1988 propounded: "We have to get away from this growing tendency towards foreign goods . . . I am not on the same wave length as the policy makers, I don't feel that since we work so hard to earn the foreign exchange that we have to buy Budweiser or Miller Lite" (*Money Index* June 14, 1988, 5; *Money Index* June 23, 1987, 7).

Here, then, the JEA was closer to what the JMA was saying than to interests of international capital being channelled through IMF and World Bank programmes. Occasionally, foreign investors were reminded by the government of the principle of good corporate citizenship to which they were expected to adhere (*DG* 24/6/1985, 2).

The organizational strengthening of the private sector (with the negotiated support of the USAID), including joint representation with state trade promotion agencies overseas, the ideological levelling of the trade union movement, the curtailment of workers' rights, the state's interference in the free collective bargaining process and the soft-pedalling of the labour unions on these issues were the major aspects of the political class struggle in Jamaica during the 1980s. These developments can only be adequately understood in terms of a limitation of pluralism and even exhibit tendencies towards an increasing corporatization of the Jamaican society.[22]

7
EXTERNAL DYNAMICS:
1981–1989

The Debt Crisis

One of the most salient economic factors determining the position and policies of international capital towards underdeveloped social formations was the rather unexpected onslaught of the global debt crisis. In August 1982, Mexico imposed a moratorium on its debt service repayments. This unilateral step raised the spectre of an international illiquidity crisis, with further possible individual or even collective debt default, threatening the very existence of a number of banks which had overstepped their lending capacities in the 1970s. The lending spree of the 1970s had come to an end. Between 1977 and 1983 the total debt of non-oil-exporting developing countries increased from US$ 300 billion to US$ 782 billion (Schubert 1985, 123). The average debt servicing quotient for developing countries, which had been less than 19 percent between 1973 and 1977, increased to 24 percent in 1982, or even 50 percent if short-term credits are added (Büttner 1984, 145). The Mexican case set into motion a fundamental reorientation of international capital transfers, transforming Latin American debtor countries into net capital exporters (Altvater and Hübner 1987, 15ff; Mugglin 1989, 47–50). The necessity to keep the international finance system afloat meant for the debtor countries that any room for sovereign manoeuvrability in foreign policy contracted palpably. Nowhere has this constraint become more evident than in the way the industrialized countries and international finance capital handled the management of the crisis.

International finance capital became primarily concerned with increasing its securities for the possible case of further instances of illiquidity or even insolvency. Thus, private banks increased their securities, sharply reduced their lending and, through negotiated rescheduling of principal and interest payments, tried to secure the steady flow of repayments in order to have a basis for the credibility of the whole debt business. Through various instruments such as secondary markets for debts, debt-to-equity swaps, increased disbursements of international public finance (through the IMF and the World Bank), they sought to salvage the debt service of debtor banks.

The huge US budget deficit exerted additional influence on the world credit system which was under severe pressure from this debt crisis. In order to finance their own deficit and secure repayments from increasingly indebted social formations in the Third World, US banks attempted to maintain their threatened hegemonic position in the world monetary system, which was now being instrumentalized to reverse the capital flows from debtor nations to the various creditors. The US and international banks had a vital common interest to support political regimes in the debtor states which were committed and able to enforce the economic arrangements deemed necessary by international capital to induce this reversion of capital flows (Schubert 1985, 117–18). These regimes mostly consisted of those socioeconomic elites (or their political representatives) who were expected to be the winners of structural adjustment programmes. With only a few exceptions therefore (e.g. Peru in 1987; Brazil in February 1987), all debtor states kowtowed to externally drafted economic reform programmes which even prescribed a number of the micro-economic details of their industrial development policies. It is hardly surprising that some economists concluded that these aspects of the debt crisis represented a "new dependency" (Furtado 1982, 259–84).

In the process of renegotiation of the debt repayments the creditor countries applied a sophisticated case to case approach which sought to prevent a cartel of debtors. In the classical divide and rule fashion, they offered some debtor countries special concessions and arrangements, thereby creating the illusory impression that each country could maximize its benefits by utilizing a bilateral approach (Taylor 1986, 41).

The need to administer the debt crisis in the 1980s gave rise to a new development orthodoxy which the industrialized countries promoted through IMF and World Bank programmes. The reality was that within the framework of the existing development structures there was no way for effective debt repayment. Thus, international financial institutions such as the IMF were instrumentalized for the purpose of implementing a new development model which was supposed to guarantee the continuation of debt repayments. However, this neoconservative "structural adjustment" vision based on an export-oriented growth model fell short of an elementary precondition:

The IMF compels the debtor countries to bring their economic policy completely into line with debt amortization. In this process, however, the repayment is prevented by the creditor countries themselves by not allowing a negative balance in their trade balance as it actually ought to result from the payment obligations of the debtor countries (Hinkelammert 1989, 109; see also Sweezy/Magdoff 1984).

Structural adjustment recipes are prescribed on the basis of the concept of comparative cost advantage which stipulates that every country in a free world economy would and should define its own productive niche through the natural resource advantages with which it is endowed. But, as some authors rightly point out, it is very questionable whether it does not in effect reduce them "to the status of raw materials producing low-wage countries, for this, in the words of the economists, is their 'natural factor advantage'" (Körner et al. 1986, 58; see also Depelchin 1989). Moreover, the most fundamental question is: Who is going to buy all these goods produced for export? At this historical conjuncture where all countries want to increase their exports, while growth in the world economy is generally slow and uneven, and major industrial countries are applying protectionist measures against each other and the developing countries, one is hard-pressed to answer the question of where all the additional buyers should come from (see also Foxley 1984, 31–32).

As more and more developing countries pushed into the global markets with comparable goods and services, the excess supply caused by this movement led to a stagnation and (since 1986) decline of the commodity terms of trade between the North and the South. Hence, despite increases in the real amount of exports there were no comparable increases in their value (Osterkamp 1984, 100). Consequently, the debt crisis and its proposed remedy, structural adjustment, led to a situation in which developing countries transferred an increased amount of values, without receiving a comparable transfer of its trade surplus in the form of money and without the desired effect of improving their debt repayment capability. One author rightly summarized this Catch 22 situation in the following way:

For many, the capacity to diversify exports in an increasingly competitive international market is purely notional, while their traditional exports are being squeezed both by sluggish demand, and by the increased supply resulting from the generally intensified pressure to export, so that their ability to attract commercial international funds declines. In essence they are being forced back to a more self-reliant pattern of growth but under circumstances where the difficulty of sustaining a more self-reliant strategy economically or politically has risen dramatically (Bienefeld 1982, 53).

From a discursive point of view, the adoption of the notion of structural adjustment was a clever move which on the surface seemed to reflect a renewed and serious interest in genuine economic and social development of the social formations of the Third World. However, international capital did not adopt the label of structural change, which formerly had been advocated by the Latin American Left as a programme for socioeconomic development, without subjecting it to a complete revision of its original meaning. Structural adjustment now meant a radicalization of capitalism at the expense of precisely this intended socioeconomic development of the debtor nations. Being heavily indebted already and in dire need of further immediate and substantial financing, the debtors hardly had any alternative short term choice than to accept this redefined version of change. Thus, the Cancun conference in late 1981 between representatives of developing and developed countries effectively ended the advance of the New International Economic Order. As Michael Manley noted in 1987 "the defenders of the system were clearly not yielding significant ground in response to the strategy of negotiation and compromise" (Manley 1987, 114; Ruggie 1982, 508–14; Krasner 1982, 503–08; Solomon 1982, 587; Kuczynski 1982, 1022–37; *DG* 13/5/1982, 1; *DG* 9/11/1981,15).

On the other hand, the economic dynamics and imperatives of a structurally changing world economy were a positive incentive for the developing countries to follow this trend. The import-substitution strategy had exhausted itself by the mid 1970s and for Jamaica there was certainly a need to consider new industrial policies and directions. The profitability of raw material and primary product exports was increasingly losing ground while new, albeit capital-intensive, export industries (e.g. data processing, services, photonics, software production) were now achieving the highest growth rates in the world economy (Harker 1989, 11–47; Pearson and Mitter 1993, 49–64; Kenney and Buttel 1985, 61–91; Griffith-Jones 1983, 53–87)

To take full advantage of these newly opened developmental windows of opportunity demanded, however, that the developing countries become sufficiently attractive for foreign investment to flow into the economy. In turn, this meant that, both politically and economically, international capital was able to reaffirm its presence within developing social formations. Here, its main interest was to delimit its space of economic action and transactions by influencing the economic decision making of the host countries as far as possible.

The Revival of Neoconservatism and Interventionism in Global Politics

Economic structural adjustment recipes were but one slice out of a larger cake of a comprehensive renaissance of neoconservative economic and political values. In essence their criticism was a reaction to the civil assertions in developed countries during the late 1960s and early 1970s, as well as unexpected setbacks in the West's anti-communist Cold War strategies (e.g. Angola, Vietnam, Nicaragua). A number of international events at the end of the 1970s marked the termination of a decade which had witnessed attempts to make severe changes on the global political and socioeconomic maps. In Latin America and the Caribbean, two new revolutionary governments had attained and consolidated their power in Nicaragua and Grenada. In Iran, the United States experienced another traumatic setback in the wake of a failed military operation to liberate American hostages, held there by the new religio-revolutionary Shiite theocracy under the leadership of the Ayatollah Ruhollah Khomeini. The outbreak of the Iran-Iraq war again brought into focus the volatility of Middle East peace and the supply lines for the West's single most needed energy source, oil.

These and other events gave rise to a new wave of political reassertion and economic neoconservatism in the industrial countries, particularly the US. With remarkable precision the political pendulum swung to the neo-conservative side in all major industrial countries. The new political mood of the 1980s manifested itself basically on two levels: first, the socioeconomic discourse which elevated social Darwinism cum free market capitalism to a new height and, second, the politico-ideological level which reasserted the universal validity of Western conservative, status quo oriented values of family, individualism, pluralism and human rights (as opposed to socialism).

This decade (particularly the first half) witnessed increased West-East tensions along ideological, political and military lines. The deepening chasm between the United States, her allies and the Soviet bloc exerted a severe influence on the relations among Third World countries, between the latter and the industrialized countries, and on the position of the Soviet Union (and what was perceived as her proxies) within global and Third World affairs. The so-called Reagan Doctrine, which was a direct derivative of the neoconservative political discourse in the United States, defined the political parameters of United States relations with the Third World, particularly in the Caribbean and Middle America. For the latter, failure to take notice of this matrix in the establishment of foreign relations would automatically have triggered extremely negative political repercussions in Washington and economic dislocations resulting from retaliatory actions taken by US and international capital.

Low intensity conflict and global containment policies of the Reagan administration (and its allies) effectively circumscribed the room for political manoeuvre and search for alternative development options in the Third World. Thus, even within the Non-Aligned Movement the conservative members (to which Jamaica belonged now) asserted themselves and pressed for a change of direction in the Movement.[1] At their Seventh Summit, the foreign minister of Singapore took the lead and warned that the Movement was in danger of being hijacked by the Soviet Union (Singham and Hune 1986, 310–15). Introduction of staunchly anti-communist and pro-Western notions into the Non-Aligned Movement during the 1980s contributed to the political asphyxiation of its former impact on global affairs.

US Policy in the Caribbean and Latin America

Although regime changes in developing social formations will hardly ever be very consequential for United States strategic interests, the perception that this would precisely be the case was, and continues to be, a powerful determinant in United States foreign policy (Farer 1988, XIV). This became clear in the reports of two commissions evaluating the causes, extent of and possible solutions to the Central American crisis. Both reports were designed for public discussion and promotion of the Reagan administration's perceptions of the region and the policies which it intended to implement. Thus, the hysterical "Secret Document of the Santa Fe Committee for the United States Interamerican Security Council" stated that Southeast Asia and Latin America would constitute the venue for the overture to the third World War and that the Caribbean was in danger of becoming a "Marxist-Leninist sea" (Schramm and Sülberg 1983, 1 – my translation). Reviving the somewhat discredited trickle-down thesis, the authors suggested the creation of political and economic systems compatible with free entrepreneurship as the solution to the continent's socioeconomic problems. The Committee, in the tradition of the Monroe Doctrine, openly supported interference in the foreign affairs of Latin American countries, in cases where they are conducted in a way "which supports and endorses the imperialist penetration of extra-continental powers" (Schramm and Sülberg 1983, 2).

Similarly paranoid perceptions also permeated another, much more influential report which the Reagan administration commissioned. Under the chairmanship of former Secretary of State Henry Kissinger, the Kissinger Commission delivered a report which also emphasized the security aspects of the Central American crisis. Among other things, the Commission urged that increased economic assistance be connected to economic reforms (Kissinger Commission 1984, 36–37). Besides a legitimate concern for prudent and efficient usage of US taxpayers' foreign assistance money, the Kissinger Commission (on behalf of the Reagan administration) promoted the fortification of the regional bourgeoisie via development and aid.

The ambivalent oscillation between various competing foreign policy goals in US relations with the region was given a neoconservative interpretation by Reagan's new UN ambassador Jeane Kirkpatrick. Her Manichean interpretation of US foreign policy priorities had considerable influence on the president himself and gave the security issue prevalence over both human rights issues and questions of economic development in the Third World. Completely unconcerned with the structural causes of social turmoil and revolution in Central America, her solution boiled down to military and economic assistance. Money, she wrote in one article, "is quite probably the key to the viability of the region's non-Communist governments" (Kirkpatrick 1984, 169). The bottom line for her, as well as for the Santa Fe and Kissinger Commissions and the president himself, was that the region was again a testing ground for US credibility (Farer 1988, 33; May 1987, 165).

International capital was (and continues to be) also interested in fostering closer formal and informal international relations between the bourgeoisie and policy makers of the region and North America. One such institutional device was the annual conference in Miami of the US private sector organization Caribbean/Central American Action (C/CAA). Founded in April 1980, the C/CAA soon aligned itself with David Rockefeller's Americas Society and involved itself in the revitalization of the Caribbean Chamber of Industry and Commerce. C/CAA's executive director, Peter Johnson, in a moment of frivolous candour, spelt out his view about the role the Caribbean social formations ought to play in the future. As if there had not existed any economies before the arrival of Columbus in the region, he claimed: "Alone they are not viable; they will in the end have to become something like *offshore states of the United States*"(quoted in Thomas 1988, 333–34 – emphasis added).

A very visible policy instrument directed at the Caribbean region was the Caribbean Basin Economic Recovery Act (CBERA), better known as the Caribbean Basin Initiative (CBI). During the course of its implementation, restrictions and limitations with regard to accessibility to the large US market made it abundantly clear that the US by no means intended to create a string of independent and competitive export producers in its "backyard". It is therefore absolutely justified when some observers express the view that "the CBI and related USAID programmes were a bold attempt to cordon off the Caribbean region from the United States' global economic rivals" (Cypher 1989,69).

The whole CBI programme was imbued with an ideological and military bias which clearly pointed to the fact that US national security considerations had been its *accoucheuse*. Thus, not only Cuba, but also Grenada and Nicaragua, were excluded from the programme, while Eastern Caribbean countries, Haiti, and Guyana only attracted very marginal attention. Clearly, CBI was less intent on fostering economic development in the Caribbean region than on stabilizing the socioeconomic crisis in some countries considered to be of strategic importance to the US. The programme's economic aspects were meant to open the CBI countries' economies to greater political influence via the link between the local bourgeoisie and international (primarily US) capital.

The US also attempted to coerce the regional development bank, the Inter-American Development Bank (IDB), into a neoconservative policy when it contributed a significant portion to the replenishment of the bank's reserves. Washington consequently pressed for more stringent and market-oriented conditions to be attached to the bank's credit and also demanded a greater say in its management. According to US Secretary of the Treasury James Baker, "more discretion and policy influence should be with the parties that contribute the lion's share of resources" (*DG* 24/3/1987, 4).

A factor operating in favour of the JLP government in Jamaica was the amount of advanced trust and confidence it enjoyed in the mirror of the international press (cf *Frankfurter Rundschau*,10/11/1980; *Neue Zürcher Zeitung*, 31/1/1981; *Guardian*, 27/10/1980; *Le Monde*, 19/1/1981; *Handelsblatt*, 22/6/1981; *Frankfurter Allgemeine*, 15/10/1981; *Blick durch die Wirtschaft*, 25/11/1981; *Financial Times*, 2/3/1981). This initially allowed for (and reflected) greater room for manoeuvre, although it also reinforced the neoliberal parameters to which this flexibility was confined. The close, albeit positive, scrutiny of the international press would have reverberated negatively at any foreign policy digression of the Seaga regime. In other words, the positive echo was not just an appraisal but also contained an obligation.

Conclusion

In summary, it can be said that the defining factor for the economic relations between industrialized and developing social formations in the decade of the 1980s was the precipitate debt crisis. Far from being the crisis of a few single countries, it reflected a deep structural problem of the global financial system. Although there can be no doubt that a majority of debtor countries urgently needed to make adjustments in their productive structure, their budgetary and fiscal arrangements and their power relationships, there can equally be no doubt that the pace and the socioeconomic instruments utilized in World Bank/IMF type structural adjustment programmes often badly mismatched the realities of the countries affected by them.

The fact that socially and economically extremely weak states were urged to export vital resources in the midst of a severe socioeconomic crisis was not an entirely new phenomenon within the history of global capitalist development. Although some economists apologetically try to play down the abyss which opened itself before a number of structurally weak and indebted developing social formations, it should not be forgotten that in the heyday of the great Irish Famine (1845–1850) in which one to two million people perished, Ireland, the oldest British colony, exported large amounts of wheat and meat to England. The difference today is that, while foreign capital is still there and continues to come in, formally independent states in the Third World are forced to export capital, which amid an economically as well as socially costly adjustment exercise could be a critical prerequisite for the prevention of social instability and the continuation of a minimum level of meaningful social development. To the extent that this necessity was not acknowledged, quackish parols such as "Development without Aid" represented ideological rather than economic concepts.[2]

Considering these macro-economic strains, heavily indebted countries such as Jamaica hardly had any realistic alternative than to kowtow to these programmes allegedly designed to restore growth, but in reality aimed at securing debt repayments. Thus, the international environment in the 1980s contributed to a significant extent to reduced room for manoeuvre in the conduct of foreign affairs, especially where strategic economic decisions were concerned. In this scenario there was also no room for a special relationship with regional middle powers which might possibly have allowed small indebted states additional latitude as international actors. Even Latin American middle powers such as Venezuela, Colombia and, to a lesser extent, Brazil and Mexico in the 1980s again pursued foreign policies which have been characterized as "pilot fish behaviour", staying close to the shark (i.e., the US) to avoid being eaten (Hazleton 1984, 160; Drekonja-Kornat 1986, 16–60).

In the revived Cold War scenario with its renewed application of the domino theory, it was to be expected that US policy makers would be particularly pleased by explicitly subordinate policies on the part of Latin American and Caribbean states. In this context, a "minion foreign policy", i.e. joining the US anti-communist and anti-statist bandwagon, could easily earn a country an "extra carrot". In other words, applying excessively free-market and anti-communist rhetoric was likely to maximize economic opportunities in terms of foreign investment, trade quotas, technology transfer, foreign aid, etc. However, these opportunities only became available within a larger framework of dependent capitalism which just allowed marginal economic development, caused severe social and political instability, and gave rise to a subordination to the political imperatives of the industrialized countries.

Indeed, in the early 1980s it became a preeminent necessity for economically weak social formations to reposition themselves along a rapidly changing global assembly line. Export orientation cum internal liberalization became the new global economic orthodoxy which rendered dissociative "alternatives" a highly unlikely route to travel. Particularly in what the US perceived as its sphere of interest, the Caribbean, any economic or political programme which only slightly resembled socialism or even communism would inevitably be exposed to strong political opposition.

8

Jamaica and the Caribbean in the 1980s

The Assertion of Democracy as Regional Norm

Immediately after assuming power in October 1980, Prime Minister Seaga engaged in a number of public appearances, both locally and abroad, at which he propounded his views on regional and international affairs and on the role which Jamaica ought to play therein. His speeches to American business persons, opinion leaders and decision makers repeated a number of well-rehearsed arguments which in part had already been set out at earlier occasions and in the JLP's election manifesto. The thrust of his arguments was unambiguous. Jamaica was determined to join again the regional "family of nations" under the paternal leadership of the US. Two general themes loomed large in his message: democracy and liberal market economy. Both topics, of course, were also favourites of the new Reagan administration as they served as levers for the realization of US interests, being broadly defined as the reassertion of global influence.

Seaga took pains to portray Jamaica and his government as the regional beacons of anti-communism, democracy and free entrepreneurship. Thus, he frequently emphasized that "no other geographical sphere can attest to 28 practicing democracies" (Seaga 1981a). This somewhat simplistic picture was not problematized by a critical analysis of the historical genesis and consequent nature of Caribbean democracy, which would only have complicated the convenience and purpose of the argument. Seaga's abridged understanding of democracy entailed only the following elements: "By our definition the term 'democratic' would mean the expression of the will of a people in open elections with universal suffrage. This is how we understand and practice the democratic process" (Seaga 1987a). For the political purpose for which the notion of democracy was utilized in Seaga's conceptualization of regional affairs, it was not necessary to engage in a critical evaluation of its breadth and depth. The notion was mainly employed as a demarcating label which was allowed to discredit the concurring "notion of revolutionary democracy which gives legitimacy to the seizure of power in the interest of the people" (Seaga 1987a).

Frequently warning against the examples of Cuba, Nicaragua and Grenada, Seaga insisted that the 'natural choice' of Caribbean people, democracy, was still in danger of being overtaken by misled ideologists who were manipulated and supported by the Soviet Union and its regional proxy, Cuba. In Seaga's view, a regional struggle was going on for democracy and against Marxism. At the very root of this "historic confrontation" he saw a "battle . . . for the minds of men" (Seaga 1982a). The prime minister saw Jamaica and, by implication himself, in the front line of this ideological struggle, which was now turning in favour of freedom and democracy:

Alien ideologies have penetrated the political system of the Caribbean. At first the success was marginal, then it grew stridently, led by the advocacy of Jamaica. It was only after a protracted struggle against the alien system, in which Jamaica again played a lead role, this time on the other side, that the political will of the people was summoned to decisively defeat the intruders (Seaga 1981a).

Thus, Seaga portrayed democracy as the regional norm and the Caribbean's own historical political choice. He, however, did not ponder the possibility that its present form was either historically imposed or, at least, being instrumentalized to serve the political and economic ends of a local elite which had grown out of the patronage of their colonial mentors. Seaga also neglected the possibility that alternative models of democratic organization and economic structuring had been suppressed and not been given a fair chance to prove their viability *as a choice of the people at a particular historical conjuncture*. Latin America and the Caribbean have abundant testimony of alternative thinkers and practitioners whose ideas and plans were suppressed from within and outside, because they challenged the existing capitalist or hegemonic order. Names like José Martí, José Enrique Rodó, Emiliano Zapata, Augusto César Sandino, Pedro Albizú Campos, Salvador Allende, Juan Bosch and others, come readily to mind.

As a consequence of what Seaga coarsely defined in terms of a unified Caribbean identity, there also existed – in his view – a common regional foreign policy tradition:

Because we share in common what I call the Caribbean political tradition, I submit that there is equally a traditional Caribbean foreign policy which we largely share. In brief terms, it is a policy which blends our interests inoffensively in a mix of balances. It is a policy by which we avoid the unilateral advocacy of singular directions and particular causes as we try to envelop the broad spread of our range of interests (Seaga 1986b).

It is not readily apparent what foreign policy attitudes were concealed by this flowery language. Presumably it referred to a superficial, moderate pluralism in Caribbean affairs, inoffensive to the regional hegemon US, or, as Seaga submits at another point, an attitude which allowed the region to earn "the enviable perception in the eyes of the international community of being a zone of moderation" (Seaga 1986b). It is evident here that Seaga's view of a regional foreign policy tradition is externally defined. It leaves little or no room for names such as C.L.R James, Toussaint L'Ouverture or Maurice Bishop, the history of events such as Grenada's liberation from the oppression of Gairy, or Cuba's liberation from the US supported dictator Fulgencio Batista. Equally, it excludes the Roosevelt Corollary or US interventionism in Haiti before and after 1915.[1]

More importantly, Seaga's conceptualization of Caribbean foreign policy seemed to circumvent the CARICOM treaty which stipulates the coordination of foreign policy as one of its objectives. Obviously, this latter scheme seeks to increase the Caribbean's diplomatic leverage in controversial international disputes, rather than to blend different foreign policies into an opaquely defined "inoffensive mix of balances". Seaga was speaking here in the somewhat isolationist *Jamaican* tradition of "basic apprehensions about becoming absorbed into an Eastern Caribbean dominated West Indian neo-federalist regional revival" (Manderson-Jones 1990, Preface). His concept of Caribbean foreign policy, therefore, did not seek to enhance the collective bargaining power of the Caribbean vis-à-vis other international economic and political entities.

This general view directly translated into concrete policy. Thus, on May 5, 1981, the Jamaican prime minister, in a speech held in Miami, proposed the organizational amalgamation of like-minded conservative parties in the Caribbean, under the umbrella of the International Democratic Union (IDU). According to Seaga, this political interdigitization had the following purpose:

Our purpose is to strengthen international bonds by fostering the development of our common ideological positions, enhancing our fraternal relationships, and mutually reinforcing the drive to political goals . . . From this base we will reach out to strengthen relations with like-minded parties to the North, the Republican and Democratic parties of the United States and the progressive Conservatives and Liberals of Canada (Seaga 1986a).[2]

While the Caribbean Democratic Union (CDU) was operating on the party level, the organization naturally provided a conduit for informal contacts between party members involved or uninvolved in government affairs. Particularly close relations developed between the Jamaica Labour Party, which had assumed leadership within the CDU through Seaga's role as initiator and chairman, and the US Republican Party. Thus, Frank Fahrenkopf, chairman of the Republican Party, was the guest speaker at the launching of the CDU. In his speech, blurring the distinction between party and government levels, he pledged "our continued support for the parties *and nations* which have formed the Caribbean Democrat Union as neighbours and partners in the economic, social and political development of the Western Hemisphere" (*DG* 20/1/1986, 20 – emphasis added).

The CDU's charter clearly speaks in favour of the local bourgeoisie's interests. Thus in section 4a, the members "regard a free and competitive market as an important safeguard against the erosion of basic rights and freedoms" (Caribbean Democratic Union 1986). However, material support for the group from local or regional private sector groups came, according to its former general secretary, only sporadically for "operational costs" of seminars or election observer missions, but did not take the form of regular subsidies.[3] Similarly, support by US-based sources through the CDU's membership in the IDU came in the form of flight tickets and per diems which allowed CDU members to observe elections in Europe and travel as far as to the Pacific region.[4]

Although the whole scenario of party-to-party cooperation is strongly reminiscent of the PNP's relations to Socialist International and the ruling party in Cuba, it has to be noted that there was no divisive debate about this aspect of Jamaica's foreign relations in the 1980s. Presumably this was so because the CDU was a venture operating with the absolution of the major regional power and its objectives matched the ideological value system not just of the Reagan administration, but the entire US foreign policy tradition. The CDU suggested in no way any challenge to US predominance in the region. *Au contraire*, it was a new communicative conduit, allowing a subdiplomatic flow of information and ideological legitimacy from the US to Jamaican (and Caribbean) policy makers.

The prime minister's advocacy of regional democracy, which was one of his favourite topics during the first three and a half years in office, was related to his understanding of order and change, or more precisely, orderly change. In democratic communities, this orderly change would be guaranteed by the pluralist balance of everybody's preferences. Seaga's idealization of the democratic process and its dynamic potentialities was clearly inspired by conservative and gradualist premises. Thus, change essentially meant "change by reforms within the system in order to build the new society" (Seaga 1981a). This kind of change was not intended to challenge the reproduction of the social conditions of accumulation.[5] In other words, Seaga's vision of orderly change at the conceptual level implied at best a marginal, *quantitative* transformation of the status quo.

Gradualism apparently also informed Seaga's development aid diplomacy. In one of his rhetorically most polished speeches on this topic, Seaga declared:

The authority of the liberal idea, however, can only be assured by the evidence of accompanying actions that demonstrably improve the conditions and quality of people's lives . . . This is why the future of liberal democracy in the Caribbean can, in the long run, be assured only by development. And all effective development strategies today must take into account the reality and the process of interdependence (Seaga 1983d).

Although this view will be easily accepted by every liberal and may in many cases be the cornerstone of their concepts of socioeconomic development, one has to ask how far the prime minister could have claimed the pursuance of a liberal foreign policy. His highly profiled role in the Grenada intervention would – as shall be seen below – tend to disprove such a claim. The unfortunate dismissal of the executive secretary of the CDU, who claimed to have been subjected to political surveillance by a confidante of Mr. Seaga working in her office, and tutored by the prime minister himself, would also tend to underline this point.[6]

Finally, one needs to put into perspective the frequent use of the notion of interdependence introduced by the prime minister. Apart from the fact that it suggests an interactive (economic) relationship with an approximately even distribution of costs and benefits for the parties involved, and that consequently a relationship between unequal powers such as Jamaica and, say, the US simply cannot be characterized in this way, the notion of interdependence served two distinct purposes: 1) it sought to be an argument for increased assistance for the Jamaican government and 2) at the political level, it immunized the related notion of sovereignty against critics who claimed that it was being eroded by the government's excessive use of foreign assistance. Seaga expressed these sentiments in the following way:

The respect for individual nations' sovereignty and independence and a people's right to self determination is a necessary prerequisite for stable international relations . . . Because the developed world is in fact led by the democratic market economies of the West, they now have the opportunity to lead in the management of economic interdependence . . .

we both have to regard ourselves as shareholders in a mutual enterprise of interdependence (Seaga 1983d).

The antagonistic notions of sovereignty and interdependence mentioned here are not traded off against each other. This shortcoming resulted in recurrent and often unfair criticism of the Seaga administration's "selling out" to foreigners. On the other side, supporters and protagonists of the government's policies insisted on their independence of judgement and decision taking in the context of global interdependence.

The discussion missed the point. It does not make any difference whether a decision is taken in favour of either "dependence" or "independence". "Interdependence", which in Seaga's view obviously constitutes the realist nexus between the two diametrically opposed notions, is itself an ideological notion that is being used *by metropolitan countries and international capital* to shroud their dominance in social formations which are dependent on them. By introducing the notion of interdependence as a broad and general label, Seaga simply facilitated the influx of ideas on socioeconomic development whose gestation lies in the context of hegemonic thinking. Ironically, the government later found itself in a position where it had to criticize the inappropriateness of certain aspects of these economic programmes "mutually agreed upon" by the government of Jamaica and the representatives of international capital (see Chapter 9).

Seaga's emphasis on economic liberalism and democracy almost inevitably called for the incantation of the spirit of interdependence. Indeed, it appears as if the notion of democracy and its (real or perceived) potential to create internal consensus are an important precondition for the successful management of cooperation among capitalist states (Wariavwalla 1988, 263ff). However, the repeated invocation of the notion alone does not bring about real interdependence, which even the relatively powerful newly industrializing countries enjoy only to a limited extent.

Given the Jamaican economy's need for external finance capital, the prominence of this notion in the Jamaican government's foreign policy did not serve an affirmative purpose but rather had an aspirational function. As such, the notion of interdependence was supposed to pave the way ideologically for an increasingly corporatized foreign economic policy. This is to say that the JLP (particularly Seaga) intended to build fora for, and close institutional linkages between, players in the Jamaican economy (particularly the bourgeoisie), the Jamaican state, and foreign investors.[7]

Seaga's Caribbean policy established a firm logical nexus between democracy, anti-communism and economic development. By introducing the ideologically laden notion of interdependence he hinted at the need for special economic support mechanisms, if Jamaica was to be successful in her regional and (through the Non-Aligned Movement) international crusade for democracy and market liberalism. Ultimately, therefore, Jamaica's depleted international reserves position was the *primum mobile* of the JLP government's mimetic foreign policy in the Caribbean region.

Relations with Cuba

The first diplomatic step taken by the Seaga administration was the fulfillment of an election campaign promise – the extradition of the controversial Cuban ambassador, Ulises Estrada. Despite it being Saturday, the new administration presented its request that the ambassador should be "immediately" replaced on November 1, 1980.[8] It was emphasized that the government wanted a continuation of the relationship with Cuba and, indeed, it did not unilaterally terminate all the Cuban support programmes in Jamaica. Cuba did not send a new ambassador, although the *Daily Gleaner* reported Cuba's intention to do so (*DG* 1/7/1981,1).

However, this extradition did not settle the case. Thus, in early 1981, Seaga suggested that it was not just containment of Cuba that was being sought, but actually a roll-back of its alleged regional influence (*DG* 7/4/1981, 1). While in November 1980 Jamaica had signalled interest in maintaining relations with Cuba, the prime minister for no apparent reason now took a tougher stance, indicating that Jamaica was "watching to see if they so conduct themselves that normal diplomatic relationships are possible" (*DG* 7/4/1981, 1). The foreign policy commentators in the Jamaican and international press hailed the prime minister's move and – issuing a carte blanche – asked for more (*DG* 10/4/1981, 8; for international reactions see *DG* 7/8/1981, 8). According to *Newsweek* magazine, representatives of the Jamaican business community apparently saw a trade-off being involved; one of them was reported saying: "The United States will take care of us. We just have to say how much we hate Castro, and salute Wall Street now and then" (*DG* 1/11/1981, 12). The prime minister himself saw the issue in a more differentiated way and did not want to give Castro all the credit for any increase in US assistance to Jamaica and the region (*DG* 17/7/1981, 10). However, his actions seemed to belie his words.

In late 1981, while the US government and Congress were involved in yet another offensive against Cuba, the Jamaican government broke off diplomatic relations.[9] Posing an extremely short ultimatum of only twenty-four hours to deliver three Jamaican criminals suspected to be in Cuba, the government was apparently determined to terminate all relationships with Cuba under any circumstances.

The US reacted quickly on the following day. Jamaica, the fifth country in the Western Hemisphere which broke relations with Cuba in 1981 (after Colombia, Peru, Costa Rica and Venezuela), was commended by a spokesperson of the US government for a sovereign decision "essential to its own interest" (*DG* 31/10/1981, 1). Just how essential it really was, has never been told or even asked. This statement also raises the question of when and by what remarkable initiative the US government had acquired the faculty of assessing what Jamaica's national interests in foreign affairs are. After all, this definition, even in Jamaica, is by no means an uncontested territory of political discourse. The US, however, had another opportunity to note complacently the growing isolation of Cuba in the Caribbean.

In Jamaica, the break with Cuba was generally regarded as being overdrawn. Both the public and the Opposition, as well as several nongovernmental organizations (e.g. the Press Association of Jamaica; Independent Trade Unions Action Council) rejected the move, sometimes simplistically suggesting that it was initiated by the US (*DG* 15/11/1981, 1; *DG* 3/11/1981, 12; *DG* 6/12/1981, 18). While even the conservative *Wall Street Journal* saw Jamaica moving closer to the US, Foreign Minister Hugh Shearer emotionally repudiated the allegations of subservience as being "stupid, vulgar and impertinent" (*DG* 20/11/1981, 16; *DG* 4/12/1981, 8).

Again the dispute missed the point. Breaking relations with Cuba did neatly fit into the US Caribbean policy scheme which traditionally had sought to isolate revolutionary Cuba from its regional neighbours. From this perspective it is a completely irrelevant question whether there actually was a phone call by Ronald Reagan or Alexander Haig to Seaga *before* Jamaica moved. Jamaica's Cuba policy supported the US cause and, representing an influential regional state, the JLP government served US regional interests more than Jamaica's own.

After 1984, Cuba no longer played a strong role either way in Jamaica's foreign policy. However, Seaga warned a number of times against the Cuban menace, mainly in order to score points in upcoming elections or to remind the US of the importance of economic viability and vibrancy in the Caribbean (*DG* 11/10/1984, 9; *DG* 19/1/1987,1; *DG* 24/5/1987, 1; see also Payne 1988, 98).

THE RELATIONS WITH REVOLUTIONARY GRENADA AND THE INVASION

In the US-led invasion of Grenada in 1983 the Jamaican prime minister figured as one of the regional protagonists. His government's active and vigorous support of the intervention, however, was not completely unexpected. Thus, the JEA's president, Prakash Vaswani, in 1981 had spoken of "new tensions" within CARICOM; without directly mentioning Grenada, he had expressed his organization's hope that political trends "in at least one of the member countries of the region which have raised doubt about the democratic future within that country, will be normalised" (*DG* 10/10/1981, 6).[10] The Jamaican bourgeoisie clearly was worried about the image of the Caribbean (and Jamaica) in the perception of international capital. Thus, Vaswani pointed out: "Grenada send a message: . . . If the communists wanted another toe-hold in the Caribbean, the Americans will defend their position. So it means: the Caribbean a more favourable place for . . . long term investment."[11]

The revolutionary Grenada was – like Guyana – an issue in talks between the Jamaican government and the local bourgeoisie. To the extent that the government was itself concerned about the influx of foreign investment, it could be expected to chime in with the bourgeoisie's concern. It might even be considered a legitimate question to ask, to what extent its subsequent plea for security concerns emanating from revolutionary Grenada served as a political camouflage for far more immediate and material economic and political concerns.[12] Thus, national economic considerations did play a greater role in Jamaica's offensive against the Bishop government than has ever been publicly admitted.

Although on a formal level Jamaica treated Grenada just as any other CARICOM country, there was a clear tendency on the part of Seaga (as well as the Adams government in Barbados) to isolate the Bishop government and keep it out of CARICOM under political pressure.[13] Thus, in March 1982, he indicated that Jamaica would try to forge a multilateral position on Grenada and the "different system involved" in this country (*DG* 14/3/1982, 11).

During this preparatory phase of the CARICOM meeting in Ocho Rios (November 1982), the member countries were also pressured by regional media to investigate the human rights situation in Grenada (*DG* 16/11/1982, 16). During the conference, Jamaica tried to sideline Grenada by promoting the introduction of a human rights clause into the CARICOM treaty and a declaration describing the Caribbean as a zone of moderation (Seaga 1982b).[14]

Guyana and Grenada opposed this move and proposed that the concepts of the region being a "zone of peace" and "ideological pluralism" in the Caribbean be acknowledged by the conference. Through the intense mediation of Trinidad a compromise was found. As a result, the treaty was not amended, the conference reaffirmed its commitment to the political, civil, economic, social and cultural rights of the peoples of the region and recognized that the emergence of ideological pluralism in the region was an irreversible trend which should not be allowed to "inhibit the processes of integration" (Caribbean Community Secretariat 1982, attachment II, 1–4).

Significantly, Jamaica also accepted the right of economic, political and social self-determination of all peoples without external interference. Thus, the Declaration's point eight said that the leaders "reaffirm and call on all States to respect the principles of non-interference and non-intervention in the internal affairs of other countries" (Caribbean Community Secretariat 1982, 3). However, shortly before the invasion occurred, Jamaica invalidated this commitment in a speech by the Jamaican representative to the UN General Assembly (United Nations 1988, 514). Jamaica's participation in the invasion was therefore the culmination of an increasingly souring relationship between the two governments.

Within a week after the Ocho Rios conference, the contentious issues came up again and Jamaica-Grenada relations deteriorated gradually – just as in the case of Cuba – within the course of one year (*DG* 27/11/1982, 1 and 20; *DG* 8/7/1983, 1; see also Payne 1988, 94). Only seven months after the Ocho Rios meeting, CARICOM held its fourth Heads of Government Summit in Trinidad and Tobago. Here, the membership question was brought much more bluntly into the focus of public attention. This reflected the PSOJ's political line which since 1980 had been calling for a suspension of Grenada from CARICOM (*DG* 18/11/1983, 25). Seaga now narrowed his acceptance of "ideological pluralism" significantly: "The wider democracy of our community, by which we meet and relate to each other as equals, demands that no system be found acceptable to us which is not chosen by its citizens in elections that are free and fair and free from fear" (Seaga 1983b).[15] Both Guyana and Grenada, who had obviously been the addressees of this message, repudiated in quite blunt terms, causing one observer to comment that the deliberations had been "bordering on personal insults" (*DG* 22/7/1983, 14; *DG* 7/7/1983, 2; *DG* 8/7/1983,1; *DG* 10/7/1983, 1). The atmosphere at the Summit was tense. When Grenada voted against Jamaica's proposal to enlarge CARICOM, the Jamaican delegation circulated a draft resolution which questioned CARICOM's membership criteria and the unanimity rule (*DG* 17/7/1983, 12). On behalf of the Jamaican bourgeoisie, the Jamaican prime minister was commended by a *Daily Gleaner* editorial for his tough stance (*DG* 9/7/1983, 6). Other CARICOM partners, however, were concerned about the high levels of rhetoric. Thus, Trinidad's Prime Minister Chambers expressed his fear that ideological differences might retard progress within the community.

It is, of course, correct to claim – as the JLP did – that the normal democratic process in Grenada was interrupted after the revolution in 1979. However, the ruling New Jewel Movement (NJM) made attempts to broaden popular participation (e.g. the 1981 wage agreement with agricultural labourers). It was certainly a tactical error of the Bishop government to delay new elections for such a long time, which invited the kind of criticism that came out of the US, Barbados and Jamaica. In any case, under Bishop's predecessor, Eric Gairy, democracy in Grenada had not been more than a facade. Considering that the People's Revolutionary Government was just about to start the drafting of a new constitution when Jamaica heightened its criticism, one is tempted to wonder whether the Seaga administration could not have given the benefit of doubt and some more time to one of its CARICOM partners with which it also cooperated in other areas (e.g. ACP group). However, due to its own ideological bias, the US outrage about this tiny island, and the Jamaican private sector's explicitly stated political opinion, the JLP government (particularly Seaga) obviously regarded this partnership as a woebegone *mésalliance*.

The broader perspective of the Grenada issue, however, was that international and regional capital were opposed to Grenada, as well as to Cuba and Nicaragua, because it had opted for a different model of *economic development*. This model did not emphasize the development of a few with subsequent "trickle-down" effects, but rather a popular form of development, by and for the people and with their integration into national decision making and planning processes. This model operated not according to, and even against, capitalist development. The assumed demonstration effect of the first successful revolution in the English-speaking Caribbean was a thorn in the side of the regional bourgeoisie. Both US and Jamaican foreign policy towards Grenada had been influenced by these strategic-economic considerations and curtailed their governments' level of tolerance towards the Grenadian revolution.[16]

The contradictions grew once the revolutionary process in Grenada disintegrated into suppressive political adventurism. After Maurice Bishop was overthrown and killed in a bloody coup, the Jamaican prime minister issued the following statement. "It did not come as a surprise to us to learn of Mr. Bishop's overthrow because it was well known that the Cubans were displeased that he was not moving at a fast enough pace to transform Grenada to a Cuban-type society" (*DG* 21/10/1983, 1). However, from Seaga's speeches within CARICOM and on other occasions, one had the impression that Grenada was already the outgrowth of the Cuban system, and ergo its satellite, *before* Bishop had been killed. At this point, the Jamaican prime minister's arguments definitely began to become incoherent.

On October 20, 1983 the government broke off diplomatic relations with Grenada until constitutional government would be restored. On the other hand, it called on the Inter-American Commission for Human Rights to investigate human rights violations "of the present *Government* of Cuban-trained Generals" (*DG* 21/10/1983, 1 – emphasis added). Consequently, the Jamaican government appeared to be prepared to regard the junta of General Hudson Austin at least as a de facto government. Nevertheless, it called for a restructuring of "CARICOM without Grenada" and dramatically appealed to the regional "obligation to do everything" to ensure that the people of Grenada would be able to live freely again (*DG* 21/10/1983, 1).

The Jamaican bourgeoisie was very vocal immediately before and after the invasion of Grenada. Thus, the PSOJ asked the government to call a CARICOM emergency meeting which would assess the situation, take steps "to bring about a speedy return to democracy", and discuss "what needs to be done to ensure that no other CARICOM country will ever find itself in similar circumstances in the future" (*DG* 21/10/1983, 10). After the actual invasion, the PSOJ was quick to congratulate Prime Minister Seaga, noting: "We cannot close our eyes to the reality that these actions and the stance of the military regime posed a threat to the democratic Governments of the Region and particularly to our neighbours in the Eastern Caribbean" (*DG* 28/10/1983, 30; see also *DG* 3/11/1983, 1; *DG* 18/11/1983, 25).

Besides the ostensible security concerns, however, the Jamaican comprador bourgeoisie may also have been in favour of the invasion for quite different reasons. Since the JLP's popular support by mid 1983 would not have secured it a second term in office, some figures in the private sector had started to think several years ahead of the current scenario. By late 1983 it had become apparent that economic growth would not be sufficiently high to offset the economic hardships resulting from the structural adjustment process. Hence, it could be expected that the JLP would not win the election constitutionally due by the end of 1985. In other words, from the point of view of the local bourgeoisie the danger of a new PNP regime loomed large. Thus, Leslie Ashenheim, financial supporter of the JLP and head of one of the largest business families in the island, called, in the same edition of the *Daily Gleaner* that reported the invasion of Grenada, for an early election. Promising a sweeping victory to Seaga, he outlined the rationale of his suggestion:

All the hardships of lack of foreign exchange, all the gross mismanagement and corruptions which have vexed our community and made business all but impossible, all the horrors of the parallel market and increases in costs would be forgotten in the face of a glimpse of what Grenadaism or Bishopism or Austinism could bring to Jamaica (*DG* 26/10/1983, 10).

Since by 1983 the PNP had not shown any sign of major programmatic changes, the JLP clearly continued to be the preferred choice of the bourgeoisie. More important to note, however, is the fact that the entire bourgeoisie was in favour of the intervention which Ashenheim, after it had occurred, attempted to legitimize as "the only steps which were possible if the complete Russianisation and Cubanisation of Grenada was to be avoided" (*DG* 12/11/1983, 12).

As elaborated elsewhere, the Jamaican government (together with Barbados and the OECS states) bypassed established CARICOM mechanisms in order to secure a quick and as broad as possible consensus about mutual invitations for the participation in the intervention.[17] However, in the light of international law there was not sufficient legal justification for the intervention and all post hoc attempts to legitimize the intervention were based only on political and emotional appeals. This has prompted at least one observer to ask whether Jamaica's decision to participate in the intervention was made after legal advice had been sought (Manderson-Jones 1990, 151).

Of course, not only was Jamaica's international reputation jeopardized, but also the United States was very concerned about the perceptions of its own role in the intervention. Jamaica was quite functional in providing arguments for the subsequent attempt to justify the invasion. In the United Nations forum, US Ambassador Kirkpatrick was conveniently able to draw extensively on the exegetic, contentious explanations of the prime minister of a country that had participated in the invasion of a country with which it had close bonds in the United Nations, the Non-Aligned Movement, the ACP and the Caribbean Community. In this context it should also be noted that on October 16, i.e. between Bishop's arrest and the intervention, US Vice President Bush had visited Jamaica and praised Seaga for his role as regional promoter of democracy (*DG* 20/10/1983, 8). Although no official statement was made, it can virtually be taken for granted that, at a time when some Caribbean nations were already pondering the possibility of a "rescue mission" for Maurice Bishop, Bush and Seaga also discussed the situation in Grenada and the viability of various forms of intervention there. Subsequent to the Bush visit Jamaica severed its diplomatic ties with Grenada.

In particular, some of the Eastern Caribbean states (i.e. Barbados, Dominica and St. Lucia) were inclined to intervene on Bishop's behalf.[18] Seaga was also "determined to do it" (i.e. intervene militarily). Two factors account for this: first, there were the JLP government's close political links through the CDU with the above mentioned governments and second, the risks of intervening without American help, an option which had been discussed extensively, were deemed too high. Initially, however, and despite their opposition to the Grenadian revolution, the US apparently were cautious about the invasion. Thus, the Department of State "flatly" rejected the Caribbean leaders' initial call for military support.[19] Only after Seaga undertook "to get through to the White House" and tried to change the US policy, did President Reagan finally overrule the Department of State.

The lawyers of the Caribbean governments involved in the invasion drew the "best legal scenario", which they intended to present to the world public after the invasion. The best way to justify the invasion was construed as the recognition of the demoted governor general of Grenada, Paul Scoon, as the legitimate government and an attempt to elicit from him a formal invitation for external assistance (i.e. intervention). The details of this scenario were delivered to Scoon on the very day of the intervention by two emissaries of the Jamaican government who were secretly flown from Barbados into Grenada. On the basis of this draft, Scoon issued the well known invitation letter which was later produced to the world public. The two examples demonstrate how deeply the JLP government was involved in both the planning and execution of the Grenada invasion. Its function within the unfolding scenario was critical to the efforts to convince the US government of the necessity to intervene militarily and in the preparation for the post-invasion legitimation exercise.

The JLP was also instrumental in promoting the Grenadian parties which it favoured in the elections after the invasion (*DG* 3/12/1984, 1; *DG* 23/12/1984, 9). Although it avoided sending government officials, the help for the New National Party (NNP), a coalition of several moderate parties, would not have occurred without the approval of the party leader *and* Prime Minister Edward Seaga. The distinction between government or party level was further blurred when the prime minister congratulated the NNP, as opposed to its leader and prime minister elect, Herbert Blaize, for its victory at the polls (*DG* 5/12/1984, 1). During the pre-election phase, the Jamaican prime minister maintained close cooperation on the state of affairs in Grenada with several industrial nations, especially the US (*DG* 8/11/1983, 1; *DG* 2/10/1984, 3).

Although the Jamaican government did not take any direct orders from representatives of either international or local capital, its role and involvement in the handling of the Grenada intervention, as well as its relations with Grenada prior to the intervention, were fully congruent with their vision of what the Caribbean as a political and economic community ought to be. Especially in the case of US Caribbean policy, parallels are obvious. It has been suggested more than once that the US "invited" the OECS invitation for the invasion of Grenada. Indeed, even one of the main protagonists and advocates of the intervention, Barbados Prime Minister Tom Adams, later revealed that the US government had put pressure on Caribbean governments. While American officials, including President Reagan, took pains to depict the US involvement as a response to a plea for assistance from Eastern Caribbean nations, Adams revealed that "an unnamed US official approached Barbados on October 15, more than a week before the invasion, suggesting that Mr Maurice Bishop . . . should be rescued" (*Times* 28/10/1983; 5; Wöhlcke 1984, 41).[20]

The Relations with Haiti

The Jamaican government took a high profile in the diplomatic handling of the forced departure of the Haitian dictator Jean-Claude "Baby Doc" Duvalier and the subsequent political instability in Haiti. There were both similarities and dissimilarities in the government's involvement to the Grenada crisis, as well as in the accompanying internal and external power constellations. The most striking dissimilarity, from the viewpoint of this study, was the notably higher level of indifference towards the instability in Haiti on the part of both the Jamaican bourgeoisie and the US government. This, however, does not mean that they were completely oblivious to the developments, or had no idea about what the state of affairs in Haiti ought to be. The high profile of the Jamaican government, in turn, appears to have been to a larger extent more "self-generated" than in the case of Grenada, where the ideological opposition in Kingston and Washington strongly suggested a mutually agreeable solution. In other words, the fact that Haiti did not immediately project an ideology inimical to the Reagan administration's West-East focus and the relative indifference on the part of the local bourgeoisie, suggest that the Jamaican government's relative autonomy was considerably greater in the Haiti imbroglio.

Similarities existed nevertheless and ought not to be overlooked. Particularly, the conflict between CARICOM and the regional leadership role Jamaica tried to assume during the Haiti crisis are strongly reminiscent of the bypassing of CARICOM and certain of its members (e.g. Trinidad and Tobago), which were perceived as "stumbling-blocks" to Seaga's preconceived designs of crisis management during the Grenada crisis.

Prior to Duvalier's departure, Seaga was hardly concerned with the dictatorial nature of Haiti's government as far as allowing Haiti into the Caribbean Community was concerned. Thus, he stated in early 1982:

I . . . would very much like to see the Caribbean look at Haiti have relationships that would tend to bring Haiti into the system . . . At the same time the CARICOM group would find it difficult to have to deal with Haiti as a member because of the difference in the standard of living there, and what would result from industries established in Haiti being able to export freely throughout the CARICOM region (*DG* 14/3/1982, 11).

It is indeed a striking contrast that at the same time that the Jamaican government espoused the greatest concerns about the *political* nature of the regimes in Grenada and Cuba, the only problem it appeared to have with dictatorial Haiti was for *economic* reasons. Clearly, the Jamaican prime minister exhibited the same ideological bias as the US administration to which Haiti was no problem at that point. In fact Haiti, together with Suriname and the Dominican Republic, was granted observer status to several Standing Committees of CARICOM in July 1984.

During the early 1980s, Jamaica maintained a low keyed relationship with Haiti through a number of formal and informal contacts. Thus, "Baby Doc" Duvalier's wife, Michelle, in 1981 paid a visit to Jamaica. The visit, which had been arranged by the minister of state in the Ministry of Foreign Affairs, was so secret that not even the US Embassy in Kingston was aware of it (*DG* 12/5/1987, 1). In December 1985, Cabinet member Oswald Harding visited Haiti in order to strengthen bilateral relations in the economic, cultural, and technological fields as well as in education, science and commerce (*DG* 6/12/1985, 2). The minister of state in the Ministry of Foreign Affairs, Neville Gallimore, had close personal contacts with the Duvalier family and had seen the dictator on a number of occasions.[21]

The Haitian crisis unfolded in several acts. The first act of this imbroglio, in which Jamaica undoubtedly played a constructive role, was the time of the departure of Jean-Claude Duvalier in early 1986. In January of that year, the Haitian dictator was faced with increasingly violent popular protests which were the direct result of IMF austerity measures. On January 31, the White House Speaker, Larry Speakes, "erroneously" announced that Duvalier had fled Haiti. On the same day, Gallimore, who was then in Miami, was contacted by Duvalier's sister-in-law, Joyce Thiesfeld, who asked for his and the Jamaican government's assistance.[22] After consultation with his prime minister, Galli-more went to Haiti on Sunday, February 2, in order to talk with Duvalier about his options, but with the intention to convince him to depart. Duvalier himself probably sought Jamaican mediation with the West in an attempt to save his leadership in Haiti, since Western support for his regime had consid-erably decreased.

Although there may have been high level contacts between the Jamaican prime minister and the US administration, both the US Embassy in Kingston and Gallimore pointed out that the mission was purely a "Jamai-can initiative":

The first time the US knew that we were doing anything about it, was when I arrived in Port-au-Prince and I saw a man in the diplomatic lounge and . . . I asked him if he was the US Ambassador and he said yes . . . And I asked him what the situation was there, to give me a briefing, and his response was: I have no instructions . . . The US Ambassador was then a persona non grata, so Duvalier would have nothing to do with the US Ambassador, wouldn't see him . . .[23]

The independence of the Jamaican initiative seems to be plausible, even though a number of commentators suggested that it had been triggered by the US. In light of the diplomatic embargo imposed on the US, the Jamaican government possibly saw a chance to profile again as a regional force to be reckoned with. The American ambassador, indeed, had no access to the Presidential Palace subsequent to the 'erroneous' statement by the White House. He, therefore, had little or no information about what was going on within Haiti's power centre and how Duvalier had reacted to the unfolding crisis. Moreover, a statement given by Secretary of State Shultz indicated that the US essentially adopted a wait-and-see attitude (*DG* 16/2/1986). The subsequent impression that the US had promoted Duvalier's departure was created because he later fled Haiti in a US Air Force cargo plane. It is however more reasonable to assume that, at first, the US would have preferred Duvalier to remain, since they essentially perceived Haiti – as one Haiti expert put it rightly – "as a Caribbean Taiwan, the low-wage capital of the West, with no trade unions and a 'stable' dictatorship".[24]

Although Seaga claimed publicly that humanitarian issues were the main focus of his government's concerns about the situation in Haiti, economic considerations seem to have played a greater role. Thus, ". . . the spin-offs were that developments in Haiti would generally reflect on, impact on the region as a whole and it would have side-effects in terms of deferral of travel and deferral of investment or cancellations . . ."[25] To the extent that foreign investment was regarded as a major source of economic growth in Jamaica, these economic considerations were very important, albeit underemphasized, motives for the Jamaican government's approach to the Haitian crisis.

According to Gallimore's report, the Jamaican government gave Duvalier three alternatives: 1) He could stay in Haiti and suppress the popular revolt by means of force and the risk of lives. This, however, would be condemned by Jamaica and the international community. 2) He could pack and quickly leave the country which would be dangerous, in case the Tonton Macoutes heard of it. They would feel exposed and helpless, since his departure would leave a power vacuum. This could lead to a blood bath between the Macoutes and rivalling factions of the army and he, Duvalier, would be held responsible for this too. 3) The prime minister's option: Duvalier could appoint an interim government before leaving the country (*DG* 16/2/1986, 10). The three "alternatives" had been cleverly put together. The first two were designed to look quite unattractive and lead logically to the third, seemingly most rational, option. Since the interim government was the preferred option of the Americans, once they had convinced themselves that Duvalier could not reasonably hold on to power, the first two options were almost pseudo-options.

When Duvalier attempted to stall, Gallimore gave him an "ultimatum", indicating that he would leave Haiti the following day. On that day he received (from Minister Supplice) Duvalier's decision to leave the country on Saturday. Gallimore then called Seaga who "dictated on the phone to the Minister (Supplice) a part of what the farewell speech should say" (*DG* 16/2/1986, 10). However, it is questionable whether the Jamaican account of Duvalier's departure reflects the full truth. Not only could Duvalier not have clung to power by virtue of the use of the paramilitary Tonton Macoutes and/or the army, but it also seems that the Haitian bourgeoisie and even parts of the army itself had begun to turn away from him. According to one insider report, General Namphy resisted Duvalier's order to shoot on the demonstrators and disarmed him after he had informed him of his refusal to obey the shooting order (Abbott 1988, 325–26). In this case, Jamaica's role would have been more than that of an invited mediator and might rather have resembled that of a conniving "wire-puller" who gave the face-saving impression to a toppling dictator that he would give up power voluntarily.

After Duvalier had finally fled the country on February 7, 1986 the American media and officials of the Reagan administration heaped praises on Jamaica (*DG* 10/2/1986, 1; *DG* 8/2/1986, 1 and 3). Obviously, this meant a political windfall for the Seaga administration. The US government, emphasizing that "the decision to leave Haiti was Duvalier's", was quick to recognize the military-civilian National Council of government (CNG) led by Lieutenant-General Henri Namphy (*DG* 8/2/1986, 1 and 3). It was certainly helpful for the US administration that there prevailed, with the help of Jamaican crisis diplomacy, the impression that the Namphy junta had been installed by Duvalier himself and that the dictator chose freely to leave the country. This reduced whatever factional fighting between rivalling power groups might have occurred, if these groups sensed that there had been a struggle for power and some kind of a power vacuum. In this case, prolonged violence would have endangered US investments in Haiti. In summary, therefore, it can be said that, in this first act of the Haitian crisis, Jamaica again intervened in harmony with US interests as well as with what it perceived to be its own national (economic) interest.

With the departure of Duvalier the crisis was not over. Indeed, in retrospect it seems as if it was only the overture to the traumatic second act, the odious rule of the army and General Namphy. Within less than a week, popular protests against the military government were again the order of the day as the army tightened its grip on power (*DG* 14/2/1986, 1; *DG* 19/2/1986, 1; *DG* 25/3/1986, 7; *DG* 27/4/1986, 30).

But despite this state of affairs, the Jamaican government was determined to work together with the Namphy government. Jamaica led the efforts of the international community to reintegrate Haiti into the fold of nations. Thus, she supported Haiti's application for observer status in the ACP meeting in Barbados in early 1986. As Foreign Minister Shearer pointed out, the JLP government also sought to strengthen economic ties with Haiti: "Our private sector should also consider the Haitian market and public and private sector missions could demonstrate Jamaica's willingness to assist. The earlier, the better" (*DG* 8/5/1986, 6). In June 1986, Jamaica extended technical help and expertise to Haiti for a reforestation project of its severely deforested hillsides.

Around this time CARICOM started to direct its attention to the issue. However, the Jamaican government jealously guarded its regional leadership, which it had acquired through its high profiled role during the management of Duvalier's departure. The JLP leadership was very aware of its stewardship position in the Haitian crisis.[26] A closer look reveals that, although Jamaica was the leader of the fight for the Haitian cause within CARICOM, it was by no means the only country that was pressing for CARICOM action. Following a joint statement of Jamaica and Trinidad and Tobago, CARICOM urged its member states to consider inter alia: quiet diplomatic mediation between varying political interests in Haiti; provision of economic support through CARICOM; and promotion of Haiti's interests in a number of international economic, political or financial institutions (e.g. OAS, IDB, ECLAC, SELA)

(CARICOM 1986a, 6). Initially, however, due to a lack of first hand information, CARICOM appears to have been cautious and sought to avoid precipitate or overly ambitious initiatives (CARICOM 1986b, 64). Jamaica kept a low profile in these initial steps of CARICOM.

Both Jamaica and the US were pressing Namphy for elections, despite the fact that a number of observers had predicted Haiti would not be prepared to have meaningful elections for another two to three years, due to its undemocratic tradition and the prevailing political and social instability. Jamaican diplomats and the political directorate, however, were prepared to show an exceedingly high amount of goodwill and optimism regarding the Namphy junta's professed intention to hand over the power to an elected civilian government. The Jamaican emissary, who visited Haiti in September 1986 for eleven days, placed his conviction on record that the election could be held as planned in November 1987 (*DG*, 10/9/1986, 31). Compared to Jamaica's attitude to the revolutionary government in Grenada, a rather significant difference was that the government did not press the Namphy government in public for elections to the same extent that it had pressured Grenada. The matter was kept low-key and was handled largely through bilateral backstage diplomacy.

Jamaica's diplomacy regarding Haiti clearly suffered from a lack of publicly voiced reservations and cautiousness. Jamaica, perceived by the Haitian government as the junior partner of the US in the Caribbean, by its accommodative diplomacy sent the wrong signals to the Haitian leaders and military. The impulse of the optimistic Jamaica-Haiti policy emanated from the very top of the government, more precisely the prime minister himself. At the lower levels, however, there existed a greater awareness about the fragility of the democratization process and the authoritarian traces of the Haitian political system. Jamaican emissaries to Haiti received clear signals, which indicated that Namphy was not as determined to hand over power to an elected government as Seaga pretended to believe. Thus, Namphy ambiguously referred to the newly drafted constitution (see below) as a "poisoned flower".[27] Gallimore expressed his reservations about the way Namphy was campaigning in the Haitian countryside, promising the people better infrastructure in the event of his victory at the polls.[28] However, with a truly "Kirkpatrickan" bias Seaga steadfastly continued to support the Namphy regime.

Because of, or rather despite, an awareness of the undemocratic political culture prevailing in Haiti, the JLP government remained deeply involved in Haitian political affairs after Duvalier's departure and prior to the November election. In fact, Jamaica led several missions of a political-educational nature to Haiti which, in cooperation with US-based institutions, sought to instill democratic values into the political landscape of Haiti:

We continued with a very active programme of political education. I was on many trips with the NDI (the National Democratic Institute), which is the international arm of the [US] Democratic Party, and we had sessions with the leaders in Puerto Rico, and we had several sessions in Haiti, and seminars trying to train them to democracy and politics as we do it in our side of the world.[29]

During these "sessions" Gallimore "taught" Haitian party leaders political probity and harmony. There exists some evidence that political tutelage of this kind was not as uncontroversial as some Jamaican sources chose to portray it (*DG* 12/5/1987, 1).

Meanwhile in Haiti, calls for democracy continued and were being pressed for in the streets. When the Namphy government called an election for a constituent assembly to draft a new constitution in November 1986, merely five percent of the electorate responded and all the major opposition groups refused to participate. However, when the referendum to approve the newly drafted constitution was held in March 1987, more than 50 percent of the electorate voted. The new constitution was accepted by more than 99 percent of the voters. During and after this process, violence and public protest partly subsided, and partly were contained by a strong show of force.

With regard to CARICOM, it can be said that by early 1987 Haiti was increasingly pressing for full membership. The organization's secretariat had its reservations, as the use of slightly pejorative terms such as "instant democracy" and "instant development" for the legitimate demands of the Haitian people indicates (see CARICOM 1987a; CARICOM 1987b). It is also worthy to note that CARICOM was aware that further violent upheaval in Haiti might be in the offing and actually foresaw the brutal violence of the November 1987 general election. In congruence with the Jamaican comprador bourgeoisie's view that Haiti's admission should rather be considered in the long term than in the short term, Seaga did not intervene in Haiti's favour at this particular point, although he also was inclined to see the country admitted ultimately (for the private sector's view see *DG* 19/4/1987, 8 and 15; see also 28/6/1987, 8).

When the election date approached, violence flared up in Haiti and the army was apparently unwilling to effectively protect offices of candidates or the electoral council and its members, who became objects of frequent attacks and arson. While human rights groups in and outside of Haiti complained about this situation, Seaga issued lukewarm statements urging for "an atmosphere conducive to allowing the people of Haiti the opportunity to freely choose their own Government . . ." (*DG* 27/11/1987, 2).

It was in this immediate pre-election period that Seaga also started to actually circumvent CARICOM as the forum which ought to be dealing with the crisis. The fact that Haitian authorities were pressing very hard to gain full membership in the organization would have given it greater leverage than Jamaica alone to demand a speedy and smooth transition to democracy. Already in late September, however, the Jamaican prime minister had reportedly suggested to an IDU meeting in West Berlin that regional leaders establish a committee to study the procedures for a facilitated return to democracy in Haiti (*DG* 29/9/1987, 1). A similar ambivalence with regard to Jamaica's commitment to regionalism was evident when the government sent Gallimore on CARICOM's request as an election observer to Haiti. Gallimore described the nature of his visit ". . . firstly, as a Caribbean Community (CARICOM) representative, and as a resource person to the National Democratic Institute, based in Washington" (*DG* 28/11/1987, 3).[30] At the same time, Seaga announced that "several countries of the Caribbean region" had formed a committee on the level of the heads of government which planned to meet the new elected president (*DG* 27/11/1987, 2). This was a clear sign that Jamaica was not utilizing CARICOM as a mechanism through which the Caribbean could try to influence developments in Haiti in a positive way.

Apparently two reasons led Seaga to calculate that a "go-it-alone strategy" (with the help of some like-minded regional leaders) was the most befitting approach to his government's Haitian policy. First and most important, considering that some US observers were excluded by the Namphy regime, Jamaica's eminent mediation in the Haitian imbroglio was likely to enhance both her international prestige and – demonstrating the strength of geopolitical motives in Seaga's foreign policy considerations – its role as a regional ally of the US. A delegation or subordination of this role to CARICOM would have served only to detract from this potential political asset. Second, it was in Jamaica's own interest to contribute to a stabilization of Haiti. CARICOM's failure to deal more decisively with the situation may also have contributed to Seaga's relative neglect of the regional institution.[31]

The subsequent bloody abortion of the November 29 election which had been tolerated and facilitated by the Namphy regime, led to the institutionalization of ad hoc consultation groups. Seaga, who at this time was in Miami at the annual C/CAA conference, quickly called an informal meeting of a small number of Caribbean leaders (the earlier mentioned heads of government committee?) under the label of Concerned Caribbean Leaders (CCL). While the US government plainly voiced its disgust "that the [Haitian] army failed in its duty to protect the electoral process", the CCL under the Jamaican prime minister's leadership came out with a rather nonchalant statement (*DG* 2/12/1987, 1). Thus, their communiqué stated:

It was the view of the CCL that the cancellation of the elections could be attributed to as many motives as there were interest groups. [. . .] The CCL felt that at this point in time the most important task was to assist Haiti in whatever way possible to establish a firm time-table for Elections and to provide such support and encouragement as is required to ensure that the Elections are held and are fair and free from fear . . . the CCL agreed to establish contact with the government of Haiti to offer support for the holding of new Elections and for the preparedness of the group thereafter to provide assistance to the new government's programme for the development of Haiti.[32]

From the viewpoint of bargaining theory, the US's condemnation and the CCL's "carrot" complemented each other perfectly. While the US led the international chorus of condemnation of the Namphy junta, the CCL's statement set the direction for the future course to be taken. It exhorted the Haitian junta to pursue the culprits of the bloody massacre of peaceful voters and urged it to set in motion again the electoral process (*DG* 2/12/1987, 1). The US Deputy Assistant Secretary of State for the Caribbean, Richard Holwill, was heard saying: ". . .You can't, at this point, go to Namphy with a stick. We could go with a stick, and everybody would feel good, but it ain't going to change anything" (quoted in Abbott 1988, 361).

The Caribbean partners, foremost of all Jamaica, spared the Namphy government the criticism it would have deserved in order to reanimate the US proposal for new elections. Hence, while the US had the role of the initiator, Jamaica and a handful of other Caribbean states played the role of executive supernumeraries of a subtle game plan. At the same time the latter were left open to a two-pronged criticism: first, they ran the danger of being accused of interference in Haiti's internal affairs and second, they risked being criticized for their forbearing stance on the issues of human rights violations in Haiti and the Namphy regime's brutal violence leading to the abortion of Haiti's first free election in over 30 years. The JLP, therefore, had to submit to being frequently reminded of the second criticism, particularly in light of its role in the condemnation and isolation of the Bishop government in Grenada. The US, on the other hand, was able to complacently indulge in keeping up the moral aspect of its foreign policy tradition without having to fear the loss of influence over Haitian affairs (see also *DG* 2/12/1987, 31).

Subsequent to the Miami meeting of the CCL, Seaga led a CCL mission to Haiti to establish contact with the Government of Haiti. In their meeting with Namphy a new election date was set for January 1988. One of the contentious issues was the composition of the new electoral council, as the old one had been dissolved by Namphy on a flimsy pretext. After four independent organizations had refused the government's offer to nominate candidates for this council, the regime intended to fill the posts itself, thereby putting the electoral administration effectively under its own control. At a press conference on December 22, Seaga made it clear that the CCL had rejected this procedure and urged Namphy to have the majority of the council's seats filled with independent candidates (Seaga 1987e; Smith 1988, 5). Publicly, therefore, Seaga presented himself and the CCL as being critical of Namphy and dedicated to an internationally acceptable election. At the same time he had to concede that "recent developments indicate that the CNG have chosen to ignore the CCL's cautions" (Seaga 1987e).

Quite contrary to the public impression he tried to evoke, however, the Jamaican prime minister continued to go out of his way to accommodate the Namphy regime's provisions. Thus, in a letter to Roderick Rainford, CARICOM's secretary general, he pointed out that a political solution would still not be out of question and that consequently the door should not be closed to the possibility of further dialogue (Seaga 1987d).

A few days earlier, but after the CCL mission to Haiti, Seaga had even criticized the old electoral council which, in conformity with the Haitian constitution, had barred several Duvalierists from the November election (*DG* 17/2/1987, 3). However, to criticize publicly this perfectly prudent measure was at best a diplomatic lapse and at worst an offense against the Haitian people who had expected nothing different from the old electoral council. It also undermined the CCL's public condemnation of the appointment procedure of the new council.

Seaga's apologetic diplomacy did not stop here. While observers driven by less egotistical motives (e.g. the Caribbean Conference of Churches) had clearly blamed the military junta for failing to prevent the violence of the November election, the Jamaican prime minister opined that it was "not true to say that the (Haitian) army terrorized people. One or two units might have been involved, but that does not make the army as a whole culpable" (*DG* 17/12/1987, 3). Closer to the truth would have been to say that one or two units did *not* condone the violence which, however, did not make the army as a whole innocent.

Following the CCL's Haiti visit, the rift within CARICOM began to widen. Not only did disagreements within the CCL (which in part overlapped with CARICOM member countries) emerge, but also CARICOM itself voiced its criticism of the CCL's failure to relate any information about its Haiti visit to the Secretariat and other member countries.[33] Caribbean countries which did not rely as much on the US as the Seaga government had grave reservations about the role of the CCL, its negative impact on the Caribbean integration movement in general and CARICOM in particular (cf *DG* 23/12/1987, 1; for a similar account see Manderson-Jones 1990, 171ff).

On January 6, 1988 CARICOM leaders met at an Emergency Summit in Barbados to discuss the organization's position on the upcoming election in Haiti. However, prior to this meeting Seaga announced that he would not participate in the meeting; which was offically explained with the inconvenience of the original date, January 4. CARICOM managed to change the date to accommodate the Jamaican prime minister, but there is evidence which suggests that Seaga's real concern was the inclusion of non-CARICOM leaders who were members of the CCL (*DG* 1/1/1988, 1). After the date had been changed, Trinidad's prime minister, who had called for the meeting, indicated that he could not attend and would be represented by his foreign minister.

Several CARICOM leaders, including the then chair of CARICOM, St Lucia, were pressing for a condemnation of the aborted election, the second Namphy regime, and the modalities and legitimatacy of the values of the coming election. Thus, the St. Lucian prime minister expressed the view that CARICOM would not recognize the new government in Haiti if the administrative provisions for the election would not be rectified (*DG* 29/12/1987, 1; see also *DG* 30/12/1987, 1; *DG* 2/1/1988, 2). After Seaga had forced the inclusion of other CCL leaders, a serious disagreement about the nature and scope of the meeting developed, with Trinidad and Tobago charging the Jamaican prime minister with putting pressure on CARICOM. Haitian presidential candidates participating in the meeting expressed their expectation that CARICOM would attempt to prevent the Namphy regime "from going ahead with its scheduled illegal elections on January 17" (*DG* 5/2/1988, 2). The different sentiments voiced before the Barbados Summit greatly increased the horizons of expectations and, at the same time, pointed to an extremely difficult process of finding a unified position on the issues at stake.

The barren ambiguity which surrounded the meeting was mirrored in the final communiqué which the leaders agreed upon only after very difficult talks. (see Appendix) The communiqué, based on Jamaica's draft, was extremely ambiguous and weak. While attempting to urge the Namphy government to hold peaceful, credible and democratic elections, it also made it clear that it would accept an election that would not necessarily meet all standards. The communiqué, which, due to the explicit participation of a number of CCL leaders, was hardly a pure CARICOM position, produced very mixed reactions. While the US, which was holding naval exercises offshore of Haiti, supported it, most other commentators, including a number of CARICOM states and some Haitian candidates, criticized it as too weak (*DG* 10/1/1988; *DG* 8/1/1988, 2).[34] In Jamaica, however, Seaga's policy was criticized only very mildly, and for the most part was approved of by the influential *Daily Gleaner* (*DG* 15/1/1988, 1; *DG* 16/1/1988, 24; *DG* 11/2/1988, 6).

Clearly, Jamaica had hijacked the CARICOM meeting and given the communiqué its own handwriting. The Seaga government rejected calls for a postponement of the election, as well as an explicit condemnation of Namphy's role in the bloody abortion of the November election (*DG* 7/2/1988, 1). Thus, Jamaica's position again complemented the US position and the presence of the US Assistant Secretary of State for Caribbean Affairs at the Bridgetown CARICOM meeting certainly was no coincidence.

The Namphy government made some cosmetic changes to the electoral process, but the procedure was by no means satisfying in terms of demo-cratic standards. Consequently, not only did a number of CARICOM countries keep their distance from the January election, but only a minority of the Haitian people (between 10 and 15 percent) voted (*DG* 15/1/1988, 1).[35] While a number of countries (e.g. Canada, Barbados) rejected the results of the poll (i.e. the election of Leslie Manigat), Jamaica again held out its hand instantly. In a telephone interview before the polls had closed, the Jamaican "observer" indicated that "as long as things are done properly, they will have our support" (*DG* 18/1/1988, 1; *DG* 19/1/1988, 7). This rather early statement pointed to a preparedness on the Jamaican side to further support the corrupt political process in Haiti, even though the election was popularly rejected.

Indeed, the government lent its support to the Manigat government, thereby recognizing it (at least de facto) (*DG* 29/1/1988, 2). It can be argued, therefore, that the JLP government violated its own promise, given in public and in private, to take the level of participation by the Haitian people as the ultimate yardstick of deciding the legitimacy or illegitimacy of the January election.[36] Hence, it misled the public as well as other CARICOM members regarding its real attitude towards the Haitian imbroglio.

After the subsequent overthrow of President Manigat by General Namphy, the Jamaican government suspended normal relations with Haiti, but still did not see "a reason to sever or suspend observer status with the Namphy government" within CARICOM (*DG* 7/7/1988, 3). Again, this position tied in perfectly with the US attitude which, according to the State Department, was "not contemplating" a break in diplomatic relations (*DG* 23/6/1988, 4). *Au contraire*, the US indicated that it would continue to cooperate with the

Namphy regime. In the following months, Jamaica's Haitian policy waned into nothingness.

Although the *Money Index*, a magazine of and for the Jamaican bourgeoisie, critically covered the events in Haiti, they were far removed from the concerns of local business circles. This left the Jamaican government with a significant degree of relative autonomy in the handling of this affair. Indeed, the prime minister with respect to his other CARICOM colleagues primarily followed "his own agenda" (Smith 1988, 11). This agenda, in turn, was apparently influenced by geopolitical considerations, i.e. by the Jamaican government's perception that its active role in the settlement of the Haitian crisis would improve Jamaica's profile as a reliable regional ally of the United States. Thus, it ought to be remembered that at this point Jamaica was involved in difficult negotiations with the IMF and constantly seeking rescheduling of its debt repayments. Washington's deeper concerns regarding the instability in Haiti were aptly captured in an editorial of the *Daily Gleaner* on the situation there: "The communists, through Cuba . . . will make their bid and those who believe in democracy, that is parliamentary democracy, will also make their bid" (*DG* 19/2/1986, 8).

By implication, this view was also meant to influence the public discourse in Jamaica on the crisis. Even though the government never voiced similar sentiments, it would have been well aware that this kind of thinking was prevalent in influential circles of the US administration and that the US was primarily concerned with keeping a potentially eruptive and revolutionary situation in Haiti under control (*Money Index* 19/1/1988). Jamaica's position was congruent and partially overlapping with the US approach to the crisis.

Conclusion

Although the JLP government's positions and actions in both the Grenadian and Haitian crises were essentially determined by its own assessments, they were tailored to fit the body of US Caribbean policy. Thus, Seaga pointed to the inherent "naturalness" of his Caribbean policy:

This has been the natural foreign policy for this region because of the levels of compatibility . . . that exist in terms of political system, the type of economic system by which we all operate, the market system economy which gives the opportunity to the natural vent of the people as . . . entrepreneurs and to the value systems and all the other things we share in common. So, it is only logical that there should be a wide range of areas of commonality between the two countries.[37]

Although in this role Jamaica certainly was an integral component of the US foreign policy approach in the Caribbean, the role it played was not without costs. Jamaica's high profile role in both the Grenadian and the Haitian crises led to serious irritation among its CARICOM colleagues, especially Barbados (in the case of Haiti) and Trinidad and Tobago. The Jamaican prime minister's tendency to keep his colleagues uninformed strained the Caribbean integration movement unduly and undoubtedly was not in conformity with CARICOM's goal of harmonization of the member countries' foreign policies.

The extent to which the accommodative US-Jamaican approach to the Haitian crisis backfired was ultimately demonstrated when President Leslie Manigat was ousted in June 1988. No other event could have brought home better the point that there was no way that one could reasonably negotiate democracy with Duvalierist generals in Haiti, without simultaneously applying severe economic and political pressure.[38] As demonstrated above, Jamaican diplomats had received early signals that Namphy was not prepared to hand over power, but decisions made at the prime minister's level neglected these warnings.[39] The approach of the de facto US-Jamaican diplomatic axis to negotiate a simulacrum of democracy in Haiti proved to be unsuitable to the realities of the internal affairs of this country. The real losers, however, were the same people Seaga had purported to help – the Haitian people.

Judging from Jamaica's role in the two crises, her very vocal advocacy of freedom, democracy and free enterprise in the Caribbean did not mean much in practical terms. It was therefore a reminder of the high levels of rhetoric under the PNP in the 1970s. As a symbolic foreign policy, it attempted to create a strong ideological bridge to Washington, thereby maintaining a readily open line of communication with the US government. It also paved the way for some corporatist aspects of the government's foreign policy. Thus, the JLP government's defence of ideological and economic interdependence in the region was supposed to directly and indirectly extract the large material benefits from international private and public finance capital, which were deemed a precondition for the continued reproduction of the social conditions of accumulation that the Jamaican bourgeoisie had perceived to be fundamentally threatened by the end of the 1970s.

The symbolic side of the ideological fraternity between the US and Jamaican governments regarding regional affairs was complemented by Seaga's initiative of founding the CDU. The CDU was apparently less a Caribbean party issue for Seaga, than a means to further cement his government's ties with the US administration. In his own words: ". . . we will continue to have that strong inter-party relationship that we have enjoyed over the past few years, which has been one of the basic strengths of the relationship between the Government of Jamaica and the Government of the United States" (*DG* 10/11/1988, 1).

The Jamaican bourgeoisie fully approved the JLP government's Caribbean policies examined in this chapter. The JLP's regional policies were therefore in harmony with bourgeois capitalist interests, which allowed the government to seize some amount of initiative. However, this regional activism was only granted on the premise and tacit understanding that the Jamaican government operate in harmony with US foreign policy objectives *which in the 1980s allowed for a considerably smaller freedom of strategic choice than in the 1970s*. The relative autonomy of the Jamaican state to act with regard to regional issues was smaller than in the 1970s, allowing only policies which did not fall out of the ideological and geopolitical framework of the US-Jamaican bourgeois coalition.

9

Jamaica's Relations with International Capital and the US in the 1980s

The external relations which the JLP government pursued in the 1980s were to a large extent of an economic nature. With regard to the US in particular, Jamaica vigorously tried to insert itself into the global economic concept of the new Reagan administration in Washington. In a wider sense, Seaga presented his government as an adherent of the free global movement of the factors of production, especially capital.

Restoring Confidence and Attracting Foreign Capital

The Seaga government was preoccupied with courting US finance and commercial capital, which is only understandable given the fact that North America is both Jamaica's largest market and foreign investment source as well as bilateral donor of official aid. In many of its investment promotion initiatives it sought to incorporate the particular interests of the wider Caribbean, the US capital itself, and developments within the global economy.

With regard to the latter, Seaga, who as minister of finance and prime minister controlled most of Jamaica's external economic relations, displayed a keen interest in the global economic trends which affected the US economy. In all his attempts to attract US investment to Jamaica, he emphasized his understanding of the legitimate concerns of the American industry, workers and taxpayers, as well as the concerns of the US legislators. At the same time he promoted his proposals by suggesting their supposed mutual beneficence for all parties involved. In the face of global economic changes, thus Seaga's argument usually proceeded, it would be of eminent importance to readjust regional economic arrangements between the US and the Caribbean. On the most general level, this argument was certainly welcomed by economic interests in North America who sought to evacuate uncompetitive links in their production chain to more profitable sites. Likewise, US geopolitical considerations under President Reagan demanded a stronger economic concatenation of the US and Caribbean social formations.

Seaga's concern for developments in the world economy was clearly exposed after the breakdown of American stock markets in late 1987. Lecturing his North American business audience about the educational and economic virtues of Japan and Germany, he concluded that religious, cultural and social disparities were the root causes of "problems manifesting themselves in the financial dislocations which threaten the global economy today":

. . . it is as well to recognise that treating the financial dislocations which are merely symptoms, does not address the real fundamental gaps which are socio-cultural. And while these real gaps which produce technological superiority exist, financial gaps will emerge periodically as expressions of the uneven capabilities of East and West (Seaga 1987c).

With this argument Seaga tried to play out the cultural affinity of the Caribbean against the economic prowess of East Asia.

The JLP government's relations with international capital in its first two to three years in office stood very much under the banner of intensive lobbying for loans and investment. To a large extent this effort was aided by the extremely cordial personal relations which Seaga developed with the new US president. His widely reported visit to Washington in early 1981, as the first head of government being received by the new US president, set the tone of the further development of US-Jamaican relations. Thus, Reagan remarked that the US would "find ways to strongly support Jamaica" and Seaga "could count on American support for his objectives, especially in his efforts to expand his Private Sector" (DG 7/2/1981, 11).

The absolute economic priority in the early months of the new Seaga administration was the negotiation of a new loan agreement with the IMF. The IMF, which against all its conventions had started to negotiate with Seaga even before he was elected, granted Jamaica an agreement with extremely mild conditionalities attached to it.[1] Under the new three-year Extended Fund Facility (EFF) Jamaica received US$ 650 million, of which she was allowed to draw 40 percent during 1981/1982, as opposed to the usual one-third. Under the agreed Compensatory Financing Facility the government could draw an additional US$ 48 million, so that it got approximately US$ 308 million for its first full financial year. The following have to be considered as particularly favourable features of this programme: no devaluation of the Jamaican dollar; no quantitative wage guidelines; no cutback on public sector employment. The level of funding and the nature of the related conditionalities suggest that this first IMF agreement of the Seaga government reflected a far greater generosity and flexibility of the IMF and its member states than just a few months earlier when the PNP had been in power. The macroeconomic indicators of the Jamaican economy were the same, but international capital obviously felt much more comfortable with the Seaga government's economic and political approach.

The agreement was based on excessively optimistic forecasts of economic growth. Thus, projections of 3, 4, and 5 percent real growth in the fiscal years 1981/82, 1982/83, and 1983/84, respectively, were quite unrealistic figures, considering the impending global recession and the structural adjustment exercise the Jamaican economy was going to be subjected to. Despite much lower forecasts by his own experts, Seaga presented vastly exaggerated forecasts in bauxite, sugar and banana production to his financial mentors in the IMF (Stephens and Stephens 1989, 2). The apparent propensity of the upper administrative echelons in the IMF to accept the Jamaican prime minister's projections is proof of the considerable political goodwill he enjoyed at this point in the corridors of international financial power. It is by no means a secret that the IMF has some degree of latitude which varies from client to client, a fact which it is readily prepared to admit and client governments can influence conditionality through various means, such as the nature of their political relationship with the United States (Bernal 1988, 245–48). Seaga sought to establish this relationship by his proactive regional policy which represented strategic economic and political US interests in the Caribbean Basin (see Chapter 8).

To some extent, Seaga's optimistic forecasts may have been premised on an overestimation of the levels of foreign investment capital coming into Jamaica. This capital was expected to come from two sources: the return of Jamaican investment capital which had left the island in the 1970s and new foreign capital searching new business opportunities. Throughout his term of office, Seaga vigorously promoted Jamaica as a lucrative and safe investment site for foreign investors. Thus, he emphasized that differences between international corporate business and the Jamaican state "are seldom entrenched and yield to amicable and constructive solutions in almost every case" (Seaga 1983c). In a speech at the important annual conference of the US bourgeoisie's Caribbean/Central American Action (C/CAA) which he regularly attended, his great expectations regarding foreign private investments became quite evident: "The only source of big financing are private investment inflows which, aside from magnitude reach the sectors which generate most of the real productive growth" (Seaga 1980b). This broad statement was more clearly defined on a later occasion when Seaga pointed out that "Jamaica is now particularly interested in the investor who is a practicing businessman wishing to carry out a project himself . . . and who comes to us with the know-how, the markets, and some capital" (Seaga 1983c). Obviously aware that after the experience of the 1960s and 1970s no international support for large prestige projects would be forthcoming, complex and capital-intensive large-scale projects were not made a priority of the government.

The government's verbal commitment was supported by a number of practical initiatives. Among the most visible and published of these was the US Business Committee on Jamaica, which was better known as the Rockefeller Committee, named after its chairman David Rockefeller. This committee, consisting of the chairmen of a number of influential US multinational corporations (e.g. Exxon; United Brands; Alcoa), explored the chances for investment ventures in Jamaica. The Rockefeller Committee was a direct result of the consultations which Seaga had held with Reagan.

As a counterpart of the Rockefeller Committee the Jamaican government instituted the "prime minister's Committee on Foreign Investment and Employment". This committee comprised about a dozen chairmen/presidents of Jamaica's most important private sector associations (e.g. JEA; PSOJ; JMA; CoC; Jamaica Bankers' Association), a small number of state corporations (e.g. National Hotel and Properties Ltd.; Jamaica National Investment Corporation; Jamaica Development Bank), as well as a private banker and the chairman of the Petroleum Corporation of Jamaica (PETROJAM). Labour interests were, despite the innuendo in the committee's name, not represented.

Rockefeller and his Jamaican counterpart Carlton Alexander met on a number of occasions both in Jamaica and the US. Although the Rockefeller Committee dedicated time and staff to the exploration of potential business ventures which brought some successes (e.g. the establishment of a private sector development bank – the Trafalgar Development Bank), by and large, it did not fully meet the expectations of either the private sector or the government. Thus, after 1983 activities of the Rockefeller Committee were being phased out.[2] While the Jamaican private sector was not in a state of readiness, many projects of the Rockefeller Committee were too grandiose and unmindful of the lack of appropriate infrastructure, capital and management skills on the part of Jamaica. The committee's greatest success was probably to change international capital's perception of Jamaica. This, in turn, exerted a positive influence on the Caribbean Basin Initiative (CBI).

The Caribbean Basin Initiative

The CBI came as a result of Seaga's personal lobbying efforts in Washington for a Caribbean "Marshall plan". The original CBI as proposed by the Jamaican prime minister, however, differed considerably from the diluted version which the US Congress eventually passed. This proposal envisaged an aid injection amounting to US$ 3 billion. This meant that in addition to $1.3 billion already assigned to the region, an additional $1.7 billion had to be mobilized. In Seaga's view, half of this sum could have been provided by Venezuela, Mexico and Trinidad, another $400 million by the US, $300 million by Europe and Japan and $200 million by multilateral institutions. As it turned out, the US was not interested in such a multilateral scheme and CBI became essentially a bilateral programme with an insignificant aid component of just US$ 300 million.

Despite this, Seaga extended the greatest compliments to CBI and sought to grasp every potential advantage that might result from it. Utilizing the same emphatic and prophetic language US President Reagan used to indulge in, Seaga described CBI as a "God-send" (*Insight* June 1982). This policy was fully consistent with the avowed political priority (pertaining to Jamaica's external relations) of the Jamaican comprador bourgeoisie which was "markets".[3] It is arguable that the strongest (emergent) sector of the Jamaican bourgeoisie in the 1980s, the exporting sector, delegated to the state, albeit not *expressis verbis*, what eventually became a primary occupation of Jamaican foreign policy, i.e. the search for investments, markets, and bilateral and multilateral aid (in this order).

At the political level, the government made it explicitly clear to the United States that it would comply with the terms under which a country became eligible for the CBI. Thus, in a letter to William Brock, the US special trade representative, Jamaica's minister for foreign affairs and trade, Hugh Shearer, pointed out:

The Government of Jamaica expresses its willingness to cooperate fully with the United States of America in the administration of the arrangements under the act in order to ensure that it operates to the mutual benefit of our two countries; and Jamaica is prepared to notify and consult with the United States in event of changes in any of the policies or practices discussed above which may prove to be inconsistent with any of the designation criteria of the United States law (United States Congress 1983, 28).

This statement suggests that a considerable portion of the Jamaican government's discretion to change its trade policies was through the CBI legislation being tied to the US political and legislative assent. The apparent trade-off involved was again psychologically mitigated by the implicated notion of mutual dependence.

US Secretary of Commerce Malcolm Baldridge, meanwhile made it quite clear that the CBI was of economic importance to the US and an integral part of its own export strategy:

Jamaica is a natural for our investment in some very fundamental ways. For countries like the U.S., Canada and others, it is not just a replacement of investment from one country to another. It is a way to gain access to European markets with duty advantages under the LOME agreement, a way to gain access to other Caribbean countries with duty advantages, a way to export to the US with the new advantages under the CBI and another way to export to the South American market (*DG* 18/10/1983, 1).

Hence, the CBI was not only an instrument to "cordon off" the Caribbean, but also a means for international capital to penetrate Caribbean (including Jamaican) markets. But, while the initiative created only marginal low wage employment in the region, foreign investors posed stiff competition to regional producers by virtue of the greater capital and technology resources at their disposal and the tax benefits which they enjoyed in countries such as Jamaica.[4] In retrospect it is perhaps not surprising that even the already diluted version of the CBI became subject to further protectionist measures on the part of the United States. Thus, for example, the Thurmond-Jenkins Bill passed by the US Congress in 1985 sought to limit textiles imports from all over the world and clearly ran counter to the spirit of the CBI. Seaga and other Caribbean leaders spoke out strongly against this legislation (*Insight* December 1985, 1).

At the same time, the prime minister suggested an alternative plan based on a "production-sharing" arrangement in the textile industry. According to this plan, the US should increase the import quota for textiles from the Caribbean in order to compensate for the reductions from the Far East. The increased imports, in turn, were to be generated from materials produced in the US. This would have the following advantages for both the Caribbean and the US: the US textile industry would increase its production in order to satisfy increased demands; US workers would profit from the "value-added segment" of the clothes produced in the US under the 807 programme; Caribbean workers would profit; and Far East producers would increasingly utilize the Caribbean as a production platform, but produce with textiles originating from the US. This certainly was an attractive proposal for US lobbying groups and lawmakers which was subsequently accepted by the US in February 1986 as the "Super 807" programme. Both the Jamaican manufacturers and exporters were quick to congratulate the prime minister for this "tremendous break-through" (*DG* 24/2/1986, 3; *DG* 28/2/1986, 1).

The Jamaican garment producers were directly affected by the tight fiscal and monetary policies which resulted from IMF austerity programmes. According to a government study, small and medium-sized producers were lacking modern equipment and personnel, but found it extremely hard to find technical and financial assistance from either the government or the banks (*DG* 15/4/1986, 6). This situation was again evidence of the "classic" discrepancy between industrial and fiscal policies which are exogenously generated and an inadequate productive infrastructure, incapable of taking full advantage of these policies and in need of a combination of concessionary loans and temporary and selective insulation from the sudden onslaught of superior and established external competition. However, although in the early 1990s the sector had not yet reached its full estimated employment potential (i.e. 40,000 to 50,000 workers), the performance of the garment industry can be seen as a moderate success, even though it largely rested on US initiatives.

The continued application of non-tariff protectionist barriers by the US induced the Jamaican prime minister to voice some criticism which was clearly fuelled by frustration. At the 10th C/CAA conference, he warned that CBI benefits were in danger of being eroded by "narrow restrictive policies":

. . . we are concerned that having restructured our economies to make them attractive production locations better suited to address our myriad problems, having made some head-way in encouraging number of areas, having demonstrated the sensitivity that has resulted in new mechanisms . . . – with positive results to the mutual benefit of the partnership between industrialized and developing worlds – we do not go on to find that the rules will be changed mid-way in the game (Seaga 1986c).

This and similar criticisms were repeatedly rebuffed by spokespersons of the US government who – like the US Trade Representative Yeutter – cynically argued that the Caribbean's "expectations have been unrealistically high and progress will come in time" (*DG* 10/3/1986, 1; *DG* 28/2/1986, 19; *DG* 28/2/1988, 1; *DG* 13/7/1988, 1; *DG* 16/4/1988, 3).

One example of how new investments in Jamaica were jeopardized by protectionist sentiments in the US Congress was a project in ethanol distillation. The project, which was set up in March 1985, was to become the largest foreign investment under the CBI for which it even received an award by the US president. Before the investors set up the plant, they applied to the US customs and received approval that their product (utilizing raw material from

Spain) would be eligible under the CBI ruling.[5] The duty-free ruling gave the company, Tropicana, a clear competitive advantage over other foreign suppliers to the US market which was pivotal to its decision to establish production in Jamaica. After the company started exporting its product, the US Congress enacted the Tax Reform Act of 1986, imposing restrictions on the duty-free treatments of ethanol imports to the US. Only after protracted negotiations and intensive lobbying by both Tropicana and the Jamaican government was the company granted an exemption (the so-called grandfather status). Besides the direct effect on the regional ethanol industry, this incident, about which the Jamaican government was "very upset", had much more far reaching implications.[6] Thus, it clearly sent a very mixed signal to all potential investors who were planning to invest in the Caribbean under the CBI.

According to the prime minister, the Tropicana experience subsequently influenced the Jamaican government's decision not to grant Free Zone status to another ethanol joint venture (see *DG* 15/2/1987, 9). In the case of Allied Ethanol Ltd., the Jamaican partner company (Wray & Nephew Ltd.) had already made substantial investments when the Jamaican government indicated in late 1985 that it would not grant Free Zone status to the project. However, apparently it had agreed earlier to grant this status. As a consequence, Allied Ethanol pulled out of Jamaica virtually overnight. This incident reportedly had two disadvantageous consequences for Jamaica: first, Allied's departure made the controversial US Tax Reform Act of 1986 a fait accompli and secondly, PETROJAM, a Jamaican company which was also trying to establish alcohol production, was the only company the US Congress subsequently did not grant "grandfather status", which diminished the profitability of its new venture significantly (*DG* 15/2/1987, 9). Additionally, in the case of PETRO-JAM, the fact that the company was state owned was perceived in Washington as violating the spirit of CBI.

It is interesting to have a look at the implications of the Jamaican government's decision to refuse Allied Ethanol the desired Free Zone status. The official reason given was that: "... it was Government's view that the profitability of simple dehydration operations without any backward integration into the domestic industry was sufficiently profitable not to justify the provision of the Free Zone status" (*DG* 15/2/1987, 9). Indeed, Allied had planned to utilize raw materials from the US, but not from the region. Hence, Allied's project was less integrated than PETROJAM's which utilized locally produced sugar. However, probably the most important reason was that the state-owned PETROJAM, which did not operate under Free Zone status and used the more expensive local sugar, could not have borne the competition of another major ethanol producer producing in the Free Zone and with cheaper 100 percent non-Caribbean raw materials. In other words, PETROJAM had to be protected from foreign investment endangering its operations. It is in this context that the above quoted explanation has to be read. Moreover, there certainly was consternation in the Jamaican government that in the case of Tropicana the US government had increased its taxation, while Jamaica was waiving its rights to collect taxes in order to give an investment incentive to foreign capital.

However, as already mentioned, the Jamaican government's attempt to shelter PETROJAM was repudiated by Allied Ethanol, which had powerful allies in Washington. It is also interesting to note, that in its attempt to protect a state-owned enterprise, the government actually moved against the interest of a big local private company (i.e. Wray & Nephew) which had already invested in this venture. This example illustrates how the state exerted its relative autonomy vis-à-vis international capital and the local bourgeoisie. However, it can be safely assumed that Seaga would not have retracted the Free Zone status from Allied and Wray & Nephew (against the spirit of the CBI) if it had rendered their venture unprofitable. Moreover, it has to be borne in mind that this incident in no way was intended to question the primary importance assigned by the government to the private sector as the engine of economic growth.

In a comprehensive appraisal of the CBI, Hyett recently argued that the initiative helped to reverse the trend toward increasing US trade deficits. This was a noticeable development, considering that in 1988 the Caribbean Basin was the only major region in the world with which the United States had a trade surplus. The author concludes that, given the continuation of US policy to prevent shifts by CBI countries towards state-directed strategies or the necessary subsidization of critical infant industries, "few opportunities will emerge for local entrepreneurs to involve themselves in productive aspects of the region's new growth sectors" (Hyett 1989, 57). Although the garment sector in Jamaica was relatively successful, it was also plagued by this disadvantage.

The JLP government's enthusiastic, if critical, embrace of this double-edged US initiative can, therefore, only be understood as a response to the local comprador bourgeoisie's call for markets.[7] However, a diplomatically more prudent approach would have exposed to a broader public the fact that Jamaica could hardly have been expected to succeed as a free-market showcase in the Caribbean, if it was faced with US protectionism and incomplete economic programmes which are primarily concerned with US political and economic expansion in the region.

The combined effect of structural adjustment, the CBI, special import schemes, and lobbying efforts of both the government and the local bourgeoisie on the inflow of foreign investment was, at best, moderate. Seaga, not surprisingly, was disappointed by this development (Stephens and Stephens 1989, 5). Investment was particularly slow in the initial three years 1981–1983, when only 202 projects with a total capital investment of J$ 402.6 million and just 15,440 new jobs were implemented (JAMPRO 1988). By March 1988 these figures had increased to 890 projects, J$ 2440.3 million and 69,431 new jobs; 66 percent of these projects were locally owned, 26 percent foreign investments and merely 8 percent consisted of the desired joint ventures (JAMPRO 1988). Similarly, the levels of gross domestic investment (as percent of GDP) averaged only 20.8 percent between 1981 and 1987 and fell far below Seaga's target of 25 percent of GDP (*Social and Economic Survey*, various years).

The examples of the ethanol industry and, to a lesser extent, the garment industry reveal a distinct, albeit not immediately obvious, shortcoming of Jamaica's lobbying efforts in Washington. There was a marked discrepancy between the government's effort to lobby at a macro-level and at a micro-level. The government, and especially the prime minister himself, was very actively promoting Jamaica as an investment site and suggesting trade programmes aimed at enhancing (or at least preserving) Jamaica's stake in international markets. However, there was a clear lack of follow-up on these proposals once they reached Congress and of lobbying for specific industries or even single investors. Thus, one feature of Jamaica's lobbying efforts in Washington was that it was rather reactive and often merely aimed at post facto damage limitation.[8]

Clearly, a stronger presence of Jamaican (or regional) lobbyists in the corridors of Congress would have sensed earlier where US economic interests were lobbying against Jamaican or regional interests. The occasional visit by the prime minister or foreign minister to Congressional representatives was certainly a welcomed photo opportunity, but not necessarily politically rewarding. Without doubt President Reagan, with his immense popularity could have pushed through the CBI in its original multilateral and extended form. If the Caribbean would indeed have had the significance which the US government ascribed to it, the prudent and effective implementation of the programme by the bureaucracy could have been requested more forcefully, provided Jamaica (or the region) had addressed the issue of lobbying in a more structured way.

Although some criticism and occasional lobbying missions came out of the Jamaican private sector, there was no substantial material commitment to an effective and sustained lobbying effort brought forward. The absence of an integrated and continuous private and public sector lobby strategy, directed at certain pivotal members of Congress (e.g. chairmen of Foreign Affairs Committees or Appropriations Subcommittees on Foreign Operations), is all the more astonishing as Seaga was well aware of the complexities of the US legislature and the intricacies of its bargaining processes. Evidently, the Jamaican bourgeoisie was either ignorant of the importance of sophisticated lobbying or it was satisfied with the efforts being made by the prime minister, the foreign minister and executives of JAMPRO (the government agency responsible for investments). Both cases indicate its essential unpreparedness to grapple with a new economic environment. However, if the political will had been there, a structured private/public sector lobbying approach could probably have been fostered in a more forceful way.

Financial Tightness and Attempts to Change Economic Emphases

With the stagnating and, according to some economic indicators, even deteriorating economic situation in Jamaica, the JLP government's relationship with international capital in and after 1985 was of a somewhat more antagonistic nature than in the early 1980s. Seaga's perception of the capability of international capital to effectively support Jamaica's economic recovery and the adequacy of its economic prescriptions became more skeptical.

Although, as argued above, the Jamaican workers and marginalized strata endured the rapidly deteriorating standards of living with remarkable calm, there nevertheless occurred protest against the social consequences of the government's austerity programme. Moreover, an election was constitutionally due by early 1989 and if the government could not fulfill its election promises it was certain to lose at the polls. Hence, in the mid 1980s the government's priority changed somewhat from austerity to the restitution of certain social and security programmes for the increasing numbers of disadvantaged and marginalized Jamaicans.

On the domestic front Seaga's criticism of international financial institutions and trade arrangements was much less explicit than his comments in the foreign policy arena. Already by 1982/83, with the Mexican debt crisis bringing the global implications of debt into much sharper focus, he had voiced some alternative ideas concerning the solution to the debt crisis, which he aptly regarded as a development crisis. Seaga usually emphasized that he did not seek to abolish old institutions or replace their functions with new institutions, but rather intended to work for solutions in the ambit of existing institutions. Nevertheless he warned that Jamaica's economic recovery was endangered by the global debt crisis and that international financial arrangements were in danger of collapsing unless creative and expansive solutions were found. In July 1983, Seaga warned US businessmen:

There is no question that there is need for greater guidance from the multilateral institutions on the whole issue of credit, debit and payments. Otherwise we face the real dangers that not only will countries proliferate protectionist associations in trade, but that they will take steps to insulate their economies in unorthodox and dangerous ways, from the heavy debt burden which they carry (Seaga 1983c).

From this point on, and in opposition to neoliberal Milton Friedman's call for its abolition, Seaga continued pressing for an extension of the IMF programmes' lending periods (to at least 12 years) and an expansion of the total disbursements being made by the international commercial banks, whose lending activities were contracting. The Jamaican prime minister even recommended to other Caribbean and Latin American leaders the "nego-tiation of meaningful moratorium periods" and the "extension of loan maturities" (Seaga 1984a). However, this appears to have been just a singular attempt to "test the waters", i.e. to find out how much solidarity on the debt issue existed.

Echoing the priority of his domestic agenda, the prime minister in 1987 introduced a more detailed proposal for the solution of the debt crisis. While in his 1983 speech in Los Angeles he had claimed that to be developing means to be in debt, this proposal was premised on the notion that debtor countries have to grow their way out of the problem rather than borrow their way out (Seaga 1987b, 4). Although both premises aimed at the resumption of growth, the latter concept certainly fitted the economic vista of the US administration and international finance capital much better. At the same time, however, it weakened Seaga's plea for an increase of intergovernmental and commercial bank lending, since the neoconservative context from which this concept had emerged was unfavourable to increases in development aid.

The following were vital elements of Seaga's approach to a solution of the international debt crisis:

1   The introduction of new resources through multilateral development banks (MDBs) and commercial banks, and the release of more disposable resources through multi-year rescheduling, all at levels consistent with generating the required performance in economic growth and debt re-demption;

2 Structuring the release of resources to attain these performance levels
   within the framework of agreed national programmes of supporting policy
   adjustments, and the utilization of the more effective surveillance capabilities of the MDBs. This monitored programme approach was expected
   to restore confidence in expanded lending and more liberal rescheduling
   (Seaga 1987b, 5–6).

However, both the rescheduling of existing debt and the expansion of loan
facilities should – according to this plan – be conditioned on a targeted
reduction of the debt service ratio. Needless to say, within the confines of its
own premises, the realization of this plan would have been of positive relevance
to Jamaica, as well as other indebted developing countries. In a situation where
exports more or less stagnated and new debts only increased the burden of
servicing old debts, the indexation of both would have amounted to an arrest
of the continuing increase of political and economic dependence.

The question of just how feasible the prime minister's proposal was can be
approached from several angles. Its elements were neither avant-garde, nor as
unique as Seaga himself claimed. In fact, after 1982 there had been a spate of
different plans addressing the global debt problem, which were also concerned
with the disequilibrium between the debtors' capacity to service their old debts
and achieve growth at the same time (Bernal 1986, 102–111; Robichek 1984,
262–63). The prime minister's emphasis on the superfluity of creating new
institutions (e.g. a version of the widely discussed IMF II) for the administration of the debt crisis, mirrored the sentiments of international finance.
Similarly, his call for new funds simply echoed the IMF's call for "involuntary
loans" by the commercial banks. Hence, Seaga's offensive against the ad hoc
management of the debt crisis carried little or no political risks. It was just one
more call for a long-term solution, emerging from the academic literature,
international banking circles and from Third World leaders.

The feasibility of long-term solutions to the debt crisis depends to a large
extent on the continuing (if not increasing) provision of funds by the international commercial banks. However, the mood among private bankers who had
incurred large losses was anything but conducive to a further expansion of
disbursements. The failure of both the Baker and the Brady plan to sufficiently
reduce the debt servicing burden for debtor countries by inducing new funds
into the international credit system, may very well be testimony to Schubert's
warning that "the US and particularly the US banks reject any disintegration
of the principle of debtor countries' 'debt slavery' because they would run the
risk of losing their hegemonic position or having to bear its costs themselves"
(Schubert 1985, 265 – translation provided by author). Considering this

situation, the relative futility of incremental debt restructuring plans such as Seaga's and the need to find a more fundamental solution to the debt crisis should be evident.

Seaga's plan for the alleviation of the debt crisis could have led to a temporary stabilization of international credit relations, since a large amount of the banks' claims would have been relegated to a multilateral, public level. This would certainly have been a relief for the commercial banks whose claims would have been guaranteed by these schemes. However, although Seaga proposed the debt service quotient to furnish a target for a country's servicing obligations, his plan did not address the real structural obstacle to a durable solution to the crisis, namely the disadvantageous position of developing social formations within the world markets which obstructs their prospects for capital accumulation. While one of the objectives of the Seaga plan was the resumption of economic growth, there was no indication of how this growth would be achieved. Clearly, this would have required a revitalization of some items on the now dreaded NIEO agenda of the 1970s. Seaga's hopes, however, rested on the blue-eyed twin assumption that, in the face of a resumption of world trade growth, to be triggered by the 'locomotives' US, Japan and Europe, the schematic readjustment of developing economies to conducive conditions for export led industrialization would be a sufficient precondition for a continuation of the growth periods of the 1950s and 1960s. This, however, was a most unlikely prospect (cf Girvan 1987, 68–72; Berberoglu 1987, 87–88).

At yet another level, the Jamaican prime minister's foreign policy offensive for a restructuring of global debt reflected the desperate gravity of the repayment problem for the Jamaican government. Like other governments, the Jamaican government had to borrow money and reschedule its amortization payments in order to keep pace with its obligations. Thus, between 1986 and 1988 alone the World Bank and the IMF received from Jamaica a surplus of US$ 654 million over disbursements to Jamaica (Levitt 1990, 17).

This directly led to an extremely precarious foreign exchange shortage, strongly reminiscent of the late 1970s, which induced Seaga to conclude dubious short-term borrowing schemes with the Bank of Commerce and Credit (BCCI) which was later indicted in the US for fraud. As the US Senate Committee on Foreign Relations concluded in October 1992, this relationship was established on a questionable personal basis between Seaga and Abdur Sakhia who handled these transactions for BCCI:

Jamaica provided BCCI a no-risk means of generating profits through international organisations and foreign governments, and BCCI in return loaned funds to Jamaica *which other banks refused to provide*, on the basis of the personal relationships involved, and BCCI's expectation that these relationships would in the long run guarantee its repayment (quoted in *DG*8/10/1992, 33 emphasis added).

How desperate the Jamaican government was to obtain these concessionary short-term loans (amounting to a total of about US$ 34 million) is evident in Sakhia's statement to the Senate Committee in which he recollects Seaga's approach:

Seaga told me, we need oil, we need seeds for planting, can we make an exception here? Finally he called me in desperation at home. He told me, there is an oil ship which is here in Kingston already, it is ready to unload the oil. If we don't unload it we will have a dark Christmas in Jamaica. Just give us an extra $4 million or $5 million an (*sic*) we will make it up to BCCI. I promise you personally (*DG*8/10/1992, 33).

These statements (the essence of which has not been repudiated by Seaga) give a clear impression of the government's dire need of auxiliary loans at very short notice. More than anything else, they portray the extent to which Jamaica was exposed to the demands of international finance capital. In the light of this evidence it is obvious that the government had absolutely no control over strategic macro-economic decision making and the essential nature of Jamaica's foreign economic relations and development path. To the extent that money is nothing but "curdled power", the JLP government's financial strait-jacket severely curtailed critical room for discretionary governmental action. The US Senate's report, on the other hand, has to be read as the tacit admission that international capital was fully aware of this financial predicament and the political dependency which resulted from it.

International capital extended some concessions to Jamaica, as can be seen by the first IMF agreement and the US decision in 1983 to buy 1.6 million long dry tons of Jamaican bauxite for its National Defence Stockpile, thereby alleviating the country's shortfall in foreign exchange earnings due to the slump in bauxite sales. However, as the Jamaican economy stagnated in the mid 1980s and with a view to the next election to be held in early 1989, the Jamaican government attempted to oppose certain technical aspects of the austerity programme which it had embarked upon in cooperation with the IMF and the World Bank. Similarly, it rejected certain details of USAID projects which led to some disagreements between officers of the agency and the Jamaican prime minister. This phase saw a test of strength between international capital and the Seaga government which now was strongly motivated by political considerations, i.e. enhancing its chances for a re-election in 1988 or 1989.

Regarding Jamaica's relations with the IMF, problems started to develop by late 1983. While Seaga had initially been able to lean on US President

Reagan, who pressured the IMF to grant Jamaica a waiver when it started to fail the IMF test, this avenue was not easily available when Jamaica failed the second test. The IMF demanded a unification of the exchange rate, a devaluation, a better balance between current revenue and expenditure, and a balance in Jamaica's foreign trade current account. Consequently, the government spoke of "stiff targets" accompanying the new Stand-by Facility (*DG* 9/6/1989, 1). When the aluminium company ALCOA closed its operations (without informing the government in advance) in 1985, the fiscal balance became even more precarious and Seaga had to admit that there had occurred a "technical lapse" in the stand-by agreement (*DG* 22/2/1985, 1). ALCOA's withdrawal meant a sudden foreign exchange shortfall of US$ 40 million and left the budget short of J$ 125 million in revenues.

Obviously in response to the emerging public criticism of the IMF's attitude, representatives of Jamaican finance capital reaffirmed that there would be no alternative to the IMF at the present stage of Jamaica's development (*DG* 28/7/1985, 2). At the same time, the PSOJ echoed some of the criticism of international capital leveled at the government, e.g. charging it for the slow pace of divestment (*DG* 20/9/1985, 18)

After the delay in the disbursement of USAID funds had caused the government to seek another "technical waiver" from the IMF, Seaga, apparently sensing that the IMF's conditions could no longer be bypassed by his good standing with the US president, attempted a forward strategy. With the full support of the private sector Seaga invited a tripartite team of IMF, World Bank and USAID economists to review Jamaica's structural adjustment programme. For at least three reasons the Tripartite Mission was a politically expedient move: 1) it reaffirmed the government's adherence to the economic prescriptions of these institutions, 2) it allowed the government to exploit disparities of view which existed between them (particularly between the World Bank and the IMF) and 3) it brought all three organizations closer together in an exchange of views on the Jamaican adjustment process, which presumably increased their flexibility. At the same time, however, it was also likely to reinforce their cross-conditionality. Therefore, whatever the outcome of the so-called 'fresh look' mission, it was obvious that any anticipated room for manoeuvre was only to occur within the gamut of their traditional economic recipes. Diplomatically the move was certainly a success in so far as it brought together for the first time these three donor agencies in an attempt to make a comparatively homogeneous assessment of a developing country's structural adjustment programme. The invitation to the Tripartite Mission aimed to get Seaga's proposed shift from austerity to growth cum trickle-down effect sanctioned by the major multilateral institutions representing the interests of international capital in Jamaica.

However, as it turned out, the Mission did not embrace Seaga's proposal for an externally financed and more demand-led approach to economic recovery. Rather, the mission suggested a self-reliant approach which was biased towards a reduction of external payments. Its goal to achieve sustainable growth in the medium term clearly contradicted Seaga's new priority of achieving short-term growth. The recommendations of the mission included inter alia, an immediate devaluation, a reduction of the overall public sector deficit (through redundancies, divestment and improved performance of public sector enterprises), and a further opening of the economy through a reduction and restructuring of import tariffs (without any preferences) (*DG* 18/7/1986, 12). While the mission emphasized savings and investment, the government opted for an increase in public expenditure.

The government was disappointed with the Tripartite Mission's report and rejected it. Seaga pointed out that his new priority was now "to increase Central Government expenditure dramatically" (*DG* 2/5/1986, 1). This would have entailed increased investment, improved incentives, reduced interest rates, a stable exchange rate, and reduced prices. Specifically, it meant, for example, that the government would utilize the US$ 107 million which it saved from reduced oil prices to subsidize basic foods, thereby directly contravening one of the Tripartite Mission's recommendations (*DG* 2/5/1986, 1). The private sector reportedly was disappointed that it did not profit from these oil savings (*DG* 4/5/1986, 14; *DG* 20/7/1986, 40).

The primary concern of the government was to avoid any further devaluation of the Jamaican dollar. To achieve this goal the government actually halted all repayments to the IMF as part of a deliberate negotiation strategy. Consequently, Jamaica was without an IMF agreement between March 1986 and January 1987. Opposing the IMF's demand of a 10 percent devaluation of the Jamaica dollar, Seaga counterproposed the introduction of an export rebate which was more specifically targeted at an improvement of Jamaica's exports to the US. Although some private sector representatives were critical of this confrontation with the IMF, they seemed to support its rationale, i.e. the prevention of a further devaluation (*Money Index* 9/9/1986, 3; *DG* 7/9/1986, 1; *DG* 23/11/1986, 6). Support for the government was particularly focused, when Seaga during this negotiation period announced his intention to resign. Seaga announced that his government had a "contingency plan" in case the IMF should insist on a devaluation.

After a protracted period of negotiations the government secured a new agreement with the IMF, which substituted devaluation with a 7.5 percent export rebate. Since the "contingency plan" would by all means not have been a viable alternative for Jamaica, it can be said that the IMF again demonstrated considerable flexibility by substituting its standard measure of devaluation with the government's combined no devaluation/low inflation approach. Similarly, the retention of price controls for basic foods certainly promoted the government's objective of delivering greater material benefits to the majority of potential voters.

However, despite this considerable success the new agreement was not as positive as it is sometimes interpreted. Thus, it provided for a considerable reduction of import duties which represented a victory for import deregulation pressures from the international donor agencies. Hence, the new agreement attempted to further open the Jamaican market, increase competition, and make the local manufacturers more export oriented by eliminating special import duty exemptions. Again, this treatment mirrored the relative weakness of the local manufacturing sector (primarily satisfying local demand), i.e. the national bourgeoisie. Thus, repeated structural discrimination of the national bourgeoisie indicated that a partial de-industrialization of Jamaica was the trade-off for keeping the economy financially afloat.

Jamaica's challenge of the IMF may also have been a contributing factor in its decision in April 1986 to remain conspicuously silent on the ignominious US bombing of Libya with which it entertained friendly relations. Although Libya was an international pariah, Jamaica could have adopted a principled neutral position. However, apparently fearing US retaliation, it chose to 'overlook' this grave violation of international law which even created diplomatic strains among European allies of the US. The fact that this incident went almost unnoticed in Jamaica is evidence of the radically altered political climate, which in the 1970s would not have hesitated to condemn the attack as an act of US imperialism.[9]

Possible further negative consequences from Jamaica's resistance against IMF conditionality were also minimized by the simultaneousness of her role in the democratization process in Haiti which had aided US regional policy. This situation, which also allowed him to point to his government's constructive role in the promotion of US foreign policy goals, facilitated Seaga's task of explaining his defiant IMF policy to US policy makers. Although in the US some observers warned of the negative implications of Seaga's IMF policy, the international press commented relatively neutrally about it and by no means used any language or innuendoes reminiscent of the late 1970s (cf *Financial*

Times 7/5/1986; *Financial Times* 12/9/1986; *DG* 25/10/1986, 3; *DG* 28/11/1986, 1; 1/3/1987, 1).

Nevertheless, officials at the US Department of Treasury felt that Jamaica should have implemented the IMF programme instead of trying to prevent a deregulation that was perceived by them to be inevitable. This view was also brought to the prime minister's attention when he had rather candid discussions in Washington with Assistant Secretary of State for Inter-American Affairs Elliott Abrams (Ashby 1989, 35). In light of the dramatic and extremely rapid devaluation of the Jamaica dollar in 1991 (US$1 = J$25), it is arguable that, in the face of pressures from international capital a further devaluation was indeed inevitable and, given the government's commitment to neoliberal economic prescriptions, it would have been economically more expedient to have this devaluation as a gradual exercise over a medium-term period. Moreover, protecting the exchange rate with tight money supply and high interest rates (while government's local borrowing increased) proved costly in terms of lost investment and production.

US Official Assistance

Following the dispute with the IMF in the second half of 1986, Jamaica received 41 percent less official aid from the US for the year 1987 (*DG* 18/2/1986, 6). Although the Kemp-Kasten Amendment of 1984 had outruled such a linkage, in practice USAID frequently conditioned its assistance on the recipient country's entering into IMF programmes and compliance with their targets. Since around 1983, USAID had become increasingly aware that the Jamaican government was slower in implementing deregulation and privatization measures than its public and diplomatic statements had suggested to them. As a consequence of this perception, US programme commitments dropped from US$ 154.1 million in 1985 (fiscal year) to US$ 118.6 million in 1986, US$ 78.0 million in 1987, and US$ 93.6 million (requested) in 1988 (AID n.d. a, 272; AID n.d. b, 253; AID n.d. c, 242). While the PL480 food programme was hardly affected by these cutbacks, the decreases were particularly severe in the Economic Support Fund (ESF) category which is a direct balance of payment support for the Jamaican treasury. Apparently, the rationale was to make Jamaica more dependent on IMF funds that would have stricter and more verifiable conditionalities attached.

The USAID, which had become heavily involved in the restructuring process of the Jamaican economy during the early 1980s, acted as an additional catalyst for already existing IMF conditionalities.[10] The agency itself had changed its priority in the 1980s from its earlier public sector support to private sector assistance, which presumably restricted the recipient government's freedom to act, to policies supporting and, to a lesser extent, regulating the private sector. As the new JLP government settled into its new tasks, USAID eventually became aware that it was, for technical as well as political reasons, not acting in concordance with mutually agreed procedures. Thus, in 1984 USAID reassessed one of its projects, finding that there had been "friction and misunderstandings" between the government and USAID because the former had appeared "less than committed to those aspects of the project USAID officials believed were important" (USAID 1984, 7).

Another problem which caused disappointment and anger among the agency's officials was that the prime minister developed a habit of bypassing local USAID officials and going directly to the White House or friends in the Republican Party, when he objected to USAID conditions. There was at least one incident where this led to a clash between Seaga and a political appointee in the USAID, Timothy Ashby. Although the Jamaican government was technically justified in defending its position on this particular issue, the incident shows that it was at times being brought under severe political pressure.[11] The Ashby episode makes it particularly evident that USAID since 1986, together with the IMF, was increasingly pressing for an accelerated pace of privatization (e.g. of hotels) and further liberalization (e.g. cutback of bureaucracy).[12]

Despite the problems Seaga faced by not fulfilling the expectations of both international capital and officials of the Reagan administration, he continued to command considerable goodwill in Washington, particularly at the highest levels of the US government. It has to be reemphasized here that this was only possible because he remained within the basic framework of "Reaganomics" and US foreign policy traditions and Jamaica basically complied with the now more forcefully presented demands of privatization of government assets and enterprises, liberalization of import restrictions, elimination of production incentives, and restructuring the tax system.[13]

The extent of international support for the Seaga government was clearly revealed toward the end of his term in office. After Hurricane Gilbert had battered Jamaica in September 1988, Seaga was able to mobilize immediate material support from the international community. Thus, the Inter-American Development Bank reportedly committed US$ 100 million, the IMF US$ 47 million, USAID US$ 45 million, the Canadian government Can$ 13.2 million and the British government £3.5 million in emergency aid, while the EEC released J$ 112 million in funds previously approved (*Caribbean Insight* Oct. 1988, 1).

The political pressure for more liberalization and privatization of the economy eventually led the Seaga government to accelerate this process. Thus, after 1986 the government-owned National Commercial Bank sold, albeit somewhat reluctantly, public shares. In 1988, the government made a second offering in which it divested the remaining 49 percent of the shares (Jones and Mills 1989, 120–23). Similarly, in 1987 and 1988 parts of the cement company and Telecommunications of Jamaica (TOJ) were privatized. Regarding the pressures for hotel privatization, Seaga claims that they first had to be made profitable and establish a track record of profits before they could be divested for a reasonable return.[14] Since this evidently required some time, the obvious conclusion would be that, due to their ideological bias, the USAID, IMF and other donor agencies tended to impose economic prescriptions on Jamaica which did not entirely match the realities of the local economy.

Informed members of Congress should have been aware of this; thus, Jamaican university professor Carl Stone, citing USAID's involvement in the coffee industry and its ill-informed attempt to eliminate the Coffee Board which had served to protect smaller farmers from exploitation by big coffee farmers, as well as monitoring competitive quality, pointed out to them:

. . . instead of adopting a policy to look at the needs of these different farmers, AID came with a big stick, saying if you don't deregulate we're going to cut off these loans and so on. What happened was that the Coffee Board people and some farmers who have vested interests in the system mobilized thousands of growers . . . and denounced the deregulation plan. So you're getting into a situation where AID is saying to deregulate on behalf of the farmers, and the farmers don't seem to want it (Congressional Research Service 1985, 46).

The Seaga administration's "problem", however, was that it relied too much on its relatively easy diplomatic access to the highest levels of the US government for its lobbying efforts, as well as for the negotiation of what it perceived to be more appropriate conditions for either the economy or its political survival. It thereby neglected two important points of exerting influence on US policy, the legislative level as well as the implementation level of the US bureaucracy which itself was willing to undergo some learning processes.

On the other hand, the Jamaican prime minister had manoeuvred himself into this position by publicly posturing as the "Caribbean Ronald Reagan". By so doing he had greatly inflated the expectations about what his government would achieve in terms of economic reform. This in turn led to unreasonable demands being directed at his government and the Jamaican private sector.

Conclusion

Similar to the United States, where the supply side economic policies of the Reagan government – so-called Reaganomics – caused socioeconomic hardships, the austerity and structural adjustment programmes in Jamaica (cooperatively devised and implemented by the Government of Jamaica and the IMF/World Bank consortium) caused severe economic and social dislocation (cf Wilber and Jameson 1990, chap. 5). As in the US, new jobs tended to be in the low wage sectors of the economy and had fewer benefits and less security. Although Seaga, especially after 1985, attempted to cushion these effects, he was prevented from effectively doing so by his own rampant free-market rhetoric of the early 1980s, which, in the perception of the US government, had elevated him to a regional champion of neoliberal capitalism and the living antithesis of Fidel Castro.

While his concern for the social consequences of the austerity programmes was not entirely neglected in his foreign policy (especially after 1985), rights and aspirations of the working class were usually just an appendage notion. This prioritization effectively reduced the multiplicity of conflicting domestic demands in Seaga's external lobbying strategy. The ambit of his government's external interest representation therefore clearly exhibited features of a limited pluralism. Although, in the short and medium term, this strategy brought tangible benefits in terms of a renewed flow of trade and foreign investments, it bound the Jamaican government for the foreseeable future to a development model which, even in the US, did not bring about the desired results and on the global scale seems to have reached its limits with the phenomenal growth and development in a handful of newly industrializing countries.

The Rockefeller Committee and a number of similar bilateral investment committees established in conjunction with other industrial countries, introduced a new dimension to Jamaica's conduct of external relations. Together with the government's intensive lobbying on behalf of the local bourgeoisie, this approach signified an important aspect of the tendency towards an increasing corporatization of Jamaica's foreign policy. For the first time since Independence, various professional associations, basically the bourgeoisie, however, became actively involved in the country's foreign economic affairs in an organized and institutionalized fashion. Similarly, the IMF dictation of the limits of wage increases and its acceptance by the government (and, to some extent, even the trade unions) reflects the high level of international capital's interference into Jamaica's matrix of pluralism. These external limitations on the tariff autonomy certainly contradicted the concept of a free market with its self-regulating mechanisms and would face the most severe resistance in industrialized centre nations.[15]

If one accepts – as the JLP government did – the limitations of the neoliberal premises, it would have been more prudent to conduct a foreign policy pointing to the potential benefits of Keynesian tenets, instead of merely talking free-market rhetoric and risk being accused by US policy makers of deception (as happened after 1986). Thus, in the second half of the 1980s the US itself had to resort to demand stimulation which accounted for whatever slight recovery the US economy subsequently experienced (Wilber and Jameson 1990, 102). Instead of upholding Reaganite 'magic of the market' generalities, the Jamaican government should have advocated other concepts which are sanctioned by mainstream capitalist pundits (e.g. the concept of 'social market economy' as practised by Scandinavian countries and West Germany or the social equality schemes in the East Asian newly industrialized countries), but by implication already introduce a stronger social component into the discourse. It also ought to have taken stronger cognizance of the capitalist experimentation in China which over the past 10 years has – according to Stanford's Ronald McKinnon – invented "a form of corporate organisation which hasn't been created before" (quoted in *The Economist* 28/11/1992, 16).

However, Seaga simply adopted an economic ideology which, like all ideologies, did not work in the real world. Needless to say, this economic ideology has assumed a hegemonic position, to the point where it has become an economic myth in Jamaica expounded by international capital and it remains painfully persistent in the 1990s. A more sober approach would have been to systematically expose the ideological content of Reaganomics and neoliberal capitalism and demonstrate why they will not work as expected in the majority of developing social formations. This remains a task that Third World leaders ought to and, inevitably, will awake to in the future.

The JLP's acceptance of exogenous economic recipes forestalled any critical discussion about whether it was actually desirable (not to mention affordable) for a social formation like Jamaica to emulate an economic and sociopolitical praxis guided by norms of the American life-style, whether the prescribed neoliberal path can really deliver such aspirations to a majority of people, or whether alternative capitalist approaches are better able to achieve and sustain genuine national development in the context of "underdevelopment." Thus, the imposition/acceptance of tight neoliberal cross-conditionality in Jamaica led to a new, "discursive" dependency which limited not just the range of available choices, but – probably the even more momentous and lasting dimension – the very perception of their availability.

Whatever marginal and temporary bargaining power Seaga's ideological posturing may have earned, his government was purchased (as demonstrated earlier) at the expense of an embarrassingly partisan foreign policy. Particularly in the Caribbean Basin, all of Seaga's major initiatives were virtually congruent with US objectives. This minion foreign policy or "hegemonic devolution", as Dominguez aptly terms it, was particularly apparent in Seaga's Cuban, Haitian and Grenadian policies where Jamaica assumed an implemental role regarding US strategic objectives.[16]

The nature of Jamaica's relations with international capital and the US during Seaga's tenure in office had a reasonable margin of choice only on micro-economic decisions, acquired at the expense of adhering to a tightly defined macro-economic approach which, exogenously designed, assumed ideological hegemony both within the government and the local bourgeoisie. This ideology of neoliberal economics necessarily excluded some major tenets and concepts, which Jamaica and the "Third World" collectively had spent a considerable amount of intellectual energy as well as foreign policy resources on during the turbulent decade of the 1970s. Indeed, the new "discursive" dependency prevented them from even perceiving any alternatives to the current neoliberal dogma.

10

Conclusion

This study examined the foreign relations of Jamaica during a period of seventeen years, from 1972 to 1989. Necessarily it had to be selective in its analysis of a number of aspects and issues circumscribing and characterizing the policies of the two governments which led the country at that time. The segmentation of this study was not effected in an arbitrary manner; rather it was subject to both compulsion and deliberate choice. The highly secretive conduct of Jamaican foreign affairs, which in itself is part of the reason for a number of inefficiencies, ruled out a research design based on the dynamics of diplomatic interaction and the analysis of diplomatic notes and bargaining processes. Moreover, this approach was considered to be inapt for the analysis of the foreign relations of a relatively small social formation. In contrast to large nations, where the particular twists and turns of external relations are often determined to a considerable extent by bureaucratic politics, i.e. action in and interaction between different branches of government, the foreign policies of smaller nations emerge primarily from their particular societal context and more direct interaction between policymakers and society (or influential sectors thereof).[1]

It was the primary objective of this study to examine the character of Jamaica's dependency with regard to her foreign policy, assuming that it is a consequence and expression of this dependency and that in addressing this dependency in one or the other way, it has, so far, not carried the country ahead in terms of either economic development and social well being, or national self-determination in the conduct of external affairs.

Survival or National Development?

Drawing a conclusion on all that has been said so far depends to a critical extent on the observer's epistemology, i.e. the point of view from which one departs. There are essentially two horizons of expectation from which one can set out to evaluate the balance sheet of Jamaica's achievements in her relations with the external environment. The first perspective would evaluate Jamaica's foreign relations in terms of a "politics of survival". Survival implies continued existence in spite of extremely unfavourable conditions or a singular, devastating event. At the same time, however, it bears a connotation of neediness, necessity and even frugality. This study rejects these notions as a basis for the evaluation of Jamaica's foreign relations, for they are suggestive of lack of ambition, need for sympathy or even charity, as well as lack of self-esteem. They are therefore rooted in a context of patronage, presumably of an exogenous origin. In the Jamaican public discourse this perspective is often employed by self-styled pragmatists who are de facto opposed to qualitative change.

The second perspective views Jamaica's relations in terms of a "politics of national development". This implies a list of priorities primarily derived from and directed at the economic and social needs of the Jamaican people. Hence, it is ultimately an endogenously derived agenda that presumes an intensive and extensive national dialogue about economic, social and political priorities which should lead to a broadly accepted definition of nationally desired goals and policies to arrive at them. This implies both evolutionary change and consensus (or, at most, *limited* conflict). Thus, this approach differs fundamentally from the study's analysis of Jamaica's foreign relations which assumes conflicting interests and antagonism between classes as the *primum mobile* of foreign policy. Both approaches, however, do not exclude each other. *Au contraire*, they may even supplement each other. If a certain political project is being pursued, it is an advantage to know exactly the adversaries' positions, essential and secondary interests, and their lines of argument.

Development implies the qualitative upliftment of the living standards and provision for social mobility of all classes of a given social formation. The notion of development relates to a process, deals with potentialities and is, therefore, to a large extent of a normative nature. It is probably impossible to provide a definition of "national development" which is universally agreeable. Nobody questions, however, that essential items such as food, shelter, and clothing are an indispensable precondition for development. But it is equally clear that development does not end with the satisfaction of basic needs. It ought to be understood that any kind of development process entails a change of values, attitudes and social organization. At least five elements should constitute an integral concept of development, namely, growth, employment, equality/justice, participation, and independence (Nohlen and Nuscheler 1982, 48–72; Todaro 1977). The agenda for development should be derived from an intensive, broad-based and ongoing discussion within each individual social formation in which both local and international capital are operating.

The question of economic survival was repeatedly asked on the eve of and immediately after the achievement of political independence of the region's states in the early 1960s. However, it still seems to inform some policy makers and observers 25 years or so later (Payne 1987, 216–23). This is already a telling sign in itself. While in the 1950s and 1960s the concern for economic viability without the patronage (and economic support) of the colonial power was understandable, an observer educated to conceptualize historical development in terms of the Enlightenment's notion of progress would not expect to find the notion of mere survival still lingering in national or regional debates.

The massive influx of foreign values and consumption patterns through the introduction and widespread accessibility of new communication media, a new wave of otherworldly missionarism, as well as the return of overseas Jamaicans, also renders the notion of survival increasingly irrelevant. The consequential explosion of expectations in the past decade has opened discrepancies between the levels of production, consumption and aspiration which threaten to destabilize Jamaica in a variety of ways. The introduction of new illegal drugs, weapons and forms of criminality are only one sign; increasing political inertia, erosion of traditional values and the adjacent inability to mobilize the population for *any* cause (including increased productivity, capital formation or reinvestment) are just other reasons for concern. Clearly, these problems can no longer be addressed with bashful ideas of "muddling through" or "belt-tightening" in mind.

It is obvious that the unassuming notion of "survival" led a number of observers and political activists to conclude that Jamaica (and the region as a whole) did fare comparatively well over the past twenty years. This kind of assessment flows naturally from this perspective's a priori assumption: in times when the environment is particularly inhospitable, survival is clearly an achievement. Indeed, survival in itself appears already to be an achievement.

Libby attempts to demonstrate that Seaga's successful diplomacy toward Washington resulted in a contravention of Washington's own policy toward Third World countries, emphasizing their reliance upon the private sector instead of large flows of US aid (Libby 1990, 109).[2] Libby's argument hinges to a large extent on the notion that Reagan's policies de-emphasized US assistance to the Third World. However, he does not support this point and his argument therefore goes only half the way. For, although US multilateral assistance decreased, bilateral assistance programmes increased from US$ 1.6 billion in 1980 to US$ 2.4 billion in 1985.[3] Thus, the situation was not quite as adverse as Libby tries to suggest.

The second portion of Libby's argument is the fact that Seaga – especially when compared with Manley in the 1970s – was able to attract large amounts of direct US assistance, as well as support in his dealings with international capital. Whatever short-term benefits this may have brought Jamaica, the more fundamental question is, how valuable were this US assistance and the IMF/World Bank loan carnival for Jamaica's medium- and long-term development? At this point, even Libby's apologetic article has to admit that Seaga's balance sheet was not too favourable. Although he concedes that with over 40 percent Jamaica's debt service ratio (as a percentage of total exports) is "virtually unpayable", that Washington's political concessions did little to address the weaknesses in Jamaica's industrial structure, that GDP growth remains very small in the 1990s (and actually declined in the mid 1980s), and that the CBI did little to stimulate nontraditional exports, these considerations apparently could not convince Libby that, after all, the official US support for the Seaga administration, far from being real concessions, was essentially only political hush-money (Libby 1990, 104/105).

At the beginning of the 1980s the US was in dire need of a credible showcase of Third World development which countered the increasingly popular Cuban model, i.e. a public sector-led economy centrally planned on the basis of self-reliance and South-South (or South-East) cooperation. What came to mind was a political resurrection of the so-called Puerto Rican model (on which the CBI was eventually based), i.e. a private sector-led, export- and free trade-oriented economy. Seaga clearly recognized this legitimate void in US foreign policy, which he had actually helped to create since the late 1970s, and on becoming prime minister he offered Jamaica's adherence to this model. From this perspective, the increased bi- and multilateral assistance was therefore obviously part of an, albeit tacit, diplomatic quid pro quo. Jamaica was to become both the most important regional proponent of the Puerto Rican model and the regional US "Q.E.D. case-study" of this model's (allegedly) universally successful applicability.

The ideological convergence between the Seaga government and international capital is also evidenced by two other constituent facts. First, like the Reagan government Seaga justified his economic approach with a repudiation of his predecessor's policies. Specifically, the JLP and Seaga claimed that redistribution jeopardized production, growth and democracy in Jamaica.[4] Second, the linkage between Jamaican and US security twisted Jamaica's priorities and, by her active participation in the Grenada intervention, tarnished her international reputation as a zealous promoter of peace and peaceful solutions to international crises. As Braveboy-Wagner (1988, 80) rightly observes: "The enlargement of the concept of security to include ideology created much conflict in the region. The assumption continues to be made by a number of states that Caribbean security is intimately linked to U.S. security, an assumption that adds more limitations to a foreign policy already circumscribed by size and resources."

In the 1970s, Jamaica's assertion of independence, non-alignment, and global support for a "third path" leading to national development, completely alienated her traditional sources of support and assistance. Internally, it contributed considerably to the steep decline in economic performance through the alienation of the comprador and "re-compradorized" national bourgeoisie, which left the sphere of production eventually without its operators and its life-blood, i.e. capital and raw materials. However, the PNP government's attempts to include the interests of the working class in decisions of national importance increased the level of internal pluralism and broadened the basis of national discourse. Initially this contributed to greater state autonomy, since the national bourgeoisie was in favour of this political project.

In a fundamental sense Jamaica's quest for economic and political space in the 1970s empowered her foreign policies and allowed the country for the first time in her history to appear as a subject and independent actor shaping her foreign relations according to her own definitions. Rex Nettleford (1993, 82–83) has described the significance of this existential reality quite aptly:

> The capacity to make definitions about oneself and to follow through with action on the basis of those definitions is the substance of power. It expressed the capability for integration of inner space, conceived as the capacity to generate knowledge and to create, and outer space perceived as the follow through to action on the basis of such thought, knowledge and creativity.

That such a state of affairs is also an essential precondition for national development, particularly in a context of peripheral capitalism, should be readily acknowledged. Both at the individual enterprise level as well as at the national level, there is little point in starting to combine capital and means of production if one does not have an original business idea or the entrepreneurial stamina and self-confidence to face even the most formidable competition. Such qualities, however, are a direct function of the political ability and determination to make these definitions about oneself and have others accept their validity. It is the PNP government's lasting achievement that in the 1970s it attempted – albeit somewhat forcefully – to bring home these fundamental principles.

Thus, it tried to ward off the undue interference in the formulation of its external and domestic affairs which the industrialized countries had been accustomed to exert in the developing world. Its (somewhat accidental) insistence on diplomatic support for the Cuban presence in Angola, the tentative exploration of non-IMF alternatives and the establishment of links with socialist countries support this. However, preoccupation with the vocal and defiant rejection of such interference hampered the search for constructive solutions and compromises. It also neglected the real necessity for a cooperative, albeit well-defined, relationship with international finance capital and the formidable role the USA has in the establishment of an atmosphere of support and confidence. The government ignored the force of the entente cordiale between the Jamaican opposition, the majority of the bourgeoisie and the strengthened hawkish elements within the late Carter administration and the US media. Clearly, the Manley government's defiance at the end of the 1970s overstretched the bourgeoisie's dependence on capital and capital goods imports.

Moreover, the PNP government neglected the dynamics of the global productive sphere which, independent from political pressures, "gently" exert economic pressures on all social formations. Thus, new management concepts, the increasing automation and "dematerialization" of production since the mid 1970s increased competition for foreign investment among low wage countries (like Jamaica) and decreased the importance of raw materials (e.g. bauxite) in the production of highly sophisticated capital goods (cf Junne, Komen, and Tomei 1989, 130).

The government got sidetracked by unrewarding political imbroglios, e.g. the high profile of Cuba in its foreign policy and intemperate anti-capitalist/anti-imperialist rhetoric. Similarly, Jamaica's NIEO diplomacy appears to have been too broad and uncompromising. This certainly contributed to Jamaica's reputation as a speaker for the Third World, but it is questionable whether it helped to find workable solutions. Economic diversification and stronger South-South cooperation would probably have been accommodated by the US, if it had been managed more carefully and avoided close political identification with Cuba. The political and economic discourse in the 1970s would also have allowed a rhetorically low-keyed, economically high-powered strategy of selective dissociation from the world market along with a development of new export products for niche markets, which, in the long term, would probably have been a more successful course than the political priorities chosen by the PNP.

One important lasting benefit was Jamaica's diversification of foreign relations; its extension into the Third World and some socialist countries. The country broke out of its relative isolation of the 1960s and explored new forms of cooperation and markets – a benefit which even its successor in the 1980s was able to bank on, as the massive sale of 200,000 tons of bauxite to the Soviet Union in 1983 and the agreement on the purchase of one million tons for a further seven years clearly indicate.

In the 1980s, the JLP government, driven by a perceived imperative of economic "survival", aligned Jamaica's foreign policy with the increasingly forceful demands of international capital. By pursuing economic and regional policies which tended to reflect US interests, it was able to capitalize on a close personal and working relationship with the top layers of the Reagan administration. This resulted in an unprecedented influx of official bi- and multilateral assistance, as well as a new (albeit much lower than expected) interest in Jamaica by foreign investors.

The substantial change in the country's foreign policy stance has to be regarded as a consequence of the reassertion of neoliberal bourgeois ideology at both the international and domestic levels. The relative strength of the social classes in Jamaican society shifted from the national bourgeoisie and workers in the 1970s to the comprador bourgeoisie in the 1980s. However, the different emphases in both governments' foreign policies were a reflection of the policies which the social class that dominated the polity and the state (i.e., the middle class) pursued in conjunction with the party (particularly the party leader) in power. Hence, the bourgeoisie's influence on the state's foreign policy was mediated and of an indirect nature, which explains why in the 1970s it was perceived negatively by the bourgeoisie, while in the 1980s it alienated some sections of the national bourgeoisie who felt that the export thrust threw them out of business. Thus, in the 1980s there was a widespread perception, even among some members of the private sector, that the government acted according to its consultations with international capital rather than according to the priorities of the whole local bourgeoisie. However, more than ever before in postindependence Jamaica, it seemed that the middle class in the 1980s (and the early 1990s) acted in accordance with the economic interests of the comprador bourgeoisie.

On the basis of the extent to which the JLP government contributed to a weakening of the labour unions and the erosion of workers' rights in Jamaica, as well as the high level to which it involved the bourgeoisie in the representation of Jamaica overseas, this study concludes that both domestic and foreign policy in the 1980s were subjected to a limited pluralism and corporatist tendencies. While labour's leadership was partially coerced and partially co-opted, the Jamaican state actively incorporated the representative organizations of the bourgeoisie in its foreign economic policy strategy and promoted institutional joint representation of Jamaica overseas.

The degree to which the JLP government in the 1980s subscribed to exogenous prescriptions for the achievement of economic growth introduced a new dimension of dependency into both Jamaica's domestic and foreign policies. This new, "discursive" dependency prevented the economic and political elite from envisioning anything else but an almost mythical export-led development path built on liberalization, privatization and absolute free trade. The fact that neither the industrialized countries themselves, nor the newly industrialized countries in East Asia, including Japan, thrived in this schematic textbook scenario was, in this discourse on neoliberal peripheral capitalism, an afterthought at the most. It left no room for a creative exploration of national idiosyncrasies and an adaptation of both these and the neoliberal concepts. With few exceptions it left Jamaican elites in a position that effectively prohibited them from taking advantage of new economic choices and opportunities which could have come along with the adjustment exercise. On the contrary, the new dependency placed external forces in a superior position to exploit any possible choices created in this new environment. National development in this scenario is absolutely subordinated to externally driven dynamics.

The Relative Autonomy of the State

As set out in the introduction, the peripheral state's autonomy is circumscribed by both the extent of contradictions within the local bourgeoisie and contradictions between the latter and international capital. With regard to the first contradiction, it has to be repeated at this point that the national bourgeoisie is, to some extent, concerned with the alleviation of contradictions within the local economy and society, which might allow the state to act *temporarily* on behalf of the marginalized and working classes. As our study demonstrated, actions in the sole or primary interest of the local bourgeoisie and/or the lower classes (vis-à-vis international capital) were temporary features of both governments. However, the intensity, duration (within the government's term in office) and particular form of these policies were primarily determined by the particular configuration of the power bloc.

It is therefore instructive to note at this point that while in 1989 the PNP won the election on the basis of a mandate primarily deriving from the votes of the lower and working class, as well as those social strata which during the 1980s had become marginalized operators in the so-called informal economy, the domestic and foreign policies of the new Manley and Patterson adminis-trations basically continued those of its predecessor.[5] However, with a massive slide of the Jamaican dollar from $5.50 in 1989 to around $26 to US$1 in 1992 and $40 in 1995, the Jamaican economy again (as in the 1960s and 1980s) appears to be in a fragile equilibrium, operating on the basis of a growing social abyss between rich and poor.

On the basis of this study it is concluded that the relative autonomy of the peripheral state in international affairs varies with the issues at stake. It may even vary within a single issue depending on the sequential development of events. The following categorization of the Jamaican state's relative autonomy regarding the various issue areas of this study can be made:

Relations with Cuba: "restricted autonomy" during most of the period 1972–76 (while the local bourgeoisie was still divided, international capital was op-posed); "no autonomy" in the last two years in office (both international capital and local bourgeoisie were strongly opposed).

Relations with the US and international capital (in the 1970s): oscillated between "relative autonomy" and "no autonomy" (both local and international capital viewed Jamaica's foreign policy either indifferently [particularly before 1975] or as offensive).

Relations with Grenada and the Caribbean (in the 1980s): "no autonomy" (both local and international capital were clearly opposed to the Bishop government and completely rejected the Austin junta); "no autonomy" (local bourgeoisie relatively in favour of international capital's affirmative political interests, e.g. democracy, secure trade and investment markets).

Relations with the US and international capital (in the 1980s): oscillated between "no autonomy" (both the local bourgeoisie and international capital were very affirmative on the basic tenets of Jamaica's foreign economic policy) and "restricted autonomy" (latent micro-economic con-tradictions between segments of the national bourgeoisie and international capital).

On balance, Jamaica's relative autonomy in foreign affairs was smaller in the 1980s. The reason the Seaga government paradoxically *appeared* to some observers to have more leverage was that it ideologically accommodated the "no autonomy" situations by an acceptance of the neoconservative political and economic narrative, and refrained from attempting to expand its relative autonomy in a way that would have seriously offended either local or international capital. In the 1970s the Manley government *appeared* to have less autonomy because it was very vocal about the constraints it faced and which it tried to revert. At the end of the 1970s, however, its relative autonomy was much more restricted in comparison to the early and mid 1970s. Its too inflexible refusal to build these constraints into its official foreign policy, resulted in its severe electoral defeat (and an uncovered army plot to overthrow the government).

The more indirect costs for the Seaga administration resulted from the complete surrender of alternative, indigenous schemes of development and the (albeit skilful) subordination of Jamaica's industrial policies to a rigid, exogenous model of economic growth. Moreover, its Caribbean policies enjoyed relative autonomy only to the extent that they anticipated, emulated or complemented US Caribbean policy designs. As such, they were limited to the incremental manipulation of relatively minor details in a larger game-plan.

Policy Recommendations

A number of lessons have to be learned from the experiences of the 1970s and 1980s. Most important perhaps, an agenda for future development will have to find its gestation in a contradictory process which is located at the nexus of external demands and internal requirements. Any strategy which does not consider and consciously trade off both inputs is likely to be a failure.

A couple of suggestions, particularly as they relate to Jamaican (and regional) diplomacy, are in order. First, to the extent that alternative development proposals rightly suggest an autochthonous, endogenous agenda, directed at the basic needs and cooperation of the Jamaican people and based on an accumulation model which "has to be founded on the logic of a dynamic convergence between social needs and the use of domestic resources", this alternative vision of development is bound to conflict with economic and social demands of international capital (Thomas 1988, 364; 1989, 290–314). Hence, to the extent that these alternative development principles are accepted and adopted by the power bloc, a principal concern for Jamaican (Caribbean) diplomacy would be their external defence and protection. With the demise and external rejection of socialist or 'third path' alternatives, the task appears to be threefold.

First, there is a need for constantly reminding US policy makers and the media that the social and economic viability and stability of their Southern neighbours is linked with and critically important to the socioeconomic stability within their own territory (van Dieren 1995). If, through economic "stabilization programmes" promoted by international finance capital and US policy makers, the marginalized and working classes of the Caribbean have to continue to bear the brunt of the debt burden, they will seek and find ways to alleviate their plight. Three "solutions" come readily to mind: a further expansion of informal economic activities; illegal migration, which neither official measures (i.e. strict immigration control) nor unofficial barriers (i.e. racism) will ever be able to curb, once vital life chances are denied to a population; and illicit drug trade which, according to the law of comparative advantage, will increasingly seek and find entrance into its largest market – the US.

Moreover, various ethnic sections of the US population are responsive to the foreign policies the US administration pursues with regard to geographic or ethnic communities with which they identify or have strong relationships (e.g., the receptiveness of African-Americans to US policies on South Africa, Haiti, Panama, among others). US foreign policy which displays contempt for the aspirations of the developing world will only emphasize the alienation dynamics which have already begun to become antagonistic in her inner city ghettos. Ultimately, these dynamics might even lead to greater terrorist activities.

Second, regional foreign policy makers have to study meticulously the various trends and aspects of capitalist development. This will enable them to point to double standards and exploit inconsistencies of the current economic orthodoxies which international capital tends to prescribe to small, dependent and indebted social formations (see also Bhatti 1992). Thus, there is, for example, a need to point to the increased state involvement in the rehabilitation of the unified Germany, as well as the steady expansion of its public service throughout the 1980s (from 3.6 million public servants in 1970 to 4.4 million in 1980 and almost 4.7 million in 1990) (*Süddeutsche Zeitung* 21/4/1991, 17; *The Economist* 23/5/1992, 5). Furthermore, there are a number of lessons – both positive and negative – to learn from the development path of East Asian countries (Wade 1990).

Systematic research would also enable Jamaica's economic diplomacy to make creative and constructive alternative proposals for profitable yet more self-reliant capitalist development (e.g. technology adaptation). It would allow for an early recognition of niche markets for highly specialized, small- and medium-scale industries which might be established as joint ventures.[6] Thus, for example, in the chemical industry (as in technology, software, etc.) there exists, besides the trend for transnationalized cartellization, a development dynamic which points in the direction of specialized smaller-scale units producing competitively for global markets. Extremely and increasingly more rigid environmental laws and duties, moreover, have German chemical/biotechnological industries migrating to other sites and could possibly be attracted, once skilled personnel are available. At the same time, questions of market access and economic and social development ought to be couched in terms of *national security*. The terminology in this kind of discourse would enhance Jamaica's ability to indicate to the United States and other economic powers the immediate urgency to square "free market" norms and procedures in a globalized economy with the necessity and responsibility of the public sector to address the interrelated issues of social development, investment climate, and levels of crime.

Third, there is the much argued need for regionalization and a regional approach to foreign economic policy (Gonzales 1991, 1–18). The choice is stark and simple. If the Caribbean does not follow the global trend for regionalization it will be left out. In an increasingly competitive international environment nobody will consider territories with two million (or even less) inhabitants as viable economic units. To pursue a highly divisive regional policy, as in the 1980s, in exchange for dubious bilateral advantages, will be detrimental to Jamaica's regional status which is already damaged by its poor economic performance.[7] Regionalization is also a desired strategy in dealing with the persistently burdensome debt problem.

Finally, the earlier mentioned need to arrive at a higher level of national self-definition has direct and tangible implications for development and economic growth. A nation without a general consensus about its developmental teleology is hardly able to foster either the national or individual political will necessary in order to achieve excellence. If, for example, the quality of primary education is substandard, tertiary education is bound to suffer. If health care is poor, productivity is unlikely to increase. If self-esteem is low because of widespread, persistent and growing poverty and increasingly weak family structures, crime is likely to increase and production will be affected negatively. Recent data suggest that one of the consequences of structural adjustment is that the "new" middle classes in Jamaica have begun to put less emphasis on what they traditionally used to regard as a valuable instrument for upward mobility – higher education (Brown 1994, 99–102). If this should indeed be the trend, Jamaica's prospects for genuine development and sustainable growth in an increasingly knowledge- and technology-driven world economy appear to be doomed to stagnation (Henke 1996).

At the same time, the historically deeply ingrained contempt of the Jamaican upper classes for the majority of its own people has been reinforced by the new "discursive" dependency of the ubiquitous neoliberal discourse. The combination of both prevents these strata from seeing that the real potential for development in Jamaica (and, by extension, in the Caribbean) is not bananas, bauxite or beaches, but fundamentally rests in the creativity and skills of the very people they are frowning upon. Thus, for example, reggae music, once regarded as the domain of "dirty rastamen" from the Kingston ghettos, has conquered the international airwaves of musical entertainment and generated hundreds of millions of US dollars for those who recognized its potential. Indeed, it is more than likely that – as has already been estimated – the income generated by a fully developed and integrated music export industry would rival that of the tourist sector which is currently the main income source of foreign exchange (*Jamaica Herald* 19/11/1993, 8A). Other fields of cultural endeavours could also generate more income, new jobs for more people, and create new levels of self-esteem which, in turn, would have positive economic spin-off effects in terms of work ethic, productivity, a general desire to strive for excellence, etc. (Guilbault 1992, 27–40). At this point, however, there are few encouraging signs for such a shift in cultural self-acceptance.

In addition to these substantive, policy-directed suggestions, the experience of Jamaican diplomacy over the past two decades also suggests the following more formal, procedure-oriented proposals. Three areas of foreign policy making in Jamaica are in clear need of improvement: flow and processing of information, professionalism and lobbying.

Processing of information: As Hans-Dietrich Genscher, the West's longest serving (former) foreign minister rightly stated, "50% of foreign policy are won in public speech." This insight points to the need for every country to have a forward-oriented thinking about, and consensual long-term conceptualization of, its foreign policy goals. Ideally, this is being achieved in the realm of public discourse. Like many countries of the Third World, however, Jamaica is lacking such a forward looking, long-term foreign policy concept. In the recent past, its foreign relations rather tended to be increasingly of a reactive nature which is in itself already a structural disadvantage in international affairs. There is a need for a much improved public discourse about the global economy and external relations, their direction, relevance and long-term objectives. A prerequisite of this, however, is a better flow of information.

The Ministry of Foreign Affairs ought to have regular press conferences and meetings with local journalists in order to keep the public informed about the current status of important negotiations, Jamaica's position, options, etc.[8] Public fora of various kinds and scope could also help to have a more relevant involvement of the public in the discourse about Jamaica's relations to the external environment.[9] The benefit of such strong interaction would be that, in cases of difficult or controversial decisions, the *volonté generale* could be played out easier against external pressures.

Professionalism in the foreign service: A professionalization of Jamaica's foreign service would not simply include a shift to new personnel with postgraduate degrees in international relations, but also a continuing programme of education for diplomatic staff which is already employed by the Ministry of Foreign Affairs. A university degree or long experience in the foreign service do not automatically eliminate the need to follow intellectually the fast-changing developments in international political and economic affairs.[10]

There ought to be a formal course programme which could be institutionalized in cooperation with the University of the West Indies' Departments of Government and Economics. These courses should cover various aspects of international affairs: history, global politics, economics, diplomatic case studies, bargaining theory, international political economy, computer simulations of difficult bargaining situations, etc.

A professionalization of foreign affairs should also entail a deliberate depoliticization of the Ministry of Foreign Affairs. This ought to come about as a deliberate and concerted attempt to keep all posts (except the minister's) free from partisans, unless they have proven diplomatic skills and/or specialized knowledge.

Lobbying: To the extent that Jamaica continues to promote its individual interest on a bilateral basis, lobbying efforts would have to be made more efficient. Thus, US Congressmen expect to be lobbied and, to some extent, draw their conclusions about the relative distribution of power and interests involved in a particular piece of legislation from the amount and quality of lobbying they are exposed to.

Efficient lobbying of the US Congress is a permanent and tedious effort which requires professionals who intimately know the inner workings of this complex institution. Ideally, Jamaica would have to engage a lobbying firm with good connections to important Congressmen or hire the services of well-known and respected Congressmen (e.g. the former Speaker of the House, Thomas "Tip" O'Neill) who know how to "pull the strings" in the US legislative process.[11] It would also be important to cooperate closely with other lobby groups which promote increases in US development assistance, e.g. the Inter-religious Task Force on US Food Policy, Randall Robinson's Trans Africa Forum, or certain ecological groups. Jamaica's lobby group would permanently be in contact with members of Congress and thereby be in the position to affect the legislation process at the earliest possible stage. This would avoid the single-track approach which has prevailed since the 1970s, when the Jamaican government sought to influence US foreign policy primarily through direct contacts with the higher echelons of the US executive. Although this approach was not unsuccessful, it was often circumvented by Congress or unfavourable political currents within the administration.

Hiring a reputable lobby firm in Washington is certainly not a cheap venture. Indeed, one would have to expend several million US dollars annually. However, a scrupulous cost-benefit analysis should reveal that much is at stake in Jamaica's biggest market, for example, continued or increased market access (such as the current negotiations for the North American Free Trade Area, NAFTA), tourism promotion, image-building (e.g. countering the negative effects of criminal activities by Jamaican citizens in the US), countering protectionism in the US, exchange of viewpoints, and better mutual understanding.

Obviously, this venture would demand the support of the local private sector which should be made aware of the eminent importance of permanent lobbying in the US. Particularly as Jamaica has embarked on a decidedly export-oriented industrialization strategy, local entrepreneurs should be motivated to financially support a venture which would operate in their direct interest. The increased rights and benefits, which the local bourgeoisie received in the wake of "structural adjustment" and liberalization programmes, now need to be complemented by an increase in their duties and obligations, as is the case in any developed market economy. Should this cooperation not be forthcoming voluntarily, a minimal "lobbying tax" could be considered. Involvement of the private sector could also include overseas investors, e.g. AMCHAM (American Chamber of Commerce in Jamaica). This organization has already indicated its willingness and ability to lobby in Washington.

Although, in the past, politics in Europe did not require and, in fact, dismissed aggressive lobbying, the unification of the European market suggests that in future trade negotiations Jamaica (and the Caribbean) should apply some of the lessons learnt in the United States. Thus, one could think of more commercially oriented lobbying which focuses on image promotion and marketing (e.g. in tourism).

Ultimately, however, the success of Jamaica's diplomacy and the degree to which it will be able to uplift itself depend on a dynamic and conscious convergence of scrupulous and self-critical historical accounts and scientific evaluation of contemporary constraints and options. Only to the extent that Jamaica comes to terms with its history, immediate and past, will it be able to draw up a blueprint for its own future.

Appendix

DeclaRation on Haiti of the Meeting of CARICOM/Caribbean Leaders, held in Barbados on January 6, 1988:

The following statement was issued in Barbados at the conclusion of the CARICOM/Caribbean leaders meeting to discuss the situation in Haiti:

"We the CARICOM/Caribbean leaders having met in Barbados on Wednesday, 6th January, 1988 to discuss the Haitian situation:

Bearing in mind our deep interest in the peace, stability and orderly development of the Caribbean region;

Considering our commitment to the promotion of democracy and human rights in the Region and elsewhere;

Taking into account our solidarity with the people of Haiti in their efforts to achieve political, economic, social and cultural development with a democratic system which scrupulously respects the fundamental rights and freedoms of the citizen;

Bearing in mind the expressed aspiration of our peoples and the people of Haiti for closer ties of friendship and cooperation;

Recalling their decision at the Eighth Meeting of the Conference of Heads of Government of the Caribbean Community in July 1987 that extension of Haiti's current observer status in certain Standing Committees of CARICOM would be conditional upon the holding of proper election;

Recalling that the people of Haiti had been subjected over the past 30 years to a particularly brutal dictatorship which came to an end on 7th February, 1986 with the departure of Jean-Claude Duvalier into exile;

Taking note of the appointment of the National Council of Government (CNG) as a provisional Government;

Noting further that a new constitution for Haiti was overwhelmingly approved by a popular referendum on 29th March, 1987;

Noting in particular the provision in the new Constitution for the establishment of an independent electoral machinery and the transitional provisions for a Provisional Electoral Council (CEP) to arrange for the holding of the first elections on 29th November, 1987;

Declare as follows:

We regret that there was a breakdown in the relationship between the CNG and CEP;

We deplore the acts of violence which took place in Haiti prior to and on November 29, 1987, resulting in a tragic loss of life and which led to the cancellation of the election on November 29, 1987, by the CEP and the immediate dismissal of the CEP by the CNG;

We are profoundly concerned that in appointing the new CEP the CNG has acted in a manner which makes it clear that the new electoral commission is not independent of the Government.

This was done despite international protests and despite the urgings of certain Caribbean Leaders, the "Group of Concerned Caribbean Leaders" (GCCL) who visited Haiti on 10th December, 1987 to emphasize the importance of preserving the credibility of the electoral process;

We consider that the new electoral decree contravenes some important democratic electoral practices and has done further damage to the integrity of the electoral process;

In summary we consider that the arrangements for the elections now scheduled to be held on 17th January, 1988 have been seriously compromised and cannot therefore be regarded as credible. They constitute an impairment to the progress toward democracy which began in Haiti in 1986;

We consider that the problem has been complicated by the decision of some leading candidates to withdraw from elections.

Should the elections proceed as scheduled in fulfillment of the express determination of the CNG to hand over power to an elected Government on 7th February, 1988, as provided in the Constitution, we urge, even at this late stage, that the offending features of the electoral process be removed.

We therefore call on the CNG and the CEP –

(a) to recognize the transcendental importance of restoring credibility to the electoral process including in particular the provision for secret balloting;
(b) to ensure that elections are conducted peacefully;
(c) to allow all persons permitted by the Constitution and willing to offer themselves for election to do so; and
(d) to conduct the elections and the transfer of power in such a manner as to ensure that support is given to the new Government in its task of fostering the democratic process, strengthening the economy, and improving the quality of life for the Haitian people;

We recognize that even in the most favourable circumstances the task will be a difficult one, and that this difficulty will be immensely multiplied if the international community including the multilateral agencies are reluctant to extend their assistance to Haiti because of a perception on their part that the electoral process was seriously flawed.

We earnestly call on the CNG, the CEP, the Church, the candidates and others that exercise authority and influence to open a process of dialogue immediately with a view to reducing differences and hostilities, and ensuring that Haiti does not lose this opportunity to commence the process of joining the family of democratic nations and establishing the international goodwill which can be the springboard for its future development.

We express our deep concern that Haiti should not slip back into a dark period of isolation, dictatorship and atrocity; that it should not lose the opportunity of a new beginning, but that it should seek with determination and good will to build a future of greater hope and justice.

We recognize that the essence of democracy lies, not only in the actions of Governments nor in the views of institutions and political aspirants, but more importantly in the perceptions and deep-seated convictions of the people themselves.

We express solidarity with the people of Haiti in their search for a better future, and commit ourselves to be guided by their interests, and to give support to initiatives in international fora for the development of Haiti.

Requested the Chairman of the Meeting to communicate this statement as a matter of urgency to the Chairman of the National Council of Government of Haiti, and to bring it to the attention of the Secretaries-General of the United Nations and the Organisation of American States."

Notes

Chapter 1

1. This study is aware that the concept of "Third World" has increasingly become inapplicable due to the various international changes over the past decade. There are now a number of formerly developing countries – the so-called NICs or Asian Tigers – which have per capita incomes comparable to the industrial world. At the same time, some of the now independent republics of the former Soviet Union have reverted to what used to be considered as "Third World" living conditions. For a good discussion of the eurocentric notion "Third World" see Nohlen and Nuscheler (1982a, 11–24).

2. The Maroons were Africans who had been enslaved by the Spanish during its occupation of the island. Having fled, they continued to live at various points in the island's inaccessible interior after the English took the island, and intermittently launched surprise attacks on the settlers and their plantations.

3. Stone (1973, 16–21), however, arrives at his definition of classes through an empirical descriptive method, which emphasizes distribution conflicts of material and social resources as opposed to the broader Marxist view of class conflicts based on the ownership of the means of production; together with Post (1981, 298), the present study prefers the notion of middle strata which comprise such different positions as lawyers, doctors, senior managers, clerks, shop assistants, etc. but do not have a "defining relation to the means of production of their own".

4. Basically we conceive structures not just as constraints to social action but acknowledge that they can also entail enabling dimensions. However, compared to industrial countries they are more constraining to the developing countries than enabling – see also Manicas (1985, 309–22).

5. See in particular, Cox's seminal article (1981, 126–53); Cox's (1981, 141) Gramscian notion of social forces derives from the insight that "power is seen as *emerging* from social processes rather than taken as a given in the form of accumulated material capabilities, that is as the result of these processes"; see also Cox (1983, 162–75); Cox (1987); Linklater (1990, chap. 7); Walker

(1993, 130–35); Elsenhans (1985, 140–50); Biddle and Stephens (1989, 1–2 and 6).

6. Together with Merleau Ponty we would actually argue that ideal factors are an integral part of class struggles – see Whiteside (1988, 87–88).

7. This study is aware that the Jamaican bourgeoisie cannot be directly compared to its continental counterpart. Not only does it espouse a much greater entrepreneurial lethargy but, as Keith (1981, 30) aptly remarks, it has "never uttered the cry of 'liberty' "; as Stone (1987, 39) points out, the core of the Jamaican bourgeoisie perceives itself "as having a natural alliance with foreign capitalist interests"; thus, although they may have their own base for capital accumulation, the strong external links of the larger part of the Jamaican bourgeoisie justify their designation as compradors.

8. Alavi (1989a, 294) is mistaken in suggesting that functionalist Marxism (e.g. Poulantzas) neglects that conjuncturally, actions of capitalist enterprises and those of the capitalist state can be out of line with the logic of the capitalist economy.

9. See also the famous debate between Poulantzas and Miliband where Poulantzas defends his approach against the criticism of Miliband's empirical elite theory approach – Poulantzas and Miliband (1976); hence this study completely rejects Thomas' (1984, 69) contention that "it is difficult for those who control the state machinery to de-termine the national interest – or even the interest of the dominant economic groups". Thomas regards this situation as the *raison d'être* of the state's relative autonomy. However, the state "knows" very well the common economic and political denominator of the bourgeoisie *in toto*.

CHAPTER 2

1. See *Social and Economic Survey,* various years.

2. Ibid.

3. Manley himself refered to this situation as a "trap" – author's interview with Michael Manley, 22/3/1991.

4. Author's interview with D.K. Duncan, 29/10/1991.

5. Author's interview with Michael Manley, 22/3/1991.

6. All indicators, however, are based on 1979 figures – see Menzel and Senghaas (1986, 126 and 127).

7. The formula provided by Menzel and Senghaas (1986, 124) for the ETQ which would have to be expected theoretically at a certain point in time is:

$$17.86 + \frac{106.48}{\text{territorial space in } 1000 \text{ km}^2} + \frac{34.63}{\text{population in million}}$$

8. The GDP as an indicator of national development and even national growth is increasingly being criticized – cf. Daly and Cobb (1991); Nohlen and Nuscheler (1982c, 457-59). For our purposes,

however, this indicator was still the most easily accessible.

9. More details of the negotiations can be found in (Manley 1982) and in Rousseau (1987).

10. As for the other reasons, Rousseau (1987, 102) has pointed out:

I still continued . . . to have the feeling he [i.e., Manley – H.H.] was now bypassing me and dealing directly with the persons who reported to me. My objection was not out of peevishness, but was to the breaking up of the team we had so successfully built. At this time rhetoric reigned . . . he had moved even further to the left in his utterances and sometimes in his actions.

11. Manley, however, is apologetically talking about concessions that "were worth making" for the overriding goal of economic diversification – Manley (1987, 253).

Chapter 3

1. According to GATT director Olivier Long, around 3 to 5 percent annually of world trade (i.e., $20 to 50 billion) was affected between 1974 and 1977. However, restrictions imposed by the industrial countries were likely to have the greater impact – see Frank (1984, 190).

2. Interestingly, US transnationals were more efficient and successful than the rest of the US economy during most of the 1970s – see Gill and Law (1989, 196).

3. See also U.S. Congressional Record (1965, 22768) and U.S. Congressional Record (1972, 37584–37594) for concerns expressed

about Castro "inciting" American blacks and the publication of a number of Americans who allegedly went to Cuba for subversive training; cf U.S. Congressional Record (1963, 4864); see also concerns about Cuba's success in conducting profitable trade with Western Europe and Japan, expressed in an article from *Forbes* (15 April 1964), "Dollars Talk Louder Than Diplomats", reprinted in U.S. Congressional Record (1964, 9883).

Chapter 4

1. Jamaica Hansard (March 21, 1972–July 27, 1972), 317; for the application of this general statement to Cuba see Manley's statement in *DG* (8/4/1973, 1).

2. Thompson's influence was described as the actions of a political "loner" – author's interview with D. K. Duncan, 29/10/1991.

3. However, the US ambassador in Kingston at the same time asserted that Jamaica's step would not change "the excellent relations between the US and Jamaica which have never been better" – *DG* (14/12/1972, 1 and 8).

4. See also *DG* 16/9/1973, 9; criticism was also voiced by independent member of parliament R. Lightbourne who asked if a "love affair" had started between both countries *DG* (17/9/1973, 12).

5. Author's interview with D.K. Duncan, 29/10/1991.

6. Ibid.

7. However, only a year earlier a *Gleaner* editorial had seen the establishment of diplomatic relations with Cuba as a "path-breaking decision." – see *DG* (30/3/1973, 10).

8. Technical Assistance Bulletin, National Planning Agency (1977[?], 2); however, this relative significance certainly changed drastically in 1977 when the US increased its economic assistance for Jamaica to US$ 32.2 million – see Stephens and Stephens (1986, 397).

9. Ibid.

10. The following paragraph draws from Valdés' article.

11. Kissinger had expressed on December 23 that there would still be room for negotiations on a coalition government in Angola and – as an example of studied ambivalence – "we have no objection to the MPLA as long as it is an African organization". He added that Soviet actions in Angola would be "incompatible with the process of détente". – *DG* (2/1/1976, 15).

12. According to Hanlon this encouragement dated back to the time of the Alvor agreement, i.e., around 1974–1975; see also Marcum (1978, 271).

13. According to Hanlon (1986, 156), by the end of October the FNLA, supported by two Zairian elite battalions, was 20 kilometres away from Luanda and began shelling the capital around this time.

14. Jamaica's former ambassador to Cuba, surprisingly, pointed out the party's unity on the Angolan question – author's interview with Ben Clare, 18/7/1990.

15. A comment in the *Gleaner* urged the government not to recognize any group before it had firmly established itself – see *DG* (30/12/1975, 10).

16. As to the schedule of the meetings Kissinger would have, there seems to have been some confusion. Foreign Minister Thompson explained that although he would have talks with Kissinger, he could not say if the latter would also meet the prime minister. Kissinger, however, self-confidently declared he would have a meeting with Manley – see *DG* (27/12/1975, 1 and 23); according to Duncan, there was a quarrel over whether the prime minister should visit Kissinger at his holiday resort or whether Kissinger would come to Kingston. Eventually the decision was taken for the latter option – author's interview with D.K. Duncan, 29/10/1991.

17. According to the MPLA spokesman, the MPLA was already recognized by seventeen African states at this point in time – see *DG* (28/12/1975, 1).

18. Hence Verzijl (1969, 582) warns: "A government that for whatever reason wants to enter into informal relations with a new State or government without recognizing it, must be on its guard that its action cannot be construed as a recognition de facto."

19. The Jamaican government's explicit and *de jure* recognition

occurred in March 1976 – see *DG* (9/3/1976, 1).

20. The JMA statement even emphasized that "it is only the workforce aspect that has been questioned . . ." *DG* (24/1/1976, 1-2).

21. Author's interview with D.K. Duncan, 29/10/1991; however, Duncan had made his statement in Cuba after Manley himself had indicated his support for Cuba to him.

22. Ibid.

23. Article was reprinted in *DG* (20/3/1976, 10).

24. See Ministry Paper No.42, as published in *DG* (7/11/1977, 12 and 15); The *Miami Herald* echoed this view by writing that "Cubans are . . . waging a low-key campaign to win influence among their Caribbean neighbours." – quoted in *DG* (16/2/1978, 6).

25. It will be remembered at this point that under the "Treasonable and Seditious Practices Act" (1795) of the British Constitution, the intention to bring the government or constitution into hatred or contempt through the utterance of seditious words is punishable. Thomas Hobbes, of course, equated sedition with the Leviathan's sickness.

26. One standard work of international law defines the limits of diplomatic intervention thus:

. . . it must be specially emphasized that envoys must not interfere with the internal political life of the State to which they are accredited. It certainly belongs to their functions to watch political events and political parties with a vigilant eye, and to report their observations to their home States. But they have no right whatever to take part in that political life, to encourage one political party, or to threaten another. It matters not whether an envoy acts thus on his own account, or on instructions from his home State. No self-respecting state will allow a foreign envoy to exercise such interference, but will either request his home State to recall him, or, in case his interference is very flagrant, hand him his passport and therewith dismiss him.

See Oppenheim (1948, 704–05).

27. Hence, Manley (1982, 175) wrongly suggests that he had said he would "be happier if the Puerto Rican people were to choose independent status"; one commentary rightly asked, "Where is the support for Georgians, Estonians and others with much more legitimate claims to freedom from Russia oppression?" – *DG* (16/9/1979, 11).

28. For Cuba's position on the question of minority support for independence within Puerto Rico – see also United Nations (1981, 826).

29. Author's interview with Alfred Rattray, 10/7/1990; Manley describes the official US reaction as "very upset" – Manley (1982, 175).

30. We have to take note, however, that Manley later produced reports indicating that the US intelligence agencies viewed Seaga's "documents" as a cheap concoction. The actual weight given to these papers by different US government agencies deserves further enquiry.

31. Author's interview with Michael Manley, 22/3/1991.

Chapter 5

1. This, of course, is not to argue that the US should not grant countries like Jamaica greater freedom in the pursuit of their foreign relations. Rather, we would argue that the US has yet to learn to accept the consequences of its oftentimes deficient diplomacy. For too many countries, US attitudes are too important a foreign policy variable to be executed in a sloppy manner and then to be "corrected" by drastic military measures.

2. Author's interview with R. B. Manderson-Jones, 8/4/1992.

3. I am indebted to Ambassador the Hon. Don Mills for raising this point.

4. Manley was fully aware that his foreign policy proceeded with a two-track approach. Thus, his UN Ambassador Mills had pointed out to him that substantial achievements with NIEO negotiations were not to be expected as long as the international monetary system (i.e., World Bank, IMF, etc.) remained a separate component of the global economy and was excluded from the negotiations. I am indebted to Ambassador the Hon. Don Mills for making this point.

5. This inference can be drawn from a broadcast interview with David Coore in which he stated that "we decided in the latter part of 1976 to seek Fund assistance". – Coore (n.d., 4); see also Henry (n.d., 25).

6. Faced with the choice and responsibility this writer would not have advised the non-IMF path due to the possible breakdown of civil order. Nor, however, would he have tolerated an election campaign which was somewhat suggestive of this path. Despite the supportive popular mood for socialism at that time, Jamaica was not in a prerevolutionary phase of transition.

7. Although Matalon may not have been controlling local capital, as Henry suggests, he certainly was a major and influential player. At a deeper level, however, this point proves to what extent Manley – despite all the rhetoric – submitted strategic foreign policy decisions to bourgeois capitalist considerations and actual influence.

8. Regarding US support in the IMF, see the statement by the US ambassador to the UN, Andrew Young, who was a close personal friend of Manley during this time – *DG* (7/8/1977, 3).

9. Author's interview with D.K. Duncan, 29/10/1991 (the following quotations in this paragraph are also taken from this interview); see also *DG* 9/5/1979, 1 and 15.

10. This optimism was still maintained in the late 1980s by former Jamaican Ambassador Rattray – interview with Alfred Rattray, 10/7/1990.

11. Interview with Hugh Small on August 25, 1982 (interview conducted by Peter Körner – retranslated by author from the German transcript), 2–3.

12. The former Minister of Finance, Hugh Small, stated that "I have no

doubt at all that they (i.e., the IMF – H.H.) tried to steer us away from an independent position in international economic and political questions." – ibid., 3.

13. Thus e.g., the US secretary of the treasury advocated stronger surveillance powers for the IMF – *DG* 4/10/1979, 9.

14. Author's interview with Michael Manley, 22/3/1991.

15. Ibid.

16. Ibid.

17. By the same token it is often claimed that, considering the essentially capitalist nature of Jamaica's economy and foreign economic policy (including the NIEO), the lack of domestic and foreign investment, capital flight and disinvestment in the bauxite/alumina industry amounted to a concerted strategy to destabilize the PNP government. However, owners of capital and/or skills are quite free to choose where they want to invest and where not.

CHAPTER 6

1. On another occasion the same author conceded that the success of adjustment hinges on the "support of all social classes" which explains why relatively more egalitarian societies "tend to manage the adjustment problem better". However, in his conclusion he fails to draw any suggestions from this insight – see Worrell (1989, 13); for a critique of the neoliberal perception of the

East Asian experience see also Henke (1997).

2. See also *South* (June 1990, 38–39), which reports on the fast growing business in technology adaption run by the Nigerian businessman of the year in 1989; see also *South* (May 1990), 39–40 for the noteworthy case of Brazilian industrialist, Ricardo Semler, who turned his near bankrupt family business into a multi-million dollar profit company by the introduction of profit-sharing, flexible working hours, workers' participation in planning and decision making, simplification of company hierarchies and substitution of assembly lines by smaller-scale manufacturing.

3. See a statement from the chairperson of Jamaica Promotions Ltd. (JAMPRO), the country's economic development agency: "We . . . do sector studies to determine the particular needs of individual sectors . . . That we regard as a critical ingredient in our attempt to structurally reform the economy." in: *Money Index* (Aug. 23, 1988, 16); see also *DG* (8/7/81, 6); *Money Index* (Oct.18, 1988, 9).

4. Author's interview with Frank Francis, 26/11/1990.

5. Figures provided by NACLA as quoted in *Jamaika Bulletin* (July 1991, 108) – the same article cites World Bank representative, Christian Del Voie, who remarked with regard to garment export production: "The only thing an investor has to consider are the labour costs. Qualifications of the local employ-

ees are unimportant since all they do is cutting and sewing." (107–108 – my translation).

6. See interview with Edward Seaga in *The Courier* (May–June 1988, 27–28).

7. Ibid., 27 – emphasis added; it has to be pointed out that Seaga's statement was an extremely euphemistic interpretation of the international financial agencies' rejection of his social plan.

8. Ibid.

9. *Social and Economic Survey* (PIOJ), various years; while in the four years 1976–79 the number of work stoppages was over 700, in the four years 1983–86 there were only 276 reported stoppages; see also *DG* (25/5/87, 1); *DG* (27/5/87, 8).

10. As one former minister of justice rightly emphasized in 1985, new legislation introduced by the government raised the fundamental question of "whether a worker not employed in the Essential Services has a right to strike"; the significance of public opinion and the so-called national interest on the practice of labour dispute settlement was highlighted when in 1981 Justice Parnell found that an award which had exceeded the quantum granted in Ministry Paper No. 22 (sic!) had been contrary to the national interest:

The national interest varies with the period. The requirement of a rapidly changing society may influence a shift in a course of action once thought to be suitable. Public opinion may play a great part in shaping or refurbishing

national interest, *but it is the Government of the day which is competent to declare it.* – Rattray (1985, 10 and 9 – emphasis added).

11. This can be inferred from USAID's action plan for Jamaica which concerns itself with "resolving constraints to private sector growth" – see USAID (n.d., 12).

12. One of the leading bureaucrats handling the promotion of investments in Jamaica described the attitude of the local bourgeoisie as follows: "They were accustomed to the Government doing everything for them and it was very difficult for them to understand that they were now expected to do things for themselves." – author's interview with Corrine McLarty, 10/10/1991.

13. Ibid.

14. The former director of JAMPRO also diagnosed the aversion of the private sector to joint ventures in the early and mid 1980s – ibid.

15. Author's interview with Anthony Barnes, 17/8/1990.

16. However, even JEA President Vaswani in 1988 expressed the view that the international agencies "are taking Jamaica for a ride in certain . . . areas" – see *Money Index* (June 14, 1988, 5).

17. This view was corroborated by McLarty – interview with Corrine McLarty 10/10/1991.

18. Author's interview with Prakash Vaswani, 9/10/1991.

19. Interestingly, the PSOJ was of the view that the merger of the Ministry of Foreign Affairs and Trade with the Ministry of Industry

would bring "positive results" – see *Money Index* (Dec. 2, 1986, 7); see also *Money Index* (Oct. 28, 1986, 3).

20. Author's interview with Edward Seaga, 25/7/1991 (emphasis added).

21. Author's interview with Paul Thomas, August 1990.

22. In this context it is also interesting to note that two trade union representatives eminently involved in tripartite commissions in the 1980s subsequently became senators in the Jamaican Parliament; the notion of corporatism utilized here is based on Schmitter's definition: Corporatism can be defined as a system of interest representation in which the constituent units are organized into a limited number of singular, compulsory, noncompetitive, hierarchically ordered and functionally differentiated categories, recognized or licensed (if not created) by the state and granted a deliberate representational monopoly within their respective categories in exchange for observing certain controls on their selection of leaders and articulation of demands and supports. Schmitter (1974, 93-94); see also Gäfgen (1987).

Chapter 7

1. With regard to Jamaica's identification with the so-called like-minded group of conservative countries, we take note of the distinction being drawn by a former senior official in the Jamaican Ministry of Foreign Affairs: although Jamaica was prepared to consult and speak with this group (e.g., in preparation of

the Seventh Non-Aligned Summit in New Delhi), it would not have considered itself as one of its members. However, together they opposed the high levels of rhetoric within the Movement reached under Cuba's chairship – author's interview with Frank Francis, 26/11/90.

2. As May (1987, 194) points out, for a great number of key members of the Reagan administration this title of an influential book was the foundation of its foreign aid philosophy; for an overly optimistic review of socioeconomic consequences of structural adjustment in the case of Jamaica, see the article of World Bank economists Behrman and Deolalikar (1991, 291–313).

Chapter 8

1. Thus, in December 1914, American Marines walked straight into Haiti's Central Bank, "withdrew" $500,000 at gun-point and went back to New York to lodge the money with the National City Bank; hardly much of a moderate tradition.

2. The original members of the CDU are the United Democrat Party (Belize), the Dominica Freedom Party (Dominica), the New National Party (Grenada), the Jamaica Labour Party (Jamaica), the People's Liberation Movement (Montserrat), the People's Action Movement (St. Christopher and Nevis), the United Workers Party (St. Lucia), and the New Democratic

Party (St. Vincent and the Grenadines).

3. Author's interview with Joan Gordon-Webley, 9/4/1991.

4. Ibid.

5. Thus, Benda (1983, 16) argues in the introduction of the 1946 edition of his important pamphlet "*La trahison des clercs*": "The state which builds on order proves thereby that it wants to be strong but not just." Similarly, Galtung (1972, 79) argued that instead of viewing democracy as either consequence or precondition of development "one can (also) regard it as the precondition for an exertion of effective control over peripheral nations" – (translations provided by the author).

6. Author's interview with Joan Gordon-Webley 9/4/1991; see also the interview Gordon-Webley gave KLAS-FM radio on 9/10/1990.

7. "Corporatist" foreign policy is defined here as a strong external interest representation by the state on behalf of or in conjunction with divergent domestic social forces, or the facilitation/support of direct cooperation between civil associations located within its national territory and extraterritorial groups, whereby the former assume authority formerly exclusively occupied or claimed by the state. The rationale, however, is the reproduction of the internal social conditions of accumulation (often disguised as "national interest"). It is not suggested here that the Jamaican foreign policy in the 1980s was completely "corporatist". However, in several aspects it moved along a line which definitively points in this direction and it is argued here that the notion of interdependence served as a supportive tool in this movement. In this context we also take note of the dictum of Mihaïl Manoïlesco, whose concept of corporatism had already in the 1930s a distinctly international dimension: "The Nineteenth Century knew the solidarity of *class*. The Twentieth will know the solidarity of *nation*" – quoted in Schmitter (1974, 118–119); see also Cardoso and Faletto (1979, 215); Stavrianos (1981, 24).

8. For the text of the diplomatic note see Manderson-Jones (1990, 140).

9. For an account of the break, see e.g., Seaga (1981b); *DG* (30/10/1981, 1); see also Manderson-Jones, (1990, 141–43); *DG* (20/8/1981, 11).

10. This conclusion was corroborated by Anthony Abrahams who had been first executive director of the PSOJ before he became a member of the JLP government – author's interview with Anthony Abrahams, Kingston 2/9/1993; similarly, the Dominica private sector asked to keep Grenada out of CARICOM meetings – see *DG* (10/2/1982, 8).

11. Author's interview with Prakash Vaswani, 9/10/1991.

12. See in this context also Wöhlcke (1984, 25–26), who points out that even the Jamaican head of the Caribbean troops intervening in Grenada expressed doubts that

Grenada posed any threat to its neighbours.

13. The formal normalcy of this working relationship was emphasized by Francis – author's interview with Frank Francis, 26/11/90; see also *Insight* (Dec. 1982, 3 and 4).

14. This study does not share Payne's contention that the human rights clause would necessarily have excluded Grenada from CARICOM – see Payne (1988, 94).

15. Only two months later a high-ranking member of the cabinet publicly rejected the notion of "ideological pluralism in the region" – see *DG* (2/9/83, 17); in the interview with the author, Mr. Seaga also gave a very limited definition of this notion – author's interview with Edward Seaga, 25/7/1991.

16. Abrahams points out that there can be "absolutely no doubt" that the PSOJ was extremely concerned about communism in the Caribbean. However, he also lists close personal relationships with Maurice Bishop as an important factor for concerns about his well-being. Thus, even well-known socialists in the region were of the view that "something had to be done" after Bishop's arrest – author's interview with Anthony Abrahams, 2/9/1993.

17. See for example, the excellent study by Gilmore (1984).

18. All quotations in the following two paragraphs are taken from the author's interview with Anthony Abrahams, 2/9/1993.

19. For the US decision making process see also DeRouen (1993). This author, however, suggests that the Department of State was very determined to intervene – ibid., 15.

20. However, Abrahams questions the authenticity of this statement – author's interview with Anthony Abrahams, 2/9/1993; for the geopolitical and strategic considerations of the United States involvement see also Henrikson (1996, 200–01).

21. Author's interview with Neville Gallimore, 14/8/90.

22. Ibid.

23. Ibid.; see also *DG* (16/2/1986, 10).

24. *Money Index* (11 Feb. 1986, 12); the notorious Oliver North, who later became "famous" as one of the protagonists in the Iran-Contra scandal which rocked Ronald Reagan's presidency, also boasted that he contributed to Duvalier's departure although details about this were never revealed. Trouillot (1990, 226) concludes the end of the dictatorship was a "multinational exercise in 'crisis management" through a "high-level coup d'etat executed with international connivance".

25. Author's interview with Edward Seaga, 25/7/1991; see also the official explanation given in *DG* (8/2/1986, 1).

26. Indeed, four years later Gallimore still maintained that "we were the leaders in this initiative" – author's interview with Neville Gallimore, 14/8/1990.

27. Author's interview with Frank Francis, 26/10/1990; when Namphy declared himself "Commander-

in-Chief of the Armed Forces" against the provisions of the constitution, the Haitian people, alluding to Haiti's first King, Henri Christophe, started to refer to Namphy as "Henri II" – see *Money Index* (8/12/1987, 22).

28. Author's interview with Neville Gallimore, 14/8/1990.

29. Ibid.

30. For the quite critical NDI report on the election see Smith (1988, 3/4); there are indications, however, that Gallimore's claim to be a CARICOM representative might not reflect the entire picture – see CARICOM (1987c, 8).

31. At least this is Gallimore's viewpoint – author's interview with Neville Gallimore, 14/8/1990; for a summary of CARICOM's lukewarm response see CARICOM (1987c, 5 and 6).

32. The full text of the communiqué is also provided in Smith (1988, 2).

33. The insecurity about the CCL's status and complaint about the lack of information from the "Seaga mission to Haiti" was voiced but not without an undertone of disappointment in CARICOM (1987, 10–12).

34. Close to the Jamaican position, the US criticized the provisions of the new elections only very mildly as being "flawed" – see *DG* (15/1/1988, 1).

35. The degree of international rejection can also be seen from the fact that, despite invitation, neither the OAS and UN, nor the EEC sent observer teams to the election. The US did not have an invitation to send observers.

36. Thus, Seaga in a letter to Roderick Rainford, CARICOM's Secretary General, emphasized that the reaction of the Haitian people should be a major determinant of Jamaica's attitude – see Seaga (1987d); see also *DG* (16/1/1988, 1 and 24).

37. Author's interview with Edward Seaga, 25/7/1991.

38. The cynicism of the army is epitomized in a remark attributed to General Namphy: "Haiti has only one voter. The army. Ha ha." – see Abbott (1988, xii).

39. Hugh Shearer, the Jamaican foreign minister, was virtually uninvolved in the handling of both crises, which demonstrates his weak position as foreign minister.

CHAPTER 9

1. In the eyes of an influential British newspaper it was Jamaica that "accepted" the IMF loan – see the *Guardian* (12/2/1981).

2. In private, off-the-record talks USAID officials now admit that Seaga asked the Committee to terminate its activities, because it demanded very far-reaching concessions from the government in exchange for its investments; similarly, JEA President Vaswani pointed out that the American private sector is not used to the type of controls prevailing in Jamaica at that time – author's interview with

Prakash Vaswani, 9/10/1991; see also *DG* (13/4/1985, 8).

3. Author's interview with Prakash Vaswani, 9/10/1991.

4. In 1986 the JMA declared that the apparel and textile sector, one of the main beneficiaries of CBI, had earned US$ 50 million in 1985, of which only $7 million remained in Jamaica – see *DG* (10/1/1986, 1); see also *DG* (28/8/86, 15).

5. Author's interview with Corrine McLarty, 10/10/1991.

6. Ibid.

7. The government's criticism of US protectionism was fully embraced by the Jamaica Exporters' Association – see *DG* (20/2/1987, 26).

8. This conclusion was corroborated by McLarty – author's interview with Corrine McLarty, 10/10/1991.

9. See the mild criticism of the government's silence in *DG* (11/5/1986, 12).

10. See also Brown (1985, 63). In his testimony on structural barriers to export Mr. Marshall D. Brown completely fails to acknowledge the role of US protectionism; in 1984 USAID withheld an ESF disbursement "to encourage the government to reach an agreement with the IMF" – *DG* (21/12/1986, 8); see also McAfee (1991, chap. 4).

11. Author's interview with Tim O'Connor, 29/6/1990; the Government of Jamaica's right to deny US auditors access to files dealing with local currency generated from PL 480 Title I commodities, was also explicitly stated in USAID (1988, 3), from which Timothy Ashby

quoted in a maliciously unscientific manner.

12. Ibid.

13. For the changes being introduced in the Jamaican tax system and the World Bank's and USAID's involvement in it – see Bahl (1989).

14. Author's interview with Edward Seaga 25/7/1991.

15. For the opposition to and functional limits of corporatist mechanisms limiting tariff autonomy ("Tarifautonomie") in West Germany – see Beyme (1980, 250–53).

16. Dominguez' (1982, 43) "hegemonic devolution" is conceptualized here as a variant of hegemonic power "in which other countries establish their own policies, which would be consistent with but not associated with US policies".

Chapter 10

1. In large nations the decision makers encounter the notion of society often only in a very mediated sense, i.e., by public opinion polls.

2. See also Ashley (1983), who sees survival hinging on order. The basic structure of Libby's argument also lingers in some accounts of regional foreign policies – cf Romero (1989, 9–18); Payne (1987, 222).

3. May (1987, 21) – although bilateral assistance in real terms stagnated on the level of the last Carter budget, the Latin American and Caribbean share of all US bilateral assistance programmes increased from 18 percent to 28 percent

between 1980 and 1986, a doubling from US$ 233 million to US$ 461 million.

4. The inherent reactionism of this argument's structure has recently been brilliantly demonstrated and need not be reiterated here – see Hirschman (1991, chap. 4).

5. For the class composition and party leanings in the 1989 election – see Stone (1989, 105).

6. Obviously, this strategy requires highly skilled personnel which, in turn, emphasizes the need for high levels of education. However, the success of this strategy can be studied in the German "Land" Baden-Württemberg which fared extremely well with it.

7. Already, representatives of friendly endowments, e.g. the German CDU-related Konrad-Adenauer-Stiftung, are considering relocation of their regional headquarters away from Jamaica into the Eastern Caribbean, where they perceive a stronger impetus towards regional cooperation.

8. This would also necessitate the urgent upgrading of the obsolete and obstructive Official Secrets Act, which conveys to public servants the misleading impression that even the most general detail is a top secret matter and that revealing it publicly is entirely counterproductive.

9. Thus, the now defunct Centre for International Affairs under the directorship of Jamaica's former UN Ambassador Don Mills would need to be revived as a (possibly regional) "think tank", which could also sponsor public symposia and conferences. Strong and creative support from the Jamaican national bourgeoisie could help it to achieve these goals.

10. Huntley's suggestions for professionalization seem to hinge on the notion of high qualification alone and neglect the need for *continuing* education – see Huntley (1991, 73).

11. The low priority given by the JLP government to its lobbying efforts in Washington was exposed when its lobbyists (Charles Marriott and Peter Kelly), who also lobbied on behalf of the reactionary UNITA movement and the Marcos junta of the Philippines, were probed in 1986 for financial irregularities. Marriott himself was closely linked to the conservative National Endowment for Democracy (NED) which in 1985 was suspected to have paid money to right-wing groups in France – see *DG* (24/5/1986, 1).

Biblioqraphy

I list here only the writings that have been of use in the making of this book. This bibliography is by no means a complete record of all the works and sources I have consulted. It indicates the substance and range of reading upon which I have formed my ideas, and I intend it to serve as a convenience for those who wish to pursue the study of Jamaica's foreign relations. The bibliography has been subdivided into the four following sections: 1) documents, speeches, manuscripts etc., 2) newspapers, magazines, newsletters etc., 3) interviews, 4) secondary sources.

1) Documents, speeches, yearbooks, manuscripts, etc.

AID. no date a). *Congressional Representation (FY 1987)*. Washington, D.C.

AID. no date b). *Congressional Representation (FY 1988)*. Washington, D.C.

AID. no date c). *Congressional Representation (FY 1989)*. Washington, D.C.

Bank of Jamaica. 1991. *Jamaica's Financial System: Its Historical Development*. Kingston.

Brown, M. D. 1985. Prepared Statement by Marshall D. Brown (Dep. Assistant Administrator, Bureau for Latin America and the Caribbean, USAID). In *Hearings and Markup before the Subcommittee on Western Hemisphere Affairs of the Committee on Foreign Affairs*. House of Representatives, 99th Congress 1st Session (Review of Proposed Economic and Security Assistance for Latin America and the Caribbean, March 5 and 19), 55–81. Washington, D.C.

CARICOM Secretariat. 1982. *Ocho Rios Declaration*. News Release No.52/1982, 22 November, Attachment II.

CARICOM Secretariat. 1986a. *"Developments in the Hemisphere: The Situation in Haiti."* (Memorandum for the Twelfth Meeting of the Standing Committee of Ministers responsible for Foreign Affairs, FP 86/12/5, April 7.)

CARICOM Secretariat. 1986b. *"Extract from the Report of the Twelfth Meeting of the Standing Committee of Ministers responsible for Foreign Affairs."* (Rep. 86/12/25 FP), June 5–6. Belize City.

CARICOM Secretariat. 1987a. *"Update on the Situation on Haiti and on Haiti-CARICOM relations."* (Memorandum for the Thirteenth Meeting of the Standing Committee of Ministers responsible for Foreign Affairs, FP 87/13/5, April 15.)

CARICOM Secretariat. 1987b. *"Extract from the Report of the Thirteenth Meeting of the Standing Committee of Ministers responsible for Foreign Affairs."* (Rep. 87/13/26 FP), May 7–8. Georgetown.

CARICOM Secretariat. 1987c. *"The Situation in Haiti – Update and Possible Caricom Responses."* Paper by Frank Campbell (Foreign Affairs Officer). December 14.

Caribbean Democratic Union (CDU). 1986. *Charter (Kingston Declaration)*, January 17.

Congressional Research Service. 1985. *"The English-speaking Caribbean: Conditions and Implications for U.S. Policy."* Report on a workshop held on December 11, 1984, for the Subcommittee on Western Hemisphere Affairs of the Committee on Foreign Affairs. U.S. House of Representatives, 99th Congress, 1st Session. Washington, D.C.: Library of Congress.

Coore, D. no date (1977?). Interview by Easton Lee. Transcript found at the Agency for Public Information. Kingston.

Department of Statistics. Various years. *External Trade*. Kingston.

Department of Statistics. Various years. *Summary Tables of Tables of External Trade*. Kingston.

International Bank for Reconstruction and Development, International Finance Corporation, International Development Association. 1976. *Annual Meetings of the Boards of Governors (Summary Proceedings)*, October 4–8. Manila.

International Monetary Fund (IMF). 1979a. *Office Memorandum from E. Walter Robichek and C. David Finch to the Managing Director*, November 14. Washington, D.C.

International Monetary Fund (IMF). 1979b. *"Briefing for Mission to Jamaica."* Prepared by the Western Hemisphere Department, November 14. Washington, D.C.

Jamaica Hansard. *Proceedings in the House of Representatives*, Session 1972–1973. Vol.1 No.1 (March 21, 1972–July 27, 1972). Kingston.

Jamaica Hansard. *Parliamentary Proceedings of the House of Representatives*, Session 1978–1979. Vol. 4 No.1 (New Series). (May 16, 1978–Aug. 1, 1978). Kingston.

JAMPRO. 1988. *Annual Report 1988*. Kingston: Jamaica Promotions Ltd.

Kissinger Commission. 1984. "The Crisis and Our Opportunity." In *Crisis and Opportunity. U.S. Policy in Central America and the Caribbean*, edited by M. Falcoff and R. Royal. Washington, D.C.: Ethics and Public Policy Center.

Manley, M. no date (1975?). Speech by the Prime Minister in Havana (July 1975). Kingston: The Agency for Public Information.

Ministry of Finance. 1977. *"The IMF Agreement."* Ministry Paper No. 28. Kingston.

National Planning Agency. no date. *Technical Assistance Bulletin* (1977?). Kingston.

Planning Institute of Jamaica. various years. *Economic and Social Survey.* Kingston.

PSOJ (Private Sector Organisation of Jamaica). 1985. *A Policy Framework for Economic Development in Jamaica.* Kingston.

————. no date. *Annual Report 1985/86.* Kingston.

Schramm, H., and W. Sülberg, eds. 1983. *Konzeption der Lateinamerikapolitik der USA für die 80er Jahre – Geheimdokument des Santa Fe-Komitees für den Interamerikanischen Sicherheitsrat der USA.* Frankfurt a.M.: Verlag für Interkulturelle Kommunikation.

Seaga, E. 1980a. *The Correct Path.* Speech by Prime Minister Edward Seaga to the 4th Miami Conference on Caribbean Trade, Investment and Development, November 23, 1980. Kingston: Agency for Public Information.

————. 1980b. Keynote address to the IV Miami Conference on Caribbean Trade, Investment and Development in Miami, November 23.

————. 1981a. *"Address to the Graduating Class of the University of Miami,"* May 5.

————. 1981b. *The Break in Jamaica-Cuba Diplomatic Relations.* Statement by the Prime Minister of Jamaica, Oct. 29, 1981. Kingston: Jamaica Information Service.

————. 1982a. *"Caribbean Development Strategy and Private Enterprise."* Speech by the Prime Minister at St. Mary's University, School of Business Administration, San Antonio, March.

————. 1982b. Welcome Address to the Third Meeting of the Conference of Heads of Government of the Caribbean Community at Ocho Rios, Jamaica, November 15–18.

————. 1983a. *"Harmonizing Host Country and Corporate Activities."* Keynote Address at a Conference on International Business in Developing Countries, Stanford University, Graduate School of Business, Jan. 14.

————. 1983b. *Address at the Opening Ceremony.* Fourth Meeting. Heads of Government of the Caribbean Community, Port-of-Spain, July 4.

————. 1983c. *"Beyond the Debt Crisis."* Address at the 6th Annual Business Conference, Los Angeles Area Chamber of Commerce at the Century Plaza Hotel, Los Angeles, July 21.

————. 1983d. *"Dependence, Independence, Interdependence."* Address at a symposium on "The Security of the Democratic World," University of South Carolina, Columbia, South Carolina, Oct. 2.

————. 1984a. *Intervention by the Prime Minister at the Latin American Economic Conference.* Quito, Ecuador, Jan. 10–14.

————. 1984b. *"Democracy in Small States - The Case of the Caribbean."* Address by the Prime Minister to the Harvard Law School Forum, March 8.

————. 1986a. Address by the Prime Minister at the Launching of the Caribbean Democrat Union, Kingston, January 16.

————. 1986b. *"Of Freedom and Democracy."* Address by the Prime Minister to the West Indies Jaycees, Port-of-Spain, March 1.

————. 1986c. Address by the Prime Minister of Jamaica. 10th Anniversary Miami Conference on the Caribbean at the Hyatt Regency Hotel, Miami, Nov. 18.

————. 1987a. *"East/West Relations Today: A Jamaican Perspective."* Address by the Prime Minister to the Aspen Institute at Rose Hall Great House, Montego Bay, Jan. 16.

————. 1987b. *"A Proposal for Coordinating and Improving Approaches to the International Debt Crisis."* July. Kingston: Jamaica Information Service.

————.1987c. *Remarks by the Prime Minister of Jamaica.* Closing Dinner, Miami Conference on the Caribbean at the Hyatt Regency Hotel, Miami, December.

————. 1987d. *Letter to Roderick Rainford.* December 23. Kingston: Jamaica House.

————. 1987e. Statement to the Press by the Prime Minister, Jamaica House, Kingston, December 22.

Sixth Conference of Heads of State or Government of Non-Aligned Countries. 1980. *Addresses.* Havana.

Small, H. 1982. Interview by Peter Körner with Hugh Small on 25 August 1982, Kingston (German transcript provided to the author by Peter Körner, University of Hamburg).

STATIN. 1981. *National Income and Product 1980.* Kingston.

————. 1988. *National Income and Product 1987.* Kingston.

Statistical Institute of Jamaica.Various years. *Statistical Abstract.* Kingston.

United States Congress. 1983. *House Document 98-151* (Letter by Hugh Shearer to William Brock, U.S. Special Trade Representative, Nov. 10, 1983), 23–28. 98th Congress 2nd Session. Washington, D.C.

USAID. no date. *Action Plan FY 1992/93 for Jamaica.* Washington: USAID.

USAID. 1988. *Audit of USAID/Jamaica's PL 480 Title I. Local Currency. Denial of Access to Records.* (Audit Report No. 1-532-88-19), June 4.

U.S. Congressional Record. 1963. *Proceedings and Debates of the 88th Congress, First Session.* Vol. 109 Pt. 4 (March 15, 1963 – April 3, 1963). Washington, D.C.

U.S. Congressional Record. 1964. *Proceedings and Debates of the 88th Congress, Second Session,* Vol. 110 Pt. 8 (May 4, 1964 – May 18, 1964). Washington, D.C.

U.S. Congressional Record. 1965. *Proceedings and Debates of the 89th Congress, First Session.* Vol. 111 Pt. 17 (Aug. 31, 1965 – Sept. 13, 1965). Washington, D.C.

U.S. Congressional Record. 1972. *Proceedings and Debates of the 92nd Congress, Second Session.* Vol. 118 Pt. 28 (Oct. 16, 1972 – Oct. 18, 1972). Washington, D.C.

United Nations. 1981. *Yearbook 1978.* New York.

United Nations. 1988. *Official Records of the General Assembly, 38th Session, Plenary Meetings.* Vol. I (20th Sept.–14th Oct. 1983). New York.

2) Newspapers, magazines, newsletters, etc.

(All references to and quotations from these sources are made in a day, month, year sequence – e.g., 29/10/1984):

Blick durch die Wirtschaft
Daily Gleaner (Kingston).
Die Welt
Financial Times
Frankfurter Allgemeine
Frankfurter Rundschau
Handelsblatt
Insight (Kingston)
International Herald Tribune
Jamaica Herald (Kingston)
Joint Trade Union Research Development Centre (JTURDC) *Newsletter,* (Kingston)
Le Monde (Paris)
Money Index (Kingston)
Neue Zürcher Zeitung
Süddeutsche Zeitung
South (London)
The Guardian
The Nation
The Times (London)

3) Interviews (conducted and taped by the author with permission of interviewees, Kingston)

Abrahams, Anthony (minister of tourism and information in 1980). Sept. 2, 1993.

Barnes, Anthony (JMA: president 1980–1990). Aug. 17, 1990.

Blades, Desmond (COC: 1st vice-president 1986–1991). Aug. 20, 1990.

Clare, Ben (ambassador to Cuba 1975–1977; ambassador to the USSR 1977–1980). May 5, 1990 and July 18, 1990.

Davis, Winston (ambassador to Cuba 1977–1980). Oct. 5, 1990.

Duncan, D.K. (PNP: general secretary 1974–1977 and 1979–1980). Oct. 29, 1991.

Francis, E. Frank (Ministry of Foreign Affairs: permanent secretary 1976–1989). Nov. 26, 1990.

Gallimore, Neville (Ministry of Foreign Affairs: minister of state 1980–1984; minister of social security 1984–1986; minister of education 1986–1989). Aug.14, 1990.

Gordon-Webley, Joan (CDU: executive secretary). April 9, 1991.

Manderson-Jones, R.B. (Ministry of Foreign Affairs: director of political affairs 1970s). April 8, 1992

Manley, Michael (prime minister 1972–1980, 1989–1991). March 22, 1991.

McLarty, Corrine (JNIP: director 1981–1988; JAMPRO: director 1988–1989). Oct. 10, 1991.

O'Connor, Tim (USAID project officer). June 29, 1990.

Rattray, Alfred (ambassador to the US and the OAS 1975–1980). July 10, 1990.

Seaga, Edward P.G. (prime minister 1981–1989). July 25, 1991.

Thomas, Paul (JMA: president 1985–1988). Aug. 29, 1990.

Vaswani, Prakash (JEA: president 1978–1981 and 1986–1989). Oct. 9, 1991.

4) Secondary sources

Abbott, E. 1988. *Haiti. The Duvaliers and Their Legacy.* New York: McGraw-Hill.

Ajami, F. 1978. "The Global Logic of the Neoconservatives." *World Politics* 30 (3): 450–68.

Alavi, H. 1989a. "State and Class Under Peripheral Capitalism." In *Introduction to the Sociology of "Developing Countries,"* edited by Hamza Alavi and Teodor Shanin, 289–307. London: Macmillan.

———. 1989b. "The Structure of Peripheral Capitalism." In *Introduction to the Sociology of "Developing Countries",* edited by Hamza Alavi and Teodor Shanin, 172–92. London: Macmillan.

Altvater, E., and K. Hübner. 1987. "Ursachen und Verlauf der internationalen Schuldenkrise." In *Die Armut der Nationen,* edited by Elmar Altvater et al., 14–28. Berlin: Rotbuch Verlag.

Amin, S. 1977. "Self-Reliance and the New International Economic Order." *Monthly Review* 29 (3): 1–21.

————. 1980. *Class and Nation. Historically and in the Current Crisis.* London: Heinemann.

Anderson, P., and M. Witter. 1991. "Crisis Adjustment and Social Change: A Case Study of Jamaica." Draft paper of Research Project on Crisis, Adjustment and Social Change conducted jointly by UNRISD and the Consortium Graduate School of Social Sciences, UWI, Mona.

Antrobus, P. 1989. "Gender Implications of the Development Crisis." In *Development in Suspense*, edited by George Beckford and N. Girvan, 145–60. Mona: Friedrich Ebert Stiftung.

Ashby, T. 1989. *Missed Opportunities. The Rise and Fall of Jamaica's Edward Seaga.* Indianapolis: Hudson Institute.

Bahl, R. 1989. "The Political Economy of the Jamaican Tax Reform." In *Tax Reform in Developing Countries*, edited by Malcolm Gillis, 5–63. Durham: Duke University Press.

Bauer, P.T. 1976. "Western Guilt and Third World Poverty." *Commentary* 61 (1): 31–38.

Beckford, G. L. 1983. *Persistent Poverty. Underdevelopment in Plantation Economies of the Third World.* Morant Bay: Maroon Publishing House.

Behrmann, J., and A. Deolalikar. 1991. "The Poor and the Social Sectors during a Period of Macro-economic Adjustment: Empirical Evidence for Jamaica." *World Bank Economic Review* 5 (2): 291–313.

Benda, J. 1983. *Der Verrat der Intellektuellen.* Frankfurt a.M.: Ullstein.

Berberoglu, B. 1987. "The Contradictions of Export-Oriented Development in the Third World." *Social and Economic Studies* 36 (4).

Bernal, R. L. 1980. "Transnational Commercial Banks, the International Monetary Fund and the Capitalist Crisis in Jamaica 1972–80." Paper presented at the Conference on Finance Capital and Dependence in the Transnational Phase: A Latin American Perspective, March 4–7, Instituto Latinoamericano de Estudios Transnacionales [ILET] and Centro de Estudios Economicos y Sociales del Tercer Mundo [CEESTEM], Mexico City.

————. 1986. "Resolving the International Debt Crisis." In *The Debt Problem in Jamaica. Situation and Solutions*, edited by Omar Davies, 82–114. Mona: University of the West Indies, Department of Economics.

————. 1988. *The Political Economy of IMF Programs in Jamaica, 1977–84.* PhD dissertation, New School for Social Research.

Beyme, K. v. 1980. "Der Neo-Korporatismus und die Politik des begrenzten Pluralismus in der Bundesrepublik." In *Stichworte zur "Geistigen Situation" der Zeit*, Vol. I, edited by Jürgen Habermas, 229–62. Frankfurt a.M.: Suhrkamp Verlag.

Bhatti, R. 1992. "Challenging 'End of Cold War' Mythology and Implications for South Asian Politics." Paper presented at the Third World Foundation Annual Conference. May 6–9, Kingston.

Biddle, J., and J. D. Stephens. 1989. "Dependent Development and Foreign Policy: The Case of Jamaica" (unpublished version of "Dependent Development and Foreign Policy: The Case of Jamaica"). *International Studies Quarterly* 33 (4): 411–34.

Bienefeld, M. 1982. "The International Context for National Development Strategies: Constraints and Opportunities in a Changing World." In *The Struggle for Development. National Strategies in an International Context*, edited by Manfred Bienefeld and G. Martin, 25–64. Chichester, NY, John Wiley & Sons.

Bosshard, P. 1987. *Endlich haben wir eine Regierung der Liebe! Demokratischer Sozialismus in Jamaica unter Michael Manley (1972–1980)*. Basel: Z-Verlag.

Braveboy-Wagner, J. A. 1988. "Caribbean Foreign Policy: An Examination of its Limitations and Needs." *Caribbean Affairs* 1 (3): 77–89.

Brown, A. 1981. "Economic Policy and the IMF in Jamaica." *Social and Economic Studies* 30 (4): 1–51.

Brown, L. 1994. "Crisis, Adjustment and Social Change. The Middle Class Under Structural Adjustment." In *Consequences of Structural Adjustment. A Review of the Jamaican Experience*, edited by Elsie LeFranc, 56–117. Kingston: Canoe Press.

Brzezinski, Z. 1973. "U.S. Foreign Policy: The Search for Focus." *Foreign Affairs* 51 (4).

Büttner, V. 1984. "Ressourcentransfer und externe Verschuldung." In *Die Dritte Welt in der Krise. Grundprobleme der Entwicklungsländer*, edited by Peter J. Opitz, 134–56. München: C. H. Beck.

Carnoy, M. et al. 1993. *The New Global Economy in the Information Age. Reflections on our Changing World*. University Park: Pennsylvania State University Press.

Cardoso, F., and E. Faletto. 1979. *Dependency and Development in Latin America*. Berkeley: University of California Press.

Chace, J. 1985. *Krieg ohne Ende. Die Machtpolitik der USA in Mittelamerika*. München: Kindler Verlag GmbH.

Chomsky, N. 1987a. "Intervention in Vietnam and Central America: Parallels and Differences." In *The Chomsky Reader*, edited by James Peck, 315–50. New York: Pantheon Books.

———. 1987b. "Vietnam and the United States Global Strategy." In *The Chomsky Reader*, edited by James Peck, 227–55. New York: Pantheon Books.

Cox, R. W. 1981. "Social Forces, States and World Orders: Beyond International Relations Theory." *Millenium* 10 (2): 126–53.

————. 1983. "Gramsci: Hegemony and International Relations: An Essay in Method." *Millenium* 12 (2): 162–75.

————. 1987. *Production, Power, and World Order. Social Forces in the Making of History*, Vol. I. New York: Columbia University Press.

Cuthbert, M. 1979. "News Selection and News Values. Jamaica and the Foreign Press." *Caribbean Studies* 19 (1 and 2): 93–109.

Cypher, J. M. 1989. "The Debt Crisis as 'Opportunity'. Strategies to Revive U.S. Hegemony." *Latin American Perspectives* 16 (1): 52–78.

Daly, H, and J. Cobb. 1989. *For the Common Good*. Boston: Beacon Press.

Davies, O, and M. Witter. 1989. "The Development of the Jamaican Economy since Independence." In *Jamaica in Independence. Essays on the Early Years*, edited by Rex Nettleford, 75–101. Kingston and London: Heinemann (Caribbean) and James Currey.

Deere, C. D. et al. 1990. *In the Shadows of the Sun. Caribbean Development Alternatives and U.S. Policy*. Boulder, Colorado: Westview Press.

DeRouen, Jr., K. R. 1993. "Foreign Policy Decision Making and the US Use of Force: Dien Bien Phu, 1954 and Grenada, 1983." Paper presented at the Annual Meeting of the Caribbean Studies Association, May 24–29, Kingston.

Depelchin, J. 1989. "Structural Adjustment and Other World Bank/IMF Strategies in Zaire: An Historical Perspective." Paper presented at a conference on "Economic Crisis and Third World Countries: Impact and Response," April 3–6, Kingston.

Dieren, W. v., ed. 1995. *Mit der Natur rechnen. Der neue Club-of-Rome Bericht: Vom Bruttosozialprodukt zum Ökosozialprodukt*. Basel: Birkhäuser.

Dominguez, J. I. 1982. *U.S. Interests and Policies in the Caribbean and Central America*. Washington, D.C.: American Enterprise Institute for Public Policy Research.

Drekonja-Kornat, G. 1986. *Grundmuster lateinamerikanischer Außenpolitik*. Wien: Braumüller.

Edie, C. J. 1986. "Domestic Politics and External Relations under Michael Manley." *Studies in Comparative International Development* 31 (1): 71–94.

Elsenhans, H. 1985. "Der periphere Staat: Zum Stand der entwicklungstheoretischen Diskussion." *Politische Vierteljahresschrift* 26 (Sonderheft 16): 135–56.

Fagen, R. 1983. "Theories of Development. The Question of Class Struggle." *Monthly Review* 35 (4): 13–24.

Farer, T. J. 1988, *The Grand Strategy of the United States in Latin America*. New Brunswick: Transaction Books.

Foxley, J. 1984. "Saving the World Economy." *Monthly Review* 36 (4).

Frank, A. G. 1984. "Rhetoric and Reality of the New International Economic Order." In *Transforming the World Economy,* edited by Herb Addo. London: Hodder and Stoughton.

Furtado, C. 1982. *A nova dependencia. Divida externa e monetarismo.* Rio de Janeiro: Paz e Terra.

Gäfgen, G. 1987. "Kooperative Wirtschaftspolitik, Neuer Korporatismus und Wirtschafts-ordnung." Paper No. 230, Faculty for Economic Science and Statistics, University of Konstanz, Konstanz.

Galtung, J. 1972. "Eine strukturelle Theorie des Imperialismus." In *Imperialismus und strukturelle Gewalt. Analysen über abhängige Reproduktion,* edited by Dieter Senghaas, 29–104. Frankfurt a.M.: Suhrkamp Verlag.

Garthoff, R. L. 1985. *Detente and Confrontation. American-Soviet Relations from Nixon to Reagan.* Washington, D.C.: Brookings Institution.

Gerster, R. 1982. *Fallstricke der Verschuldung. Der Internationale Währungsfond und die Entwicklungsländer.* Basel: Z-Verlag.

Gill, S., and D. Law. 1989. *The Global Political Economy. Perspectives, Problems, and Policies.* Baltimore: Johns Hopkins University Press.

Gilmore, W. C. 1984. *The Grenada Intervention. Analysis and Documentation.* Berlin: Berlin Verlag.

Girvan, N., R. Bernal, and W. Hughes. 1980. "The IMF and the Third World: The Case of Jamaica." *Development Dialogue* 2: 113–55.

Girvan, N. P. 1987. "Development Patterns in the Caribbean." In *The Caribbean Basin Initiative: Genuine or Deceptive?,* edited by Glenn O. Phillips and T. O. Shaw, 61–72. Baltimore: Morgan State University Press.

Gonzales, A. P. 1991. "World Restructuring and Caribbean Economic Diplomacy." In *Diplomacy for Survival: CARICOM States in a World of Change,* edited by Lloyd Searwar, 1–18. Kingston: Friedrich Ebert Stiftung.

Griffith-Jones, S. 1983. "The Growth of Transnational Finance: Implications for National Development." In *Latin America in the World Economy. New Perspectives,* edited by Diana Tussie, 55–87. Aldershot: Gower.

Guilbault, J. 1992. "Sociopolitical, Cultural and Economic Development Through Music: Zouk in the French Antilles." *Canadian Journal of Latin American and Caribbean Studies* 17 (34): 27–40.

Habermas, J. 1985a. "Die Kulturkritik der Neokonservativen in den USA und in der Bundesrepublik." In Jürgen Habermas. *Die Neue Unübersichtlichkeit,* 30–56. Frankfurt a.M.: Suhrkamp Verlag.
———. 1985b. "Konservative Politik, Arbeit, Sozialismus und Utopie heute." In Jürgen Habermas. *Die Neue Unübersichtlichkeit,* 59–76. Frankfurt a.M.: Suhrkamp Verlag.

Hanlon, J. 1986. *Beggar Your Neighbours. Apartheid Power in Southern Africa.* London: Catholic Institute for International Relations.

Harker, T. 1989. "The Caribbean in the Context of the Global Crisis." In *Development in Suspense. Selected Papers and Proceedings of the First Conference of Caribbean Economists*, edited by George Beckford and Norman Girvan, 11–47. Kingston: Friedrich Ebert Stiftung.

Hazleton, W. A. 1984. "The Foreign Policies of Venezuela and Colombia: Collaboration, Competition, and Conflict." In *The Dynamics of Latin American Foreign Policies. Challenges for the 1980's*, edited by Jennie K. Lincoln and E G. Ferris, 151–70. Boulder, Colorado: Westview Press.

Heilbroner, R. L. 1985. *The Nature and Logic of Capitalism.* New York: Norton.

Hein, W. 1985. "Konstitutionsbedingungen einer kritischen Entwicklungstheorie Globale kapitalistische Expansion, räumliche Strukturen wirtschaftlicher Entwicklung und der schwindende Einfluss nationalstaatlicher Strategien." *Politische Vierteljahresschrift* 26 (Sonderheft 16): 27–55.

Henke, H. 1996. "On the Political Economy of North American Integration: The Perspective of the Caribbean Countries." *Scandinavian Journal of Development Alternatives and Area Studies* 15 (3&4): 117–43.

––––––. 1997. "The Rise of Industrial Asia and its Implications for Small Developing Countries: A Perspective from the Caribbean." *Australian Journal of International Affairs* 51 (1): 53–72.

Henrikson, A. K. 1996. "The United States, the Caribbean Basin, and the Post-Cold War International Order." In *Choices and Change. Reflections on the Caribbean*, edited by Winston C. Dookeran, 197–228. Washington, D.C.: Inter-American Development Bank.

Henry-Wilson, M. 1977. *Institution-Building and Development. A Case Study of the Ministry of National Mobilization.* MPhil thesis, University of the West Indies.

Henry, M. no date. "Getting into the IMF." Unpublished paper (draft), Department of Government, University of the West Indies, Mona.

Herman, E. S. 1978. "Business Scholarship Fills the Bribery Gap." *Monthly Review* 30 (7): 38–44.

Hinkelammert, F. 1989. "Der Schuldenautomatismus. Wirtschaftspolitische und wirtschaftstheoretische Zugänge zur Verschuldung Lateinamerikas." In *. . . in euren Häusern liegt das geraubte Gut der Armen*, edited by Kuno Füssel et al., 79–190. Fribourg/Brig: Edition Exodus.

Hirschman, A. O. 1991. *The Rhetoric of Reaction. Perversity. Futility. Jeopardy.* Cambridge: Belknap Press of Harvard University Press.

Hofmann, L. M. 1984. *Politics of the Manley Regime in Jamaica.* PhD dissertation, University of Wisconsin, Madison.

Holzberg, C. S. 1977. *Race, Ethnicity, and the Political Economy of Entrepreneurial Elites in Jamaica*. PhD dissertation, Boston University Graduate School.

Huntley, E. 1991. "Development, Diplomacy and the Management of Foreign Affairs by the OECS in the 1990s and Beyond." In *Diplomacy for Survival: CARICOM States in a World of Change*, edited by Lloyd Searwar, 65–75. Kingston: Friedrich Ebert Stiftung.

Hyett, C. 1989. "The CBI and its Impact on the Commonwealth Caribbean in Light of the Puerto Rican Model of Export-Oriented Development." Paper by the Group for the Study of National and International Development (Donner Canadian Foundation Project on Sovereignty and Security), Queen's University, Kingston.

Hymer, S. 1972. "Multinationale Konzerne und das Gesetz der ungleichen Entwicklung." In *Imperialismus und strukturelle Gewalt. Analysen über abhängige Reproduktion*, edited by Dieter Senghaas, 201–39. Frankfurt a.M.: Suhrkamp Verlag.

James, C.L.R. 1971. "The West Indian Middle Classes." In *Readings in Government and Politics of the West Indies*, edited by Trevor Munroe and Rupert Lewis, 192–96. Mona.

Jones, E., and G. E. Mills. 1989. "The Institutional Framework of Government." In *Jamaica in Independence. Essays on the Early Years*, edited by Rex Nettleford, 105–29. Kingston and London: Heinemann (Caribbean) and James Currey.

Junne, G., J. Komen, and F. Tomei. 1989. "Dematerialisation of production: impact on raw material exports of developing countries.", *Third World Quarterly* 11 (2): 128–42.

Kaufman, M. 1985. *Jamaica Under Manley*. London, Westport, and Toronto: Zed Books, Lawrence Hill & Co., and Between the Lines.

Keith, N. E. 1981. *Democratic Socialism in Jamaica: Politics of Reform, Transition to Socialism or "Third Way" of Development?* PhD dissertation, Rutgers University.

Keith, N. W., and N. Z. Keith. 1992. *The Social Origins of Democratic Socialism in Jamaica*. Philadelphia: Temple University Press.

Kenney, M., and F. Buttel. 1985. "Biotechnology: Prospects and Dilemmas for Third World Development." *Development and Change* 16 (1): 61–91.

Kirkpatrick, J. J. 1984. "This Time we Know What's Happening." In *Crisis and Opportunity. U.S. Policy in Central America and the Caribbean*, edited by Mark Falcoff and R. Royal, 167–71. Washington, D.C.: Ethics and Public Policy Center.

Kissinger, H. A. 1979. *The White House Years*, London: Weidenfeld & Nicolson.

Körner, P. et al. 1986. *The IMF and the Debt Crisis*. London: Zed Books.

Krasner, S. D. 1982. "The Political Context of the Cancun Summit." *Third World Quarterly* 4 (3): 503–08.

Kubálková, V., and A. Cruickshank. 1989. *Marxism and International Relations*. Oxford: Oxford University Press.

Kuczynski, P.-P. 1982. "Action Steps after Cancun." *Foreign Affairs* 60 (5): 1022–37.

Levitt, K. 1990. *The Origins and Consequences of Jamaica's Debt Crisis, 1970–1990*. Mona: Consortium Graduate School of Social Sciences.

Lewis, V. A. 1977. "The Commonwealth Caribbean." In *Foreign Policy Making in Developing States. A Comparative Approach*, edited by Christopher Clapham, 110–30. Westmead: Saxon House.

————. 1979. "The Commonwealth Caribbean Policy of Non-Alignment." In *Contemporary International Relations of the Caribbean*, edited by Basil A. Ince, 1-11. St. Augustine: Institute of International Relations.

————. 1983. "The Small State Alone. Jamaican Foreign Policy, 1977–1980." *Journal of Interamerican Studies and World Affairs* 25 (2): 139–69.

Libby, R. T. 1990. "The United States and Jamaica: Playing the American Card." *Latin American Perspectives* 17 (1): 86–109.

Linklater, A. 1990. *Beyond Realism and Marxism. Critical Theory and International Relations*. New York: St. Martin's Press.

Linsley, A. 1979. "U.S.-Cuban Relations. The Role of Puerto Rico." In *Cuba in the World*, edited by Cole Blasier and Carmelo Mesa-Lago, 119–30. Pittsburgh: University of Pittsburgh Press.

Lukács, G. 1986. *Zur Ontologie des gesellschaftlichen Seins*. Vol. 2. Darmstadt and Neuwied: Hermann Luchterhand Verlag & Co KG.

Mandel, E. 1978. *Late Capitalism*. London and Atlantic Highlands: NLB and Humanities Press.

Manderson-Jones, R. B. 1990. *Jamaican Foreign Policy in the Caribbean, 1962–1988*. Kingston: Caricom Publishers.

Manicas, P. T. 1985. "Explanation, Generalisation and Marxist Theory *vis-a-vis* Third World Development." In *Marxian Theory and the Third World*, edited by Diptendra Banerjee, 309–22. London: Sage Publications.

Manley, M. 1980. "Message from the Prime Minister of Jamaica, Hon. Michael Manley, to the South-North Conference on the International Monetary System and the New International Order." *Development Dialogue* 2: 5–6.

————. 1982. *Jamaica. Struggle in the Periphery*. Oxford: Writers and Readers Publishing Cooperative Society Ltd.

———— 1987. *Up the Down Escalator. Development and the International Economy.* London: Andre Deutsch.

Marcum, J. A. 1978. *The Angolan Revolution.* Vol. 2. *Exile Politics and Guerilla Warfare.* Cambridge: MIT Press.

May, B. 1987. *Reagan und die Entwicklungsländer. Die Auslandshilfepolitik im amerikanischen Regierungssystem.* München: R. Oldenbourg Verlag.

McAfee, K. 1991. *Storm Signals. Structural Adjustment and Development in the Caribbean.* London and Boston: Zed Books and Oxfam America.

McDonald, S. 1982. "The Political Youth In The Contemporary Caribbean." Paper presented to the College of Charleston Caribbean Studies Association.

Menzel, U., and D. Senghaas. 1986. *Europas Entwicklung und die Dritte Welt.* Frankfurt a.M.: Suhrkamp Verlag.

Mesa-Lago, C. 1979. "The Economics of U.S.-Cuban Rapprochement." In *Cuba in the World*, edited by Cole Blasier and Carmelo Mesa-Lago, 199–224. Pittsburgh: University of Pittsburgh Press.

Moffitt, M. 1983. *The World's Money. International Banking from Bretton Woods to the Brink of Insolvency.* New York: Simon and Schuster.

Mugglin, M. 1989. "Alternativen sind unausweichlich." In . . . *in euren Häusern liegt das geraubte Gut der Armen*, edited by Kuno Füssel et al., 45–77. Fribourg/Brig: Edition Exodus.

Munroe, T. 1990. *Politics in Jamaica. A Marxist Perspective in Transition.* Kingston: Heinemann (Caribbean).

Nettleford, R. 1993. *Inward Stretch, Outward Reach. A Voice From The Caribbean.* London: Macmillan.

Niess, F. 1986. *Der Koloss im Norden. Geschichte der Lateinamerikapolitik der USA.* Köln: Pahl-Rugenstein Verlag GmbH.

Nohlen, D., and F. Nuscheler. 1982. "Was heißt Dritte Welt?" In *Handbuch der Dritten Welt*. Vol. 1, edited by Dieter Nohlen and F. Nuscheler, 11–24. Hamburg: Hoffmann und Campe Verlag.

————. 1982. "Was heisst Entwicklung?" In *Handbuch der Dritten Welt*. Vol. 1, edited by Dieter Nohlen and F. Nuscheler, 42–72. Hamburg: Hoffmann und Campe Verlag.

————. 1982. "Indikatoren von Unterentwicklung und Entwicklung. Probleme der Messung und quantifizierenden Analyse." In *Handbuch der Dritten Welt*. Vol. 1, edited by Dieter Nohlen and F. Nuscheler, 451–85. Hamburg: Hoffmann und Campe Verlag.

Opitz, P. J. 1984. "Statt einer Einleitung: Elemente zu einer Bilanz zweier Entwicklungsdekaden." In *Die Dritte Welt in der Krise. Grundprobleme der Entwicklungsländer*, edited by Peter J. Opitz, 11–44. München: Verlag C. H. Beck.

Oppenheim, L. 1948. *International Law* Vol. 1. *Peace,* edited by H. Lauterpacht. London: Longmans, Green & Co.

Osterkamp, R. 1984. "Der Aussenhandel." In *Die Dritte Welt in der Krise. Grundprobleme der Entwicklungsländer,* edited by Peter J. Opitz, 97–114. München: Verlag C. H. Beck.

Palmer, R. 1979. *Caribbean Dependence on the United States Economy.* New York: Praeger.

Parris, C. D. 1976. "Size or Class: Factors Affecting Trinidad and Tobago's Foreign Economic Policy." In *Size, Self-Determination and International Relations: The Caribbean,* edited by Vaughan A. Lewis, 248–63. Mona: Institute of Social and Economic Studies.

———. 1979. "From Populist Nationalism to Corporate Nationalism. Trinidad and Tobago – a Brief Overview." In *Contemporary International Relations in the Caribbean,* edited by Basil A. Ince, 242–59. St. Augustine: Institute of International Relations.

Payne, A. 1987. "Of Beauty, Vulnerability and Politics: Survival in the Caribbean." In *Third World Affairs 1987,* 216–23. London: Third World Foundation for Social and Economic Studies.

———. 1988. *Politics in Jamaica.* London and Kingston: C. Hurst & Co and Heinemann.

Pearson, R., and S. Mitter. 1993. "Employment and Working Conditions of Low-Skilled Information-Processing Workers." *International Labour Review* 82 (1): 49–64.

Petras, J. F. 1977. "President Carter and the 'New Morality'." *Monthly Review,* 29 (2): 42–50.

Petras, J. F., and H. Brill. 1986. "The Tyranny of Globalism." In *Latin America. Bankers, Generals, and the Struggle for Social Justice,* edited by James F. Petras. Totowa, New Jersey: Rowman & Littlefield.

Phillips, P. 1976. "Capitalist Elites in Jamaica." In *Essays on Power and Change in Jamaica,* edited by Carl Stone and Aggrey Brown, 18–42. Mona: Jamaica Publishing House.

Polanyi Levitt, K. 1980. *The World Economic Situation with Special Reference to the Countries of the Caribbean.* Mona: University of the West Indies.

Post, K. 1981. *Strike The Iron. A Colony at War: Jamaica 1939–1945,* Vol. 1. Atlantic Highlands and The Hague: Humanities Press and Institute of Social Sciences.

Poulantzas, N. 1974. *Politische Macht und gesellschaftliche Klassen.* Frankfurt a.M.: Athenäum Fischer TB Verlag.

———. 1979. *Classes in Contemporary Capitalism.* London: NLB.

Poulantzas, N. and R. Miliband. 1976. *Kontroverse über den kapitalistischen Staat.* Berlin: Merve Verlag.

Rattray, C. 1985. "The Worker and the Law." Public lecture. Kingston: Joint Trade Union Research Development Centre.

————. 1986. "The Recent Amendment to the Labour Relations and Industrial Disputes Act and its Implications for the Trade Union Movement." Public lecture. Kingston: Joint Trade Union Research Development Centre.

Reid, S. 1975. "An Introductory Approach to the Concentration of Power in the Jamaican Corporate Economy and Notes on its Origin." Mona: University of the West Indies, Department of Management.

Richardson, N. R. 1978. *Foreign Policy and Economic Dependency*. Austin and London: University of Austin Press.

Robbins, C. A. 1983. *The Cuban Threat*. New York: McGraw-Hill.

Robichek, E. W. 1984. "The International Debt Crisis and the Role the IMF Plays in it." Paper presented at the Inter-American Press Association Mid-Year Meeting, April 9–12, Ocho Rios.

Romero, C. A. 1989. "Pragmatic Democracy and Foreign Policy in the Caribbean." *Caribbean Affairs* 2 (1): 9-18.

Rothstein, R. L. 1977. *The Weak in the World of the Strong*. New York: Columbia University Press.

————. 1979. *Global Bargaining. UNCTAD and the Quest for a New International Economic Order*. Princeton: Princeton University Press.

Rousseau, P. H. O. 1987. *Negotiating Change. Pat Rousseau and the Bauxite Negotiations 1974–7*, Kingston: Heinemann (Caribbean).

Ruggie, J. G. 1982. "A Political Commentary on Cancun." *Third World Quarterly* 4 (3): 508–14.

Schmitter, P. C. 1974 "Still the Century of Corporatism?" In *The New Corporatism. Social-Political Structures in the Iberian World*, edited by Frederick B. Pike and Thomas Stritch, 85–131. Notre Dame and London: University of Notre Dame Press.

Schubert, A. 1985. *Die internationale Verschuldung*. Frankfurt a.M.: Suhrkamp Verlag.

Singham, A.W. and S. Hune. 1986. *Non-alignment in an Age of Alignments*. London, Westport, and Harare: Zed Books Ltd, Lawrence Hill & Co, College Press Ltd.

Smith, K. 1988. "President or puppet? Only time will show Manigat's true character." *Caribbean Affairs* 1 (2): 1–12.

Solomon, R. 1982. "'The elephant in the boat?': The United States and the world economy." *Foreign Affairs* 60 (3): 573–92.

Stavrianos, L.S. 1981. *Global Rift. The Third World Comes of Age*. New York: William Morrow and Company.

Stephens, E. H. and J. D. Stephens. 1983. "Democratic Socialism and the Capitalist Class: An Analysis of the Relation between Jamaican Business and the PNP Government." Documentos de Trabajo no.8, CISCLA, Universidad Interamericana de Puerto Rico.

————. 1986. *Democratic Socialism in Jamaica. The Political Movement and Social Transformation in Dependent Capitalism*. London: Macmillan.

————. 1989. "The Political Economy of Structural Adjustment: The Seaga Government in Jamaica." Paper presented at the XIV, Annual Meeting of the Caribbean Studies Association, May 23–29, Barbados.

Stone, C. 1973. *Class, Race and Political Behaviour in Urban Jamaica*. Mona: Institute of Social and Economic Research.

————. 1976. "Class and the institutionalization of two-party politics in Jamaica." *Journal of Commonwealth and Comparative Politics* 14 (2).

————. 1987. *Class, State and Democracy in Jamaica*. New York: Praeger.

————. 1989. *Politics versus Economics. The 1989 Elections in Jamaica*. Kingston: Heinemann.

Sweezy, P. M., and H. Magdoff. 1973. "The dollar crisis. What next?" *Monthly Review* 25 (1): 1–14.

————. 1984. "The two faces of Third World debt: A fragile financial environment and debt enslavement." *Monthly Review* 35 (8): 1–10.

Tancer, S. B. 1976. *Economic Nationalism in Latin America. The Quest for Economic Independence*. New York: Praeger.

Taylor, L. 1986. "Sovereign-debtor dilemmas in negotiating debt relief." In *The Debt Problem in Jamaica. Situation and Solutions*, edited by Omar Davies, 25–45. Mona: University of the West Indies, Department of Economics.

Therborn, G. 1980. *What Does the Ruling Class Do When it Rules? State Apparatuses and State Power under Feudalism, Capitalism and Socialism*. London: Verso Editions.

Thomas, C. Y. 1984. *The Rise of the Authoritarian State in Peripheral Societies*. New York: Monthly Review Press.

————. 1988. *The Poor and the Powerless. Economic Policy and Change in the Caribbean*, New York: Monthly Review Press.

————. 1989. "The Next Time Around: Radical Options and Caribbean Economy." In *Development in Suspense. Selected Papers and Proceedings of the First Conference of Caribbean Economists*, edited by George Beckford and N. Girvan, 290–314. Kingston: Friedrich Ebert Stiftung.

Todaro, M.P. 1977. *Economic Development in the Third World*. London: Longman.

Trouillot, M.R. 1990. *Haiti. State Against Nation*. N.Y.: Monthly Review Press.

Valdés, N. P. 1979. "Revolutionary solidarity in Angola." In *Cuba in the World*, edited by Cole Blasier and C. Mesa-Lago, 87–117. Pittsburgh: University of Pittsburgh Press.

Verzijl, J. H. W. 1969. *International Law in Historical Perspective*. Vol. 2. Leyden: Sijthoff.

Vogelgesang, S. 1980. *American Dream. Global Nightmare. The Dilemma of U.S. Human Rights Policy*. New York: Norton.

Wade, R. 1990. *Governing the Market. Economic Theory and the Role of Government in East Asian Industrialization*. Princeton: Princeton University Press.

Walker, R. B. J. 1993. *Inside/outside: International Relations as Political Theory*. Newcastle: Cambridge University Press.

Wariavwalla, B. 1988. "Interdependence and domestic political regimes: The case of newly industrializing countries." *Alternatives* 13 (2): 253–70.

Whiteside, K. H. 1988. *Merleau-Ponty and the Foundation of an Existential Politics*. Princeton: Princeton University Press.

Wilber, C. K., and K. Jameson. 1990. *Beyond Reaganomics. A Further Inquiry into the Poverty of Economics*. Notre Dame and London: University of Notre Dame Press.

Witter, M. 1989. *Higglering/Sidewalk Vending/Informal Commercial Trading in the Jamaican Economy*. Occasional Paper Series No.4. Mona: University of the West Indies.

Worrell, K. 1989. "Debt Crisis and Democracy in Latin America and the Caribbean," In *Prospects for the Economy in the Caribbean*. Reports of Seminars held in St. Kitts, April 1987 and Belize, July 1987, 9–18. Kingston: Bustamante Institute of Public and International Affairs.

Wöhlcke, M. 1984. "Die Intervention in Grenada." Unpublished paper. Ebenhausen: Stiftung Wissenschaft und Politik.

Index

Abrahams, Anthony, 183n.10, 184n.16

Abrams, Elliott, 148

ACP, 113, 119

Adams, Tom, 115

Afghanistan, 48

African Americans, 176n.3

Agriculture industry, 21. *See also* Food

Air Cubana, 33

Alavi, Hamza, 7, 10, 175n.8

Alcoa, 133, 145

Alcohol distillation industry, 136–138

Alexander, Carlton, 17, 46, 133

Algiers, 31

Allende, Salvador, 44

Allied Ethanol Ltd., 137

AMCHAM (American Chamber of Commerce in Jamaica), 168

American Bar Association, 27

Americas Society, 97

Amin, Samir, 70

Anderson, P., 77

Angola: civil war in, 42; and Cuba, 35–43, 159; and Jamaica, 35, 37–39, 41–43, 177n.14, 177–178n.19; and Kissinger, 35–36, 38–39, 43, 177n.11; and neoconservatism revival, 95; South African invasion of, 36-37, 39, 40; and U.S., 36, 42, 177n.11; and USSR, 27, 36, 177n.11

Apartheid, 36

Argentina, 31

Ashby, Timothy, 149, 186n.11

Ashenheim, Leslie, 17, 112, 113

Ashenheim family, 57

Asian Tigers, 174n.1

Autonomy: and Manley, 163; and national interest, 175n.9; private foreign investment versus, 53–54; relative autonomy, 9–11; restricted autonomy, 11–13; and Seaga, 162–163; and state's interest, 175n.9

Ayatolla Ruhollah Khomeini, 95

Baker, James, 98

Baker plan, 142

Balance of payments indicators for Jamaica, 76

Baldridge, Malcolm, 135

Bank of Commerce and Credit (BCCI), 143–144

Barbados: and ACP, 119; and Cuba, 30–31, 37; and Grenada, 109, 113, 114, 115; and Haiti, 125, 128

Batista, Fulgencio, 103

Bauxite: cartellization of, 55; and foreign exchange, 75; Soviet purchase of, 22–23, 63; and world debt crisis, 144

Bauxite Commission. *See* National Bauxite Commission

Bauxite levy: domestic programmes funded by, 15; and external trade quotient (ETQ) for Jamaica, 19; international reactions to, 55–56; overview of, 21–23; as windfall gain, 16

BCCI. *See* Bank of Commerce and Credit (BCCI)

Belize, 182n.2

Bell, Eric, 50, 62

Benda, J., 183n.5

Bertram, Arnold, 38

Bishop, Maurice, 103, 109, 111, 113, 115, 184n.16

Black Power movement, 3

Blaize, Herbert, 114

Blockades, 8

Bourgeoisie: and bauxite levy, 56; comprador bourgeoisie, 6–7; continental counterpart compared with, 175n.7; and Grenada invasion, 109; and IMF, 57–58, 89; indigenous bourgeoisie, 6; investment attitude of, 181n.12; local bourgeoisie, 8, 12–13, 54, 66, 67; Manley opposition of, 43, 56; metropolitan bourgeoisie, 7, 10; national bourgeoisie, 6, 160; and Private Sector Organization of Jamaica (PSOJ), 82–83; transnationalization of, 26–27. *See also* Comprador bourgeoisie

Boycotts, 8

Brady plan, 142

Braveboy-Wagner, J. A., 158

Brazil, 92, 99–100, 180n.2

"Bridgehead elites", 5

Brock, William, 134

Brown, Marshall D., 186n.10

Brzezinski, Zbigniew, 49

Burnham, Prime Minister, 34

Bush, George, 113

C/CAA. *See* Caribbean/Central American Action (C/CAA)

Canada, 58, 60, 77, 149

Capitalist economies, 4–5, 8

Caribbean Basin Economic Recovery Act (CBERA), 97-98

Caribbean Basin Initiative (CBI): and alcohol distillation industry, 136-139; as Caribbean "Marshall plan", 134; and Puerto Rican development model, 157; and "Super 807" programme, 135-136; and textile industry, 135–136, 138, 139; and U.S. foreign policy, 97–98, 134–135

Caribbean Cement, 57

Caribbean/Central American Action (C/CAA), 97, 132-133

Caribbean Chamber of Industry and Commerce, 97

Caribbean Conference of Churches, 124

Caribbean countries: decolonization of, 3; and democracy as regional norm, 101–107; economic nationalism in, 3; foreign relations politics in, 2–4; and U.S. foreign policies, 96-98, 186-187n.3. *See also* specific countries

Caribbean Democratic Union (CDU), 104, 105, 182–183n.2

CARICOM: and Concerned Caribbean Leaders (CCL), 185n.33; Declaration on Haiti of the Meeting of CARICOM/Caribbean Leaders, 125-126, 171–173; and Gallimore, 185n.30; and Grenada, 110, 184n.14; and Haiti, 119-120, 121, 125; and human rights, 109, 184n.14; and Jamaica, 63, 115–116; and PSOJ, 112; rift within,

124–125, 128; Seaga's circumvention of, 103

Carter, Jimmy, 27, 28–29, 57, 61

Castro, Fidel: and Angola, 36; "inciting" of American blacks by, 176n.3; and Manley, 31-32, 36; and NAM, 48; Thompson on, 40–41; visit to Jamaica, 44. *See also* Cuba

CBERA. *See* Caribbean Basin Economic Recovery Act (CBERA)

CBI. *See* Caribbean Basin Initiative (CBI)

CCL. *See* Concerned Caribbean Leaders (CCL)

CDU. *See* Caribbean Democratic Union (CDU)

Centre for International Affairs, 187n.9

Chemical industry, 165

Chile, 7, 43–44

China, 152

Classes. *See* Social class

CME. *See* Joint Committee of Commerce, Manufactures and Export (CME)

CNG. *See* National Council of Government (CNG)

CoC. *See* Jamaica Chamber of Commerce

Coffee Board, 150

Colombia, 108

COMECON, 63

Communications industry, 21

Communism, 14, 17, 32, 45, 46, 54, 175n.8, 184n.16. *See also* specific countries

Communist Party of Jamaica (CPJ), 14

Compensatory Financing Facility, 131–132

Comprador bourgeoisie: and bauxite levy, 56; and Cuban diplomatic relations with Jamaica, 46; definition of, 6–7; and foreign capital, 7; and Grenada invasion, 112; and Haiti membership in CARICOM, 121; Jamaican shift from national bourgeoisie to, 160; power of, 7; rise of, 89. *See also* Bourgeoisie

Concerned Caribbean Leaders (CCL), 122–123, 185n.33

Construction industry, 21

Coore, David, 56, 179n.5

Corporatism, definition of, 182n.22

"Corporatist" foreign policy, 183n.7

Costa Rica, 108

CPJ. *See* Communist Party of Jamaica (CPJ)

Credit, political restrictions on, 8

Crime, 78, 156, 165, 168

Cuba: and Angola's liberation, 35–43, 159; Argentina's exports to, 31; and Batista, 103; and Caribbean Basin Initiative (CBI), 98; and communist influence in Caribbean, 102; construction workers in Jamaica, 40; Cuban ambassador's expulsion from Jamaica, 47; and Guantanamo Bay issue, 46; "integral coexistence" policy, 35; international capital opposition to, 111; and Jamaica, 30–51, 63, 71, 107–108, 116, 153, 162; Japan's trade with, 176n.3; Organization of American States (OAS) embargo on, 31; and Puerto Rican self-determination, 178n.28; and subversive training, 176n.3; training police in Jamaica, 44; U.S. suppression of, 28–29. *See also* Castro, Fidel

Daily Gleaner: bauxite levy support of, 22; and communism, 17, 32; and Cuban ambassador, 107; and Cuban troops in Angola, 38, 40; and diplomatic relations with Cuba, 177n.7; and Grenada invasion, 112–113; on Haiti crisis, 127; and Jamaica Labour Party (JLP), 69; and Jamaica-U.S. relationship, 48–49; ownership of, 57; and Patterson's speech in New York, 53; and recognition of Marxist Popular Movement for the Liberation of Angola (MPLA), 177n.15; and Seaga, 111; as "ultra-reactionary", 47

De Roulet, Vincent, 54

Declaration on Haiti of the Meeting of CARICOM/Caribbean Leaders, 125–126, 171–173

Decolonization, 3

Del Voie, Christian, 180–181n.

Democratic Party (U.S.), 121

Democratic socialism, 17, 22

Dependency: "discursive" dependency, 161; and Jamaica Labour Party (JLP), 70–71; "new dependency", 92; structural dependency, 1, 4–9, 9–13, 18, 70–71, 92

Deregulation, 106, 148, 149, 150

DeRouen, K. R., Jr., 184n.19

Devaluation, 145–148, 162

Development models: definition of development, 155–156; elements of development, 156; elite class model, 3; import-substitution model, 1, 3; Jamaica Labour Party (JLP) model, 1; People's National Party (PNP) model, 1; Puerto Rican model, 157

Diplomatic intervention, 178n.26

"Discursive" dependency, 161

Distribution industry, 21

"Divide and rule" politics, 2

Dominguez, J. I., 153

Dominica, 114, 182n.2

Dominican Republic, 7, 116

Drug trade, 156, 164

Duncan, D. K.: Angola liberation support of, 38, 43, 65, 178n.21; and Jamaica's foreign policy, 63; and Jamaica-USSR relations, 58; and Kissinger, 177n.16

Duvalier, Jean-Claude "Baby Doc," 115–119, 184n.24

Duvalier, Michelle, 116

Economic Support Fund (ESF), 148, 186n.10

Economics: budget deficits, 15–16; capital inflows into Jamaica, 18; coercion mechanisms of, 8; deregulation, 148, 149, 150; devaluation of currency, 145–148; economic liberalism, 106; economic neoliberalism, 71-72; "excessive demand," 73; and exporting, 84–86, 146–147, 161; external debt statistics for Jamaica, 16; external trade quotient for Jamaica, 19; and finance capital, 24; fixed capital formation in Jamaica, 20; gross domestic product (GDP), 20, 21, 74, 175–176n.8; imports, 147; inflation rates, 77; oil crises, 18, 24; open economies, 18; political economy of Caribbean countries, 2–4; price controls, 147; privatization, 148, 149, 161; productive capital, 24–25; and protectionism, 25, 135–137, 168; societal counter-strategies and economic performance, 18–20; of structurally dependent state, 4–9; and world re-

cession of 1970s, 24–25, 176n.1.
See also Capitalist economies; Finance capital; International capital; Productive capital

Education, 15, 165, 187n.6

EEC, 79, 149–150, 185n.35

EFF. *See* Extended Fund Facility (EFF)

El Salvador, 28-29

Emergency Production Plan, 57, 59

ESF. *See* Economic Support Fund (ESF)

Estrada, Ulises, 47, 107

Ethanol distillation, 136–137

ETQ. *See* External trade quotient (ETQ)

"Excessive demand", 73

Exchange rate, 59, 145

Exporting, 84–86, 146–147, 161, 186n.7, 186n.10. *See also* Jamaica Exporters' Association (JEA)

Extended Fund Facility (EFF), 131

External trade balance for Jamaica, 76

External trade quotient (ETQ), 19, 77, 175n.7

Exxon, 133

Fahrenkopf, Frank, 104

Finance capital, and world economic crisis of 1970s, 24

Fixed capital formation in Jamaica, 20

FNLA, 36, 177n.13

Food: food farms, 15; Food Security Programme, 79; Inter-religious Task Force on US Food Policy, 168; price controls for, 147; World Food Programme, 79

Food Security Programme, 79

Ford, Gerald, 44

Foreign policy: Caribbean countries' politics of, 2–4; and comprador bourgeoisie, 6–7; "corporatist" foreign policy, 183n.7; "hegemonic devolution", 153, 186n.16; IMF and Jamaican foreign policy, 64–65; and Manley, 18, 52-53; and People's National Party (PNP), 18; and relations of production, 6; and relative autonomy, 10–11; Seaga on, 127; and structural dependency, 4–9, 13; U.S. foreign policy in 1980s, 96-98. *See also* specific countries

France, 187n.11

Francis, Frank, 184n.13

Free Zone status, 138

Gairy, Eric, 103, 111

Gallimore, Neville, 116, 118, 120, 122, 184n.26, 185n.30

Galtung, J., 183n.5

GATT, *See* General Agreement on Tariffs and Trade (GATT)

GDP. *See* Gross domestic product (GDP)

General Agreement on Tariffs and Trade (GATT), 8, 26, 176n.1

Genscher, Hans-Dietrich, 166

Germany, 164, 165

Gerster, R., 73

Global economy: debt crisis, 91–94, 140-148; and Jamaica, 24–26, 76; and labour costs, 78, 180-181n.5; neoconservatism revival in, 95–96; and stagnation, 93; and world recession of 1970s, 24–25, 176n.1. *See also* specific countries

Government services production, 21

Grenada: and Barbados, 109, 113, 114, 115; and Caribbean Basin Initiative (CBI) programme, 98; and Caribbean Democratic Union (CDU), 182n.2; and CARICOM, 110, 184n.14; and democracy, 111; and human rights, 110; and Jamaica, 105, 109–116, 120, 128, 153, 158, 162, 183–184n.12; People's Revolutionary government, 111; revolution in, 29, 109–115; Seaga's attitude toward, 102; U. S. invasion of, 109, 113–115, 184n.19

Gross domestic product (GDP), 20, 21, 74, 175–176n.8

Group of 77, 26

Guantanamo Bay issue, 46

Guatamela, 7

Guyana, 30–31, 36, 98, 110

Habermas, J., 70

Haig, Alexander, 108

Haiti: army cynicism in, 185n.38; Caribbean Basin Initiative (CBI), 98; and CARICOM, 121, 125; Declaration on Haiti of the Meeting of CARICOM/Caribbean Leaders, 125–126, 171–173; and Duvalier, 115–119, 184n.24; elections in, 120–125, 126, 185n.34, 185n.35; as first black republic, 2; human rights violations in, 123; and Jamaica, 115-128, 153; National Democratic Institute (NDI) political tutelage in, 121; new constitution for, 121; and U.S. ambassador as *persona non grata*, 117; U.S. intervention in, 103, 125–127, 182n.1

Hanlon, J., 177n.12

Harding, Oswald, 116

Health care, 77, 78, 165

"Hegemonic devolution", 153, 186n.16

Henri Christophe, King, 185n.27

Hobbes, Thomas, 178n.25

Holwill, Richard, 123

Hope Bulls, 33

Human rights: and CARICOM treaty, 110, 184n.14; Haiti violations of, 123; Inter-American Commission for Human Rights, 112; and Third World policy, 27–28

Hungary, 63

Huntley, E., 187n.10

Hurricane Gilbert, 149

Hyett, C., 138

IBA. *See* International Bauxite Association (IBA)

ICSID. *See* International Centre for the Settlement of Investment Disputes (ICSID)

IDB. *See* Inter-American Development Bank (IDB)

Ideological pluralism, 184n.15

IDU. *See* International Democratic Union (IDU)

IMF. *See* International Monetary Fund (IMF)

Imports, 147

Import-substitution model of development, 1, 3

Independent Trade Unions Action Council, 108

Industrial Dispute Tribunal, 88

Inflation, 77

Informal economy, 77, 164

Inter-American Commission for Human Rights, 112

Inter-American Development Bank (IDB), 98, 149

Inter-American Press Association, 33

Interdependence, 105–107

International Bauxite Association (IBA), 55

International capital: and Caribbean/Central American Action (C/CAA), 97; and General Agreement on Tariffs and Trade (GATT), 8; and IMF stabilization programme in Jamaica, 59–60; and Jamaica Labour Party (JLP), 140–148; local bourgeoisie tension with, 12–13; and Manley, 43; and Nicaragua, 111; and private sector commitment, 84; and social relations of dominance and subordination, 9; and world debt crisis, 92–94, 140–148; and World Trade Organization (WTO), 8. *See also* International Monetary Fund (IMF); World Bank

International Centre for the Settlement of Investment Disputes (ICSID), 55

International Communist Movement, 17, 46

International Democratic Union (IDU), 103, 104

International Monetary Fund (IMF): anti-IMF sentiments in Jamaica, 62; Compensatory Financing Facility, 131–132; and development model for Jamaica, 1; economic analysis by, 73; Extended Fund Facility (EFF), 131; and international capital, 8; and Jamaican foreign policy, 64–65; and Jamaican structural adjustment, 72–73, 141, 144–150, 186n.10; Jamaica's break with, 63–66; Jamaica's default, 60; Manley government negotiations with, 56–63; manufacturers' criticism of, 85; monetary prescriptions of, 73; Seaga government negotiations with, 131–132; stabilization programmes, 72–73; and tax reform, 73; U.S. support in, 179n.8; and USID, 148; and world debt crisis, 92-94

Inter-religious Task Force on US Food Policy, 168

Iran-Contra scandal, 184n.24

Iraq, 66

Irish Famine, 99

Jamaica: and African liberation struggles, 31–32; and Air Cubana, 33; and Angola, 35, 37–38, 41–43, 177n.14; balance of payments indicators, 76; and Bank of Commerce and Credit (BCCI), 143–144; bauxite levy, 15, 16, 21–23; break with IMF, 63–66; budget deficits of, 15-16; capital inflows, 18; and Caribbean Basin Initiative (CBI), 97-98, 134–140; and Caribbean Democratic Union (CDU), 182n.2; and CARICOM, 115–116; class relations in 1980s, 80–86; communist movement in, 14; condemnation of USSR intervention in Afghanistan, 48; and "Corporatist" foreign policy, 183n.7; and Cuba, 30–51, 63, 71, 107–108, 116, 162; default on IMF loans, 60; and democracy, 101–103; destabilization in, 43–46, 180n.17; devaluation of currency, 145–148, 162; development models for, 1; domestic policies of, 22; Emergency Production Plan, 57, 59; and ethanol distillation, 136–137; expulsion of ambassadors from, 47, 54; external debt statistics, 16; external trade balance, 76; external trade quotient for Jamaica, 19, 77; fixed capital formation in Jamaica, 20; foreign policy goals, 166–167; and global economy, 24–26, 76; and gradualism, 105; and Grenada, 105, 109–116, 120, 128, 153, 158, 162, 183–184n.12; gross domestic product (GDP), 74; and Guantanamo Bay issue, 46; and Haiti, 115–128, 185n.34; health expenditures in, 77; and Hurricane Gilbert, 149; and IMF programmes, 59-63, 72-73, 131–132, 141, 144–150; import deregulation, 147; informal economy in, 77; and interdependence, 105–107; Kissinger's relations with, 32, 55; labour movement split in, 2–3; and Libya bombing by U.S., 147; Marxist Popular Movement for the Liberation of Angola (MPLA) recognized by, 39, 42, 177-178n.19; and migration, 77; nationalization of enterprises, 58; and Non-Aligned Movement, 96; police training by Cubans, 44; policy recommendations for, 163–169; "politics of national development", 155; "politics of survival", 155; and price controls for food, 147; private foreign investment, 53–54, 84; and privatization, 148, 149; and Puerto Rican self-determination, 34, 46; secretiveness in foreign affairs of, 154, 187n.8; sectoral performance of the economy, 75; and Seventh Non-Aligned Summit, 182n.1; social activism in, 14; social indicators, 78; as speaker for Third World, 159; structural adjustment, 72–77, 140-148; and "Super 807" programme,

135–136; textile industry, 135–136; and U.S. Congress, 167–168; U.S. intelligence on, 49; U.S. official assistance to, 148–150, 177n.8; and USAID, 65, 79, 82, 98, 181n.11, 185n.2, 186n.10, 186n.11; and USSR, 63; and world debt crisis, 91-94

Jamaica Bauxite Institute (JBI), 22

Jamaica Chamber of Commerce, 15, 40, 62, 80, 86

Jamaica Development Bank, 133

Jamaica Employers Federation (JEF), 80, 81

Jamaica Exporters' Association (JEA), 15, 35, 80, 86, 185n.2, 186n.7. *See also* Exporting

Jamaica Hotel and Tourist Association, 15

Jamaica Labour Party (JLP): bauxite levy support of, 22; and CDU, 104; and dependency, 70–71; development model of, 1; and Grenada invasion, 114; and Haiti, 126; and IMF, 83, 131, 140–148; and international press, 98; and Jamaica-Cuba relations, 50; and 1980 elections, 69; and trade, 70; U.S. Congress, 187n.11; U.S. relationship with, 108; and Westminster-type democracy, 1

Jamaica Manufacturers' Association (JMA): and Caribbean Basin Initiative (CBI), 186n.4; and communism, 54; and Cuban ambassador's expulsion, 47; Jamaica Exporters' Association (JEA) merger with, 86; and National Youth Service Programme, 16; objection to Manley's travel with Castro, 31–32; opposition to Cuban construction workers in Jamaica, 40; as private sector organization, 15; and social justice, 80

Jamaica National Export Corporation (JNEC), 83

Jamaica National Investment Corporation, 133

Jamaica National Investment Promotions (JNIP), 83

Jamaica Nutrition Holdings, 62

Jamaica Promotions Ltd., 180n.3

James, C. L. R., 103

JAMPRO, 181n.14

Japan, 70, 176n.3

JBI. *See* Jamaica Bauxite Institute (JBI)

JEA. *See* Jamaica Exporters' Association (JEA)

JEF. *See* Jamaica Employers Federation (JEF)

JLP. *See* Jamaica Labour Party (JLP)

JMA. *See* Jamaica Manufacturers' Association (JMA)

JNEC. *See* Jamaica National Export Corporation (JNEC)

JNIP. *See* Jamaica National Investment Promotions (JNIP)

Johnson, Peter, 97

Joint Committee of Commerce, Manufactures and Export (CME), 86

Kelly, Peter, 187n.11

Kemp-Kasten Amendment of 1984, 148

KGB, 49

Kirkpatrick, Jeane, 97, 113

Kissinger Commission, 97

Kissinger, Henry: and Angola's liberation, 35–36, 38–39, 43, 177n.11; and bauxite levy, 55; and Duncan, 177n.16; Jamaican disapproval of,

32; and Manley, 43, 177n.16; and Thompson, 177n.16

Labour: costs of, 78, 180–181n.5; and Industrial Dispute Tribunal, 88; labour movement split in Jamaica, 2–3; strikes, 181n.9, 181n.10; as unionized, 3; workers' rights, 88

Labour Relations and Industrial Disputes Act, 62, 88

Levitt, K., 15–16, 79

Libby, 156–157, 186n.2

Liberalization. *See* Deregulation

Libya, 66, 147

Lightbourne, R., 176n.4

Lobbying, 167–168, 187n.11

Local bourgeoisie, 8, 12–13, 54, 66, 67. *See also* Bourgeoisie; Comprador bourgeoisie

Long, Oliver, 176n.1

L'Ouverture, Toussaint, 103

Luers, William H., 58

Lukács, Georg, 88

Mahfood, Winston, 35, 49

Manigat, Leslie, 126, 128

Manley, Michael: alleged contact with KGB, 49; and autonomy, 163; and bauxite levy, 22; and capitalism, 35; and Castro, 31–32, 36; communism linked with, 46; and Cuba, 31–32, 36, 42, 50, 178n.21; and economic diversification, 176n.11; and foreign policy, 18, 52–53; and IMF, 64, 65, 66; and Kissinger, 43, 177n.16; in Moscow, 63; on MPLA, 39, 42; and New International Economic Order (NIEO), 94, 179n.4; on PNP government, 175n.3; Puerto Rican self-determi-

nation support of, 34, 48, 178n.27;
and Rousseau, 176n.10; and Seaga,
178n.30; and Young, 179n.8

Manoïlesco, Mihaïl, 183n.7

Manufacturing industry, 21, 85

Maroons, 2, 174n.2

Marriott, Charles, 187n.11

Marxism. *See* Communism

Marxist Popular Movement for the
Liberation of Angola (MPLA), 36,
38–39, 41, 42, 177n.11,
177–178n.17

Matalon, Aaron, 47

Matalon, Mayer, 21, 22, 55, 57–58,
179n.7

McIntyre, Alister, 57–58

McKinnon, Ronald, 152

Meeks, Winston, 40

Melhado, O. K., 32

Metropolitan bourgeoisie, 7, 10.
See also Bourgeoisie; Comprador
bourgeoisie

Mexico, 22, 91, 99–100, 134, 140

Miami Herald, 178n.24

Migration, 77, 78, 164

Mills, Don, 179n.4, 187n.9

Mining industry, 21, 22, 74. *See also*
headings beginning with Bauxite

Money Index, 127

Monroe Doctrine, 96

Montserrat, 182n.2

MPLA. *See* Marxist Popular Movement for the Liberation of Angola
(MPLA)

Multilateral development banks,
141–142

Munn, Keble, 44

NAFTA. *See* North American Free
Trade Area (NAFTA)

NAM summits, 31, 48

Namibia, 36

Namphy, Henri: cynicism of,
185n.38; and democracy, 128; and
Duvalier, 118; and exclusion of
U.S. observers, 122; and Haiti elections, 120, 125; international condemnation of, 123, 125; Manigat
overthrown by, 126; as self-declared
Commander-in-Chief of Haitian
military, 184–185n.27; U.S. recognition as leader of Haiti, 119

National Bauxite Commission, 21, 22

National City Bank, 182n.1

National Commercial Bank, 150

National Council of Government
(CNG), 118

National Defence Stockpile, 144

National Democratic Institute (NDI),
121, 122

National Endowment for Democracy
(NED), 187n.11

National Hotel and Properties Ltd.,
133

National Workers' Union (NWU), 81

National Youth Service Programme,
16

Nationalization of enterprise, 58

NDI. *See* National Democratic
Institute (NDI)

NED. *See* National Endowment for
Democracy (NED)

Neoconservatism, 95–96

Nettleford, Rex, 158

"New dependency", 92

New International Economic Order
(NIEO), 26, 94, 143, 159, 179n.4

New Jewel Movement (NJM), 111

New National Party (NNP), 114

New York Times, 44

Newsweek, 107

Nicaragua: and Caribbean Basin Initiative (CBI), 98; and communist influence in Caribbean, 102; external trade quotient (ETQ) of, 19; international capital opposition to, 111; and neoconservatism revival, 95; U.S. policy toward, 28

NICs, 174n.1

NIEO. *See* New International Economic Order (NIEO)

Nigeria, 180n.2

Nixon, Richard, 25

NJM. *See* New Jewel Movement (NJM)

NNP. *See* New National Party (NNP)

Non-Aligned Movement, 17, 26, 46, 96, 113, 182n.1

Non-Aligned Summit, Seventh, 182n.1

North, Oliver, 184n.24

North American Free Trade Area (NAFTA), 168

North-South Conference, 64

NWU. *See* National Workers' Union (NWU)

OAS. *See* Organization of American States (OAS)

O'Connor, Tim, 186n.11

OECS, 113, 115

Official Secrets Act, 187n.8

Oil industry, 15, 18, 24

O'Neill, Thomas "Tip", 167–168

Organization of American States (OAS), 27, 31, 185n.35

Parnell, Justice, 181n.10

Pastor, Robert, 49

Patterson, P. J., 46, 53, 61

Payne, A., 184n.14

People's National Party (PNP): and bauxite levy, 55; and Cuba, 30–31, 33, 40; and democratic socialism, 17; destabilization of, 180n.17; development model of, 1; domestic programmes of, 15–16; foreign policy agenda of, 18; and global economy, 159; and illegal export of capital, 19–20; policies of, 14–15; support of Cuban troops in Angola, 38; and Westminster type democracy, 1

Peru, 92, 108

Petro-dollars, 24

PETROJAM. *See* Petroleum Corporation of Jamaica (PETROJAM)

Petroleum Corporation of Jamaica (PETROJAM), 133, 137–138

PIOJ, 181n.9

PNP. *See* People's National Party (PNP)

PNP Youth Organization, 38

Portugal, 36

Post, K., 174n.3

Poulantzas, N., 6, 7, 10, 175n.9

Poverty, 165

Power, definition of, 174n.5

Press Association of Jamaica, 108

Price controls for food, 147

Private Sector Organization of Jamaica (PSOJ): as anti-communist, 17; as bourgeoisie umbrella organization, 82-83; and CARICOM, 112; communism as concern to, 184n.16; and Cuban ambassador's expulsion, 47; and Grenada's suspension from

CARICOM, 110; Jamaica Labour Party (JLP) government criticism of, 145; as major private sector organization, 15; members of, 183n.10; on Ministry of Foreign Affairs merger with Ministry of Industry, 181–182n.19; and role of State, 87–88; and social justice, 80

Privatization, 148, 149, 161

Production, 6

Productive capital, 24–25, 176n.1

Protectionism, 25, 135-137, 168, 175n.1, 186n.7

PSOJ. *See* Private Sector Organization of Jamaica (PSOJ)

Public opinion polls, 186n.1

Public speaking, 166

Puerto Rico: model of development, 157; political education by NDI in, 121; and self-determination, 34, 46, 48, 178n.27, 178n.28

Rainford, Roderick, 124, 185n.36

Rastafarians, 38

Rattray, Alfred, 48, 179n..10

Reagan, Ronald: and Caribbean Basin Initiative (CBI), 139; and Caribbean social formations, 131; foreign aid policies, 182n.2; and Grenada invasion, 114, 115; and Haiti crisis, 118; and Iran-Contra scandal, 184n.24; and Jamaica, 108, 145, 160; and prophetic language, 134; "Reaganomics", 149, 151, 152; and Seaga, 133, 145; Third World policies of, 156–157

Reagan Doctrine, 95

Real estate industry, 21

Reggae music, 166

Relative autonomy, 9–11, 175n.9

Republican Party (U.S.), 104, 149

Reston, James, 44

Restricted autonomy, 11-13

Robinson, Randall, 168

Rockefeller, David, 97, 133

Rockefeller Committee, 151

Rousseau, Pat, 22, 176n.10

Royal Bank of Jamaica Ltd., 17

St. Christopher and Nevis, 182n.2

St. Lucia, 114, 125, 182n.2

St. Vincent and the Grenadines, 183n.2

Sakhia, Abdur, 143–144

Sandinistas, 28

Sasso, Ronald, 17

Savimbi, Jonas, 42

Schweicker, Richard, 49

Scoon, Paul, 114

Seaga, Edward: and autonomy, 162–163; and Bank of Commerce and Credit (BCCI), 143–144; and Bush, 113; Cabinet changes of, 87; and Caribbean Basin Initiative (CBI), 134, 138; and Caribbean Democratic Union (CDU), 128; and CARICOM, 103, 125; on Castro, 45, 151; on causes of financial dislocations, 131; and Cold War domino theory of communism, 45; correspondence, 185n.36; criticism of, 82; and Cuba, 153; and democracy, 101–105; and deregulation, 150; and economic liberalism, 106; and export rebates, 146–147; and Food Security Programme, 79; on foreign policy, 127; and gradualism, 105; and Grenada, 109, 153; and Haiti, 117, 118, 122, 123-124, 126, 153, 185n.33; and ideological pluralism, 184n.15; and IMF, 83, 131, 140–141; and interdependence, 105–107; and Manley, 157–158, 178n.30; NIEO challenge of, 72; and privatization, 150; programme failures of, 79–80, 181n.7; and Reagan, 133, 149; on self-determination, 105–106; and structural adjustment, 140–148; support for, 70; and USAID, 149; and U.S. capital, 130, 157; and world debt crisis, 141–143

"Secret Document of the Santa Fe Committee for the United States Interamerican Security Council", 96

Semler, Ricardo, 180n.2

Shaw, Audley, 85

Shearer, Hugh, 108, 119, 134, 185n.39

Shultz, George, 117

Simon, William E., 25

Singapore, 96

Sloterkijk, Peter, 70

Small, Hugh, 62, 179–180n.12

Social activism, 14

Social class: and debt burden, 164; definition of, 174n.3; and economic adjustment, 180n.1; elite class development model, 3; and ideal factors, 175n.6; politics as class based, 3; relations between classes in 1980s, 80-86; social relations of dominance and subordination, 9; technico-administrative class, 7, 8. *See also* Bourgeoisie

Somoza, Anastasio, 28

South Africa, 36, 39, 40, 41

Soviets. *See* Union of Soviet Socialist Republic (USSR)

Speakes, Larry, 116

Special Employment Programme, 15

State Trading Corporation, 58, 62

Stephens, 19–20

Steward, J. Todd, 88

Stone, Carl, 81, 150, 174n.3, 175n.7

Strikes, 181n.9, 181n.10

Structural dependency: and "bridgehead elites", 5; central problem of, 5–6; and development models, 1; and foreign policy, 4–9, 13; interactive loci of, 8; nature of, 70–71; and open economies, 18; and peripheral state, 9–13; perpetuation of, 5; and world debt crisis, 92

"Super 807" programme, 135–136

Supplice, 118

Suriname, 116

Taiwan, 19

Tate & Lyle, 61

Technico-administrative class, 7, 8

Telecommunications of Jamaica (TOJ), 150

Textile industry, 135–136, 138, 139, 186n.4

Therborn, G., 7, 9

Thiesfield, Joyce, 116–117

Third World: assertiveness in, 26–27; and Cold War, 95; dependency perpetuation in, 5; human rights issues, 27–28; Jamaica as speaker for, 159; Reagan's policies toward, 156-157; and republics of former Soviet Union, 174n.1; Third World Movement, 3–4; and transnationalization of bourgeoisie, 26–27. *See also* specific countries

Thomas, C. Y., 175n.9

Thompson, Dudley: on Castro, 40–41; on Cuba, 32, 43; on destabilization in Jamaica, 44; on Jamaica's support of Puerto Rican self-determination, 48; and Kissinger, 177n.16; on OAS, 31; as political loner, 176n.2

Thurmond-Jenkins Bill, 135

Thwaites, Peter, 87

TOJ. *See* Telecommunications of Jamaica (TOJ)

Tonton Macoutes, 118

Tourism industry, 75, 166

Trade unions, 40, 62, 81

Trafalgar Development Bank, 133

Trans Africa Forum, 168

Transnational productive capital, 25

Transportation industry, 21

Treasonable and Seditious Practices Act of British Constitution, 178n.25

Trinidad and Tobago: and Caribbean Basin Initiative (CBI), 134; and CARICOM, 110, 125, 128; and Cuba, 30–31, 37; external trade quotient (ETQ) of, 19; and Haiti, 119-120; and Jamaican foreign trade policies, 63

Tropicana, 137, 138

Trouillot, M. R., 184n.24

Unemployment, 25, 40, 78

Union of Soviet Socialist Republic (USSR): Afghanistan intervention of, 48; and Angola, 27, 36, 177n.11; and bauxite purchases, 22–23; and communist influence in Caribbean, 102; détente with U.S., 27-28, 36; independent republics as Third World, 174n.1; Jamaica's alumina sales to, 63; Manley contact with KGB, 49

Unions, 3, 40, 62, 81

UNITA, 36, 42, 187n.11

United Brands, 133

United Kingdom, 58, 60, 77, 149, 178n.25

United Nations, 26, 27, 34, 56, 185n.35

United Nation's Charter of Economic Rights and Duties of States, 56

United States: and Angola, 36, 42, 177n.11; anti-Jamaican press in, 44; assistance to developing countries, 25, 186–187n.3; and Caribbean Basin Initiative (CBI), 97–98, 134–140; Caribbean foreign policy in 1980s, 96–98; Central American policies of, 28–29; and Cuba, 28–29; détente with USSR, 27–28, 36; expulsion of ambassador to Jamaica, 54; fixed exchange rate termination, 24; Grenada invaded by, 109, 113–115, 184n.19; and Haiti, 103, 125–127, 182n.1, 185n.34; and IMF, 58, 179n.8; International Democratic Union (IDU) membership, 104; and Jamaica, 44, 49, 63, 77, 148–150, 177n.8; Libya bombing by, 147; neoconservatism revival in, 95; and Nicaragua, 28; official assistance to Jamaica, 148-150; and protectionism, 135–137, 186n.7; and Puerto Rican self-determination, 34; sloppy diplomacy of, 179n.1; and "Super 807" programme, 135–136; Tax Reform Act of 1986, 137; transnational interests of, 176n.2

University of the West Indies, 56–57, 71

US Business Committee on Jamaica, 133

USAID: and Food Security Programme, 79; Jamaican assistance, 65, 144, 148–150; and Private Sector Organization of Jamaica (PSOJ), 82, 181n.11; and protectionism, 98, 186n.10; Seaga termination of, 185n.2; and U.S. audit of Jamaican currency files, 186n.11

USSR. *See* Union of Soviet Socialist Republic (USSR)

Valdés, N. P., 35, 36

Vance, Cyrus, 49

Vaswani, Prakash, 86, 89, 109, 181n.16, 185n.2

Vaz, Douglas, 32, 87

Venezuela: and aluminum smelter complex, 22; and Caribbean Basin Initiative (CBI), 134; and Cuba, 108; loan agreement with Jamaica, 66; "pilot fish behavior" of, 99–100

Verzijl, J. H. W., 177n.18

Vietnam, 95

Wall Street Journal, 108

Weapons, 156

Williams, Prime Minister, 34

Witter, M., 77

WLL, 38

Wöhlcke, M., 183–184n.12

Workers. *See* Labour

Workers' Party of Jamaica (WPJ), 14

World Bank: and American partnership with developing countries, 25; and international capital, 8; and Jamaican structural adjustment, 144, 145; and labour costs, 180–181n.5; manufacturers' criticism of, 85; structural adjustment loans of, 72–73; and world debt crisis, 92–94

World Food Programme, 79

World Trade Organization (WTO), 8

WPJ. *See* Workers' Party of Jamaica (WPJ)

Wray & Nephew Ltd., 137, 138

WTO. *See* World Trade Organization (WTO)

Young, Andrew, 61, 179n.8

Zaire, 36, 177n.13